HORNBLOWER'S
HISTORICAL SHIPMATES

Hornblower's Historical Shipmates

The Young Gentlemen of Pellew's *Indefatigable*

Heather Noel-Smith
& Lorna M. Campbell

THE BOYDELL PRESS

First published 2016
The Boydell Press, Woodbridge

ISBN 978 1 78327 099 6

The Boydell Press is an imprint of Boydell & Brewer Ltd
PO Box 9, Woodbridge, Suffolk IP12 3DF, UK
and of Boydell & Brewer Inc.
668 Mt Hope Avenue, Rochester, NY 14620–2731, USA
website: www.boydellandbrewer.com

A catalogue record for this book is available from the British Library

The publisher has no responsibility for the continued existence
or accuracy of URLs for external or third-party internet websites
referred to in this book, and does not guarantee that any content
on such websites is, or will remain, accurate or appropriate

This publication is printed on acid-free paper

Designed and typeset in ITC Bodoni by
David Roberts, Pershore, Worcestershire

To Friends

'there shall ever be friendship among the good'

Plato, *Phaedrus*

Contents

Illustrations

Preface and Acknowledgements

THIS book has its origins in a wider research project that initially arose from the authors' shared love of HMS *Indefatigable*'s most famous fictional midshipman, Horatio Hornblower, and a mutual fascination with the career of his historical captain, Sir Edward Pellew. Despite the honours Pellew earned during his long and distinguished naval career, the *Droits de L'Homme* engagement still stands as the apotheosis of his career as a fighting captain so it was perhaps unsurprising that we were drawn to this iconic frigate action as the starting point for our archival research. Our original intention was to explore the lives and careers of the commissioned officers of all three ships that fought through the night and the storm off the lee shore of Hodierne Bay on 13 January 1797; the *Indefatigable*, the *Amazon* and the *Droits de L'Homme*. However it did not take us long to realise that any one of these officers warranted extensive biographical research in their own right and consequently we narrowed the scope of our research to concentrate on a single ship.

The first young gentleman we focused our attention on was the Honourable George Cadogan. Cadogan had already been the subject of an authoritative biography written in 1989; however, we were intrigued to discover that he had been subjected to three courts martial during the early years of his career, none of which were mentioned in the otherwise comprehensive biography. Cadogan became the subject of our first research paper, 'The Honourable George Cadogan: A Career in Courts Martial', which we presented at the New Researchers in Maritime History Conference in Glasgow in 2012. It was as a result of this paper that we were approached by Peter Sowden of Boydell & Brewer who invited us to submit the proposal for this book.

One theme that emerged early in our research was the high regard, mutual affection and lasting friendship that bound Pellew and the young gentlemen of the *Indefatigable* together throughout their careers and later civilian lives. The parallels with the fictional Pellew's affection and concern for Hornblower were clear. This should not have been a surprise, of course – Pellew was renowned for his patronage of junior officers; however he also had a reputation for avarice and nepotism that arose partially from C. Northcote Parkinson's influential but flawed biography. As the breadth of our research expanded, it became clear that the picture of Pellew that was emerging from the archives and the personal correspondence of his young officers was quite at odds with Parkinson's characterisation of a man who failed to gain the devotion of his officers and men and who was 'loved by few'.

In the course of our archival research, we often found ourselves one step behind the author Stephen Taylor, who we learned was writing a new biography of Pellew. A year into our research, Taylor published his highly regarded biography *Commander* and we were extremely gratified to discover that he had addressed many of the inaccuracies in Parkinson's 1934 biography and presented a much more balanced picture of Pellew. We immediately contacted Stephen who was interested in and enthusiastic about our research and we would like to thank him for pointing us towards several important sources that we might otherwise have missed.

This work has been undertaken as an independent research project; however we have benefited enormously from the support and encouragement of a wide circle of naval and maritime historians and scholars. In particular we would like to acknowledge the support of Duncan Redford, formerly of the National Museum of the Royal Navy Portsmouth. The Museum's research programmes, conferences and seminar series gave us an invaluable opportunity to meet other naval historians and seek input, comment and criticism on our research. We would also like to thank Brian Lavery for pointing us towards the O'Byrne papers at the British Library, Joanne Begiato for advice on parenting and friendship in the long eighteenth century, Peter Le Fevre, and the irrepressible Port Towns and Urban Cultures research group, for their interest and enthusiasm.

Clearly this research would not have been possible without the help of many librarians and archivists. We would like to thank Kira Charatan, Archivist and Assistant to Lord Chelsea; John Harnden, Herefordshire Archive and Records; Heather Home, Queens University, Ontario; Heather Johnson, National Museum of the Royal Navy Library; Anne-Marie Mazaud, D'Archives du Bayonne et du Pays Basque; Anna Petrie, Oxford University Archives; Mary Robertson, The Huntington Library; Martin Salmon, Royal Museums Greenwich; Stuart Tyler, Devon Heritage Centre; and the staff of the British Library and the National Archives.

We would also like to thank all those individuals and institutions who have generously allowed us to use the images that appear in this book, including Musée des Beaux-arts de Brest Métropole, the National Portrait Gallery, Royal Museums Greenwich, Herefordshire Archive and Records, and Sotheby's. In particular we would like to thank Juliet and Phil Barker for the picture of William Warden's memorial, the family of the late George Nicolle for Thomas Groube's headstone, Adam and Giles Quinan for the portrait of John Thomson, and Lord Chelsea for the portrait of George, 3rd Earl Cadogan.

Although this work focuses on the historical officers of HMS *Indefatigable*, the starting point for this research was their fictional counterpart Horatio Hornblower. This book would not have come about without the inspiration provided by those who have brought Hornblower and his shipmates to life.

Stephen Taylor commented that Pellew had a 'gift for friendship' and this research has certainly led us to make many new friends along the way.

In particular, we have been honoured to meet several descendants of two of the *Indefatigable*'s young gentlemen, Thomas Groube and John Thomson; we hope this book helps to bring their ancestors' remarkable lives to light. Among the many friends, both old and new, whom we would like to thank are Michael Nash of Marine and Cannon Books for encouragement and interest; Dr Sherry Watson for reanalysing the medical evidence relating to Richard Badcock's death; Wendy Baskett of Pinpoint Indexing for the index; Phil and Juliet Barker for taking a detour during a family holiday in India to photograph William Warden's memorial; Ann Laird for photographing Thomas Groube's headstone; Stirling Hotson for his patience and assistance driving us to and from various museums, libraries and archives; Lisa Adolf for transcribing numerous wills; Ross Hutchison for assistance with French translation; and Andy Marshall and Mike Rooke for their hospitality and for opening their home to us when we visited Portsmouth. Lorna owes an enormous debt of gratitude to Stuart and Rhuna McCartney for their unfailing patience, support and understanding. And Heather owes thanks to Wendy Baskett for listening with patience to many of the stories of these men's lives, and submitting to being diverted on holidays to locations associated with them.

Finally, for their encouragement, belief and support we would like to thank our fellow shipmates on this journey and wish them all fair winds and following seas.

Heather Noel-Smith and Lorna M. Campbell
February 2016

Abbreviations

ADM	The National Archives: Records of the Admiralty, Naval Forces, Royal Marines, Coastguard, and related bodies
Beaufort Papers	The Huntington Library: Francis Beaufort Papers
Bergeret Papers	Archives Pyrénées Atlantiques: Fonds Jacques Bergeret
Census	The National Archives: Census Returns
Exmouth Papers	National Maritime Museum, Caird Library: Papers of Lord Exmouth, Edward Pellew
Grenville Papers	The Huntington Library: Grenville Papers
LDS	LDS Family Search
Pateshall Papers	Herefordshire Archive: Records of the Pateshall Family of Allensmore
PCC Wills PROB	The National Archives: Records of the Prerogative Court of Canterbury
Pellew of Canonteign Collection	Devon Archive and Heritage Centre: Pellew of Canonteign Collection
Smyth Papers	Southampton Archive: Smyth Collection

Introduction

A GREAT deal has been written about the British Royal Navy frigate HMS *Indefatigable* and her first captain, Sir Edward Pellew, including three biographies, many accounts of actions in which the ship engaged and a number of works of historical fiction. In this last category the best-known example is the series of *Hornblower* novels by the twentieth-century author C. S. Forester, who chose Pellew's *Indefatigable* as the ship on which his eponymous antihero, Horatio Hornblower, served the majority of his time as a midshipman.[1] This book presents an examination of the lives and careers of seventeen of the young gentlemen who would have been Hornblower's historical shipmates aboard HMS *Indefatigable*; the volunteers, midshipmen and mates alongside whom he would have lived, berthed and fought.

Captain Sir Edward Pellew, later Admiral Lord Exmouth, is still highly regarded as a gifted and audacious sea officer. In a long and successful career he served as Commander in Chief of both the East Indies station and the Mediterranean Fleet, was feted as the victor of the Bombardment of Algiers and rose to the rank of Admiral of the Red and Vice Admiral of the United Kingdom. Notwithstanding these notable achievements, Pellew is most widely remembered as the quintessential frigate commander and captain of the 44-gun rasée HMS *Indefatigable*.

Pellew captained the *Indefatigable* for just over three years, from December 1795 to March 1799. It was a successful command by any measure and during this time the ship took numerous prizes and fought several notable engagements. The *Indefatigable*'s most famous action was unquestionably the dramatic *Droits de L'Homme* engagement when, on 13 January 1797, the *Indefatigable*, together with her consort the 36-gun frigate *Amazon*, took on a French 74-gun ship of the line and ran her on shore following a brutal twelve-hour engagement fought at night in the teeth of a ferocious storm on the lee shore of Audierne Bay on the Breton coast.

The *Droits de L'Homme* engagement is regarded as one of the most emblematic frigate engagements of the French Revolutionary Wars, but, despite being cited in almost every contemporary and modern naval history of this period, little has been written about the *Indefatigable*'s officers and crew. Through detailed examination of contemporary documents, private

---

[1] *Mr. Midshipman Hornblower*, first published in 1950, covers Hornblower's time as midshipman aboard HMS *Indefatigable*. Pellew also appears in several of the other books in Forester's series.

correspondence and Admiralty records held in national, public and private archives in the UK, USA and France, this book brings to light the lives and careers of the cohort of 'young gentlemen', the junior officers, who served aboard the *Indefatigable* during the iconic *Droits de L'Homme* engagement, while at the same time reassessing the legacy and reputation of their captain.

Throughout his career, Pellew was renowned for the patronage he extended to the young men who served under him; however he has often been criticised for over-exerting his influence to further the careers of his own sons and those of his friends and political allies. Pellew may indeed have been guilty of promoting his sons beyond their capabilities, but what is less well remembered is the support he offered to all his men, regardless of whether they had connections or interest to recommend them. The *Indefatigable*'s young gentlemen are typical in this respect; ranging from the son of an earl to a run-away Irish cabin boy, they all benefited from Pellew's patronage, and several served almost their entire naval career under his command. The great diversity of the young gentlemen's backgrounds and naval career paths, together with their close relationship with their captain, illustrates that Pellew's patronage extended far beyond his own sons and those of the wealthy and influential, and provides a counterbalance to the assertion of Pellew's partial but influential twentieth-century biographer, C. Northcote Parkinson, who described Pellew as a man who was 'loved by few'.[2] The large volume of moving condolence letters sent to the family on Pellew's death, from men who had served with him since boyhood, does indeed reveal a man who had gained the lasting love and devotion of his men.

The seventeen young gentlemen mustered on the *Indefatigable*'s books in 1797 present a fascinating snapshot of the commissioned officer class of the late eighteenth-century sailing navy in microcosm. Many of these young men, from diverse social backgrounds, went on to have eventful naval careers that equalled anything experienced by their famous fictional shipmate. Several reached the rank of Rear Admiral in retirement; a few served at Trafalgar and Algiers; one sailed to Australia; one became feted as a dashing naval hero in his own lifetime; another had the misfortune to suffer three courts martial in the space of four years; and an unfortunate few lost their lives during the course of the war.

Those of the *Indefatigable*'s young gentlemen who survived the war lived on to experience the transition from decades of conflict to lasting peace and were among the first generation to live at peace for many years. After leaving the service, they went on to have distinguished and diverse civilian careers; some engaged in scientific discovery and technological innovation; several took up public office in politics, the judiciary, charitable institutions and the church; others undertook diplomatic

---

[2] Parkinson, *Edward Pellew: Viscount Exmouth, Admiral of the Red*, p. 471.

service; one became noted for his radical politics. Whatever path their later lives took, many of the Indefatigables maintained ongoing personal relationships with their former captain and shipmates.

The legacy of the time these men served together aboard the *Indefatigable* and the lasting impression the *Droits de L'Homme* engagement had on their lives can be clearly seen in their obituaries and is further evidenced by the roll of the Naval General Service Medal.[3] The Naval General Service Medal (NGSM) was issued by the government in 1847 to honour those who had served their country in the many conflicts from the beginning of the French Revolutionary War in 1793. Each medal was decorated with clasps naming specific actions and one of the clasps issued commemorated the *Droits de L'Homme* engagement. Of the seventeen young gentlemen mustered on the *Indefatigable* at the time, only seven were still alive and able to exercise their claim to the 13 January 1797 clasp. The NGSM roll archive records the name and rank of each of the claimants at the time of the action; they included, amongst others, Volunteer First Class George Cadogan, by then the 3rd Earl Cadogan, Midshipman John Gaze, who retired with the rank of Commander after a long active service spent almost entirely under Pellew's command, and Volunteer John Harry. The presence of Harry, whose service on the *Indefatigable*, and indeed in the navy, lasted only from 1796 until 1797,[4] illustrates the formative nature of the young gentlemen's shared experience. Short his naval career may have been, but the night of 13 January 1797 was still a defining point in his life.

The same can be said for all the young gentlemen of the *Indefatigable*. Although their deaths occurred over a period of sixty years, from tragically early, like the unfortunate Philip Frowd, lieutenant of the *Blanche*, who died of yellow fever in Jamaica[5] in 1802, to George, 3rd Earl Cadogan, the last of the Indefatigables, who died at his home in Piccadilly in 1864,[6] from first to last, their obituaries never fail to mention the *Droits de L'Homme* engagement. Captain John McKerlie's 1848 epitaph in the *Morning Chronicle* is typical; despite the headline 'Death of Trafalgar veteran' the obituary devotes more coverage to McKerlie's years aboard the *Indefatigable* than to his service at Trafalgar, as first lieutenant of the

---

[3] ADM 171/2, Naval General Service Medal Rolls.

[4] ADM 36/13143, Muster Table of His Majesty's Ship the Indefatigable, January–October 1796; and ADM 36/13144, Muster Table of His Majesty's Ship the Indefatigable, November 1796–October 1797. John Harry joined the *Indefatigable* on 7 March 1796. The muster identifies him as a Volunteer First Class, aged seventeen, from Bodmin, Cornwall. Harry was discharged from the *Indefatigable*, and the service, on 1 August 1797 'per request'.

[5] *Naval Chronicle*, vol. 12, p. 166.

[6] *United Service Magazine*, 1864, part III, p. 292.

Spartiate.[7] Another case is that of Sir Henry Hart; by the time of his death in 1856 he was known for his diplomatic service and as a commissioner of Greenwich Hospital, but even the relatively obscure *Uckfield Visitor's Guide*, which in 1869 published an account of Hart's life, includes the almost inevitable comment that he was present at the destruction of the *Droits de L'Homme*.[8]

These young men were, at the time of the action, aged roughly between thirteen and twenty-eight, so many of them were very much at a formative stage in their lives. One of the younger boys, Nicholas Pateshall, wrote excitedly to his mother Ann on the day after the *Droits de L'Homme* engagement, as the *Indefatigable* struggled home to Falmouth for repairs: 'Sir Edward thinks that never was such an action known or even heard of ...'[9] The *Droits de L'Homme* engagement was certainly unique in the annals of naval warfare and, for those who witnessed it, those who participated in the unparalleled act of seamanship, the event bound them together and marked them out as a distinct and special group. Whatever their subsequent successes in naval or civilian life, they had just cause to be proud.

[7] *Morning Chronicle*, 1848, p. 6.
[8] *The Uckfield Visitor's Guide*, pp. 29–30.
[9] Pateshall Papers, BD 30/9/1-50, Nicholas Pateshall to Ann Pateshall, 17 January 1797.

I

Edward Pellew – Partisan and Patriarch

SINCE his death in 1833, Admiral Edward Pellew, 1st Viscount Exmouth, has been the subject of three biographies and numerous character studies,[1] both contemporary and modern, which have shaped the perception of the man, his reputation and his legacy. While Pellew's reputation as a gifted sea officer and the foremost frigate commander of his era is beyond dispute, the picture of the man that emerges from his biographies is both complex and contradictory. N. A. M. Rodger's brief but balanced assessment of Pellew as 'tough, brave, skilful, lucky and unscrupulous' illustrates the ambiguous nature of his character.[2] From his earliest days as a midshipman, Pellew's courage, activity and zeal were recognised and rewarded, but he was also criticised for being volatile, intemperate and antagonistic. At a time when naval captains were celebrated for their ability to earn enormous fortunes in prize money, Pellew was feted for his success in capturing prizes but gained a reputation for avarice and cupidity. In a system that favoured interest and patronage, Pellew was a generous and steadfast patron who nurtured the careers of many young officers and men, but at the same time he was criticised for taking nepotism to extreme lengths by over-promoting his own sons. Pellew was celebrated by the press and public for rising through the ranks on his own merits, but there were persistent sneers from some of his contemporaries that his eager pursuit of honours was undignified at best. Many of these contradictory attitudes towards Pellew arose from the social and political mores of the period, while others have resulted from the vagaries of Pellew's biographers.

Pellew's first biography, *The Life of Admiral Viscount Exmouth*, was written in 1835, immediately after his death, by Edward Osler. While Osler's work was sanctioned by Pellew's eldest brother Samuel, the rest of the family vehemently objected to its publication and refused to allow Osler access to Pellew's archive. Osler's primary aim in writing the biography was clearly to glorify Pellew's reputation and that of his family; however, much of what he wrote is ambiguous or just plain wrong, particularly with regard to the details of Pellew's naval service. This is perhaps unsurprising as his primary source was Samuel who, although he had served briefly as a naval surgeon, spent most of his life ashore as a customs official and had

---

[1] Mahan, pp. 428–76; Le Fevre and Harding, pp. 271–93.
[2] Rodger, *The Command of the Ocean: A Naval History of Britain 1649–1815*, p. 386.

1 Edward Pellew, 1st Viscount Exmouth, by James Northcote, 1804.

little experience of life at sea. After the publication of the biography, there was an angry exchange of letters in the press,[3] with Pellew's son George denouncing the work and accusations of piracy being levelled at Osler. George had aspirations to write his own biography of his father and began to assemble material and solicit letters from friends and former colleagues. The family owned a copy of Osler, which still exists, with comments and errata written in the margins[4] by George, Fleetwood Pellew and others. A manuscript copy of these comments together with further annotation of his own was prepared by Francis Pinhey, one of Pellew's many great-grandchildren.[5] Although George Pellew did collate a considerable body of material from his father's archive, together with testimonies from his shipmates and colleagues, he did not write the planned biography of his father. Consequently, although Osler's unauthorised biography is often written off as hagiography, it remained the definitive account of Pellew's life for many years.

A century was to pass before an authorised biography of Pellew saw the light of day. In 1934, Cyril Northcote Parkinson, then a recently graduated student of naval history, published *Edward Pellew: Viscount Exmouth, Admiral of the Red*, based on family papers donated to the National Maritime Museum. While Parkinson had access to the Pellew archive, which included much of the material collated by George Pellew, his use of these sources was partial at best. Several letters which shed valuable light on Pellew's character have been casually marked 'not important' in Parkinson's hand.[6] In addition, Parkinson made little use of Admiralty documents at the National Archives which, had he studied them, would have contradicted some of his assertions.

While Parkinson corrected many of Osler's errors, he introduced many more of his own. This is particularly true with regard to Pellew's punishment record. While Osler observed that Pellew 'endured no relaxation of discipline',[7] Parkinson went further and claimed 'there was much of the martinet in Edward Pellew';[8] however, subsequent authors have shown that reference to Pellew's logs proves this to be manifestly untrue. In a chapter on Pellew published in 2005, Rae shows that even

---

[3] *The Metropolitan Magazine*, 1835, pp. 40, 81; *The London Quarterly Review*, 1835, pp. 69–93.

[4] Taylor, pp. 2–3.

[5] Pinhey was a son of Mary Anne Pellew, daughter of Pellew's youngest son, Edward. He copied the annotations with page numbers and identified which comments were added by George Pellew, Fleetwood Pellew, John Gaze and the 3rd Viscount Exmouth, as well as adding some personal comments of this own. This document is now in a private collection.

[6] Exmouth Papers, Box 22, MS 92027, Spencer to Pellew, 1 October 1790.

[7] Osler, p. 262.

[8] Parkinson, *Edward Pellew: Viscount Exmouth, Admiral of the Red*, p. 58.

a cursory analysis of ships' logs reveals that the rate of punishment on Pellew's ships was distinctly average.[9] Nevertheless, as a result of Parkinson's unsubstantiated claims, Pellew's reputation as a martinet persists.

Parkinson was also responsible for the widely held belief that Pellew was unpopular with his men. In a frequently quoted passage, Parkinson referred to Codrington's unfavourable comparison of Pellew with Nelson,[10] and proclaimed:

> A great captain must be either loved or feared. Men would perform miracles in the hope of pleasing Nelson. They would do their duty from fear of displeasing St. Vincent. Exmouth was loved by few, and in later life was not greatly feared by any. It was his misfortune to combine the highest abilities with an inability to gain the devotion of men.[11]

This assertion is flatly contradicted by the considerable volume of personal correspondence from men, officers and adversaries who fought both with and against Pellew, which reveal genuine devotion to the man whom they often referred to fondly as both father and friend.

Despite its inaccuracies, Parkinson's biography is still, arguably, the authoritative account of Pellew's life; however, a 2012 biography, *Commander: The Life and Exploits of Britain's Greatest Frigate Captain*, by Stephen Taylor, has gone some way towards redressing the balance. Using Pellew's own letters and log books, and the recollections and observations of his contemporaries, Taylor reveals a more accurate portrait of Pellew's character, which challenges many of the common misconceptions that

---

[9] Rae in Le Fevre and Harding, pp. 273, 390.

[10] 'In a conversation with an old friend (on 5th December 1835), Sir Edward Codrington was describing the personal agility of Lord Exmouth, who, when a captain would defy any man in his ship to a race to the mast-head and down again, giving him to the main top. He went on to say that he was remarkable for that gift of ready resource and wonderful personal activity "which we look for in what we call a good seaman;" but he was not born to command a fleet. Lord Nelson; on the contrary, was no seaman; even in the earlier stages of the profession his genius soared higher, and all his energies were turned to becoming a great commander. He had probably been always occupied in planning manœuvres and modes of attack with a fleet – while it is equally probable that at the time Lord Exmouth was appointed to a command, the subject of the management of a fleet had never engaged his attention. Lord Exmouth was not liked by his fleet, and Lord Nelson was adored by his; he never met with a distressed sailor without assisting him with his purse, or attention, or advice; nor did he ever neglect to encourage merit; he was easy of access, and his manner was particularly agreeable and kind. No man was ever afraid of displeasing him, but everybody was afraid of not Pleasing him.' Bourchier, pp. 124–5.

[11] Parkinson, *Edward Pellew: Viscount Exmouth, Admiral of the Red*, p. 471.

have resulted from Osler and Parkinson. In particular, Taylor goes to considerable lengths to refute Parkinson's assertion that Pellew was 'loved by few', and presents compelling evidence to justify his own claim that Pellew was a man who had a real gift for friendship.[12]

Many who encounter Pellew's name do so, however, not in the pages of naval biographies but in the adventures of his most famous fictional protégé, Horatio Hornblower. C. S. Forester portrays Pellew as a larger-than-life figure, but in some ways he comes close to capturing something of the essence of his character: a renowned fighting captain feted for his reputation and success,[13] a man marked for greatness but one who attracted bitter jealousy from fellow admirals,[14] but above all, a staunch patron, devoted to his young officers.[15]

Despite the complex and ambiguous picture of Pellew that emerges from these sources, there are two characteristics, partisan and patriarch, which all Pellew's biographers identify strongly with the man, and, paradoxically, they are also the roles in which he experienced both unparalleled success and painful failure.

In the earlier part of his career, Pellew was spectacularly successful as a partisan, as the word was understood in the common parlance of the time: a commander of irregular troops operating largely independently.[16] More than any of his contemporaries, with the arguable exception of Sir Sidney Smith,[17] he excelled as a commander of light detached forces employed to harass the enemy on their own territory. Pellew was, and still is, regarded as the quintessential detached frigate captain of his day. As patriarch he was equally exceptional. To both his own family and the extended family of scores of young gentlemen who served under his command, he was a loving, generous and inspiring patron and protector. However he was not without his faults: his overindulgent treatment of his own sons and his eagerness to oblige powerful allies by promoting their sons and protégés are well-documented, and far less admirable, aspects of his character. Accusations of avarice also dogged Pellew throughout his career, though he was not alone in this regard. The appellation of partisan was not without its negative connotations and detached frigate commanders often came

---

[12] Taylor, p. 24.

[13] Forester, *Mr. Midshipman Hornblower*, p. 21.

[14] Forester, *Hornblower and the Hotspur*, p. 93.

[15] Forester, *Hornblower and the Hotspur*, pp. 124–5.

[16] Partisan *Mil.* a. A member of a small body of light or irregular troops operating independently and engaging in surprise attacks, etc.; a guerrilla. Also in extended use. b. A commander of such a body of irregular troops; a guerrilla leader. Now *hist.* and *rare* (*U.S.* in later use). OED Online, 2012.

[17] Thomas Cochrane also made his name as a successful and audacious partisan fighter; however he belongs to a slightly later generation of sea officers than both Pellew and Smith.

into conflict with admirals who were denied a cut of the not inconsiderable prize money they earned. St Vincent disdainfully described Pellew's contemporary and fellow frigate commander, Sir John Borlase Warren, as 'a mere partisan, preferring prize money to the public good at all times'.[18]

To a considerable extent, the origins of Pellew's success and failure in this regard have their roots in his childhood. Edward Pellew was born in Dover in 1857, one of twins, the second son and first daughter of an eventual six children for packet captain Samuel Pellew and his wife Constantia Langford.

The packet service was a branch of the Post Office founded in the late sixteenth century to carry government letters and despatches, but which also carried fee-paying passengers and high-value cargo, including specie and bullion. At the time his children were born, Samuel Pellew was commander of the *Dispatch*, a packet vessel based in Dover that operated the route to Flushing, near Falmouth, where the Pellews had their roots.[19]

The exact nature of Pellew's family background has been the subject of some debate and there is considerable disagreement among his biographers as to Pellew's relative poverty and access to interest and patronage. Osler, and Pellew's older brother Samuel, were at pains to emphasise the respectability of the family's history and connections. In retelling the aftermath of Samuel Pellew senior's death in 1765, Osler emphasised the story of a respectable family that had fallen on hard times but still retained an acceptable social status. Osler also intended to show how Pellew's life, and his dramatic rise from obscurity to glory, could inspire those with such aspirations: 'he began his career as an almost unfriended orphan, and rose to the highest honours of his profession without having been indebted to fortune or patronage'.[20]

Parkinson, in contrast, distanced himself from Osler's classic portrait of a penniless orphan ascending to the peerage. In his 1934 biography, Parkinson suggested that the Pellew family's poverty was entirely relative; however, he also placed disproportionate weight on the patronage that the Pellew boys received from Lord Falmouth.

> His poverty in early life was only comparative ... they [the Pellew family] were far from friendless and only improperly can Edward Pellew's career give sanction to those who like to contemplate romantic ascents from the gutter to the House of Lords. If he started life with fewer advantages than Nelson, he was far more fortunate than Collingwood.[21]

---

[18] St Vincent to Warren, Wareham, p. 41.

[19] Post Office Appointment Books for 1759, 1761 and 1764, digitised on ancestry.co.uk.

[20] Osler, p. 1.

[21] Parkinson, *Edward Pellew: Viscount Exmouth, Admiral of the Red*, pp. 4–5. Parkinson does not make it explicit, but it appears that by

In revisiting the circumstances of Pellew's childhood and entry into the navy, both Rae and Taylor have given credence to Osler's claim that Pellew joined the service with little interest and less financial support. By referring to the original sources concerning the family's relationship to Lord Falmouth, and documents relating to Pellew's entry into the Royal Navy, Rae and Taylor have shown that his initial rating on joining the service was purser's servant, as opposed to captain's servant, the usual entry rating for boys marked for advancement.[22] Furthermore money was deducted from his wages to pay for slops, leading Rae to suggest that 'he possessed few clothes and no money'.[23] Both authors present a convincing case that Pellew had no real interest and that he genuinely did rise through his own talents and endeavours.

Pellew joined the service in 1770 when he entered Captain John Stott's 32-gun frigate *Juno*, which sailed for the Falkland Islands the following year. Later in 1771 Pellew followed Stott to his next command, another 32-gun frigate, HMS *Alarm*, where he was re-rated master's mate. It was during his time on the *Alarm* that an incident occurred which has become part of the folklore of Edward Pellew's early life. In 1774 he and a fellow midshipman, Frank Cole, were thrown off the ship at Mahon[24] for a youthful 'crime' relating to the captain's mistress, who was resident on board. Cole was alleged to have either had a disagreement with the woman in question, or to have drawn a lewd caricature of her.[25] Taylor has reappraised this incident and suggested that it is likely that Pellew was more involved in the initial wrongdoing than suggested by earlier biographers who maintained that he was ejected from the ship merely for supporting his friend.[26]

Arriving back in England after this adventure late in 1775, Pellew joined the *Blonde*, a 32-gun frigate captained by Philemon Pownoll, a gifted and intelligent commander who had had the good fortune to capture

---

referring to Collingwood he is making a deliberate comparison to a contemporary officer who may have been regarded as being socially handicapped by being from 'trade'. In actual fact, although his parents were not at all wealthy, Cuthbert Collingwood had a point of entry into the service via his mother's cousin, Richard Braithwaite, who was captain of the frigate *Shannon* at the time.

[22] Taylor, pp. 22–3.

[23] Rae in Le Fevre and Harding, p. 274.

[24] Parkinson, *Edward Pellew: Viscount Exmouth, Admiral of the Red*, p. 10, says that Pellew and Cole were 'turned out of the ship at Marseilles'; however, Taylor, p. 30, states that the *Alarm* was 'at Mahon' at the time. The muster and captain's log of the *Alarm* are inconsistent: the muster records them as having been discharged in 1775 rather than 1774. The location of the ship is not recorded; at this time, however, it is more likely that she was in Mahon rather than Marseilles.

[25] Taylor, p. 30.

[26] *Ibid.*

a prize carrying bullion worth over half a million pounds and was, as a consequence, a very wealthy man. By the end of the Seven Years War, Pownoll had already earned the equivalent of many millions of pounds in prize money and was happily married and living comfortably on his estate with his family; nonetheless he had volunteered to return to the service in 1774 just prior to the outbreak of the American Revolutionary War.

Pellew was initially rated able seaman on joining the *Blonde*, but as a result of the sea-going experience he had gained on the *Alarm*, was quickly re-rated master's mate. Pownoll was soon to become a role model for Pellew and he proved to have a powerful and inspirational influence on the high-spirited and rather wayward young man. Rodger, who describes Pownoll as a 'remarkable officer', notes:

> In every generation of eighteenth century British sea officers there were one or two who were distinguished as educators of young officers. Invariably they were frigate captains, for that was the only school of seamanship; eminent themselves for their mastery of their profession, painstaking in the care of the young gentlemen, they enjoyed a reputation within and without the service which made berths with them highly desired.[27]

Pellew learned much from Pownoll that he later integrated into his own model of captaincy. With his innate character of intelligent decisiveness, warmth, and physical and mental toughness, Pellew was becoming a formidable commander in the making.

In April 1776, shortly after Pellew joined the *Blonde*, the frigate was attached to a convoy of transports carrying troops destined for North America where provincial patriots were in open rebellion and had wrested power from the colonial government. The American Revolutionary War was to prove a turning point in Pellew's career as a naval officer. Under the command of the *Blonde*'s Lieutenant Dacres, Pellew and another more senior midshipman were seconded to serve on the tender *Carleton* on Lake Champlain. In the autumn of 1776, during the Battle of Valcour Island, both Dacres and the senior midshipman were severely wounded and command devolved to Pellew at just nineteen years of age. With half his crew wounded, five enemy ships firing on the *Carleton* and two feet of water in the hold, Pellew discovered that the jib was fouled, preventing the ship from turning around. Under heavy fire, he went out along the bowsprit to free the jib, and then passed lines out to two nearby ships so that the stricken vessel could be towed to safety. This action, swift-thinking, practical and utterly courageous but with more than a hint of recklessness, is typical of Pellew the man. It is also indicative of the daring gallantry of Pellew the captain, which inspired many, and the lead-from-the-front tendencies of Pellew the admiral, which frustrated more than a few.

---

[27] Rodger, in Duffy, *Parameters of Naval Power 1650–1850*, p. 88.

A winter spent building ships with Lieutenant John Schank,[28] in the harsh and hazardous conditions on Lake Champlain, was followed by a difficult mission ashore with the army, which ended with the defeat of General Burgoyne at Saratoga. This tough and formative year was compounded by a major personal loss for Pellew when his youngest brother John was killed at Saratoga, aged only sixteen.

Pellew's dramatic first-hand experience of how suddenly a junior officer could find himself in command at the height of battle, his hard labour in shipbuilding and his bereavement of a loved brother, had a formative impact on his character. Indeed many of Pellew's character traits as an adult, both difficult and admirable, are direct reflections of his experiences as a boy and a young man. The relative poverty of his family circumstances, the early bereavement of his father and brother, and the sudden responsibility of command, undoubtedly influenced his care and affection for fatherless boys, and the generosity and opportunities he offered to those without wealth or influence, just as they certainly influenced his pursuit of wealth, honours and security for himself and more blatantly for his elder sons.

In recognition of his gallant service, Pellew was sent home as a paroled prisoner of war carrying General Burgoyne's despatches. Although he was promoted to lieutenant for his heroic actions, he was initially appointed to a guard ship in Portsmouth harbour, as he was considered bound by parole not to go to sea. Eventually in late 1778 Lieutenant Pellew was appointed to the 32-gun frigate *Licorne*, Captain the Hon. Thomas Cadogan. Cadogan, the son of the 1st Earl Cadogan, was the older half-brother of George Cadogan, who later served as midshipman aboard the *Indefatigable*. Although they were half-brothers, George and Thomas never knew each other as Captain Cadogan died when his ship foundered in a hurricane in September 1782 and George was not born until the following May. Tenuous though it may seem, this connection may explain why Lord Spencer personally asked Pellew to accept young George as a volunteer some fourteen years later.

Two highly significant events occurred in the four years between 1779 and 1783 that had a profound affect on Pellew's life both personally and professionally. In 1780 Pellew lost his patron and friend, Philemon Pownoll, and in 1782 he met his future wife, Susan Frowd.

In late 1779 Pellew was appointed to the 32-gun frigate *Apollo*, by his old captain Philemon Pownoll, who had requested Pellew as his first lieutenant. To be personally chosen by such a successful captain was a great compliment to Pellew. Serving as first lieutenant of a frigate with a famously lucky and successful commander, and the likelihood of glory and

---

[28] John Schank (1740–1823) was a Scottish naval officer, known for his skill in ship design and construction. Schank oversaw the construction of a fleet of almost thirty ships and craft on Lake Champlain in 1776. Taylor, pp. 34–6.

prize money that presented, was the type of commission that all ambitious young officers sought.

Pellew's new posting, which must have seemed like a golden opportunity to the new lieutenant, began dramatically and ended abruptly. At Chatham, where the ship was being fitted out, a violent storm almost swept the *Apollo* off her moorings and disaster was only averted by the swift intervention of her captain. It is perhaps not difficult to imagine why Pownoll and Pellew saw one another as kindred spirits. The abrupt end came in June 1780 when the *Apollo* engaged a French privateer, the 26-gun *Stanislaus*. During a running battle, Pownoll was shot and mortally wounded, and died shortly afterwards in the arms of his first lieutenant. Pellew wasted no time in taking command of the *Apollo* and succeeded in driving the enemy ship on shore. Pownoll's death had a profound impact on Pellew, depriving him of a patron, a mentor and a friend. His account of the action, sent to Lord Sandwich at the Admiralty, included a moving tribute to his captain:

> The ship's company have lost a father. I have lost much more, a father and a friend united; and that friend my only one on earth. Never, my Lord, was grief more poignant than that we all feel for our adored commander. Mine is inexpressible. The friend who brought me up, pushed me through the service is now no more![29]

The combination of loyal courage and calm assumption of duty under fire earned Pellew his promotion to master and commander. His less than shining new command was the appropriately named *Hazard*, a worn-out brig-sloop originally launched in 1749 and stationed in the North Sea where she patrolled the east coast of Scotland and northern England keeping privateers at bay. In fact the *Hazard* was so slow she was incapable of catching any hostile ships she came across, though that did not prevent Pellew from trying. During his final voyage to Sheerness in the *Hazard*, Pellew suffered the ignominy of having to throw all his guns overboard in order to keep the decrepit vessel afloat at all.

Pellew's next command, the 18-gun sloop *Pelican*, was rather more satisfying for an ambitious young officer. Though still a small vessel, Pellew took his first prizes in the *Pelican*, setting the tone for his future career. This in turn led to his appointment to temporary command of the 40-gun frigate *Artois*, in which he was similarly successful, and as a result he was made post captain in May 1782.

Around this time, Pellew met the person who was to become one of the most enduring influences in his life: Susan Frowd, a country squire's daughter from Wiltshire, whom he married in May 1783. They formed a strong and lasting partnership, which was very happy in the main. Susan was a vivacious and intelligent woman who handled domestic matters and the upbringing of their children with self-assurance and ability, allowing

---

[29] Osler, p. 47.

Pellew to have confidence that his personal and family affairs were well attended to.[30] After their marriage, the couple moved initially to Truro and then, following Pellew's older brother Samuel who had been appointed as Collector of Customs in Falmouth, they moved to a home in Flushing where all their children were born.

Susan was a true counterweight to her husband; she was loving and supportive but a strong character in her own right. She was undeterred from holding different opinions from her husband and never shrank from trying to persuade him of an alternative view.[31] Susan Pellew was instrumental in creating a hospitable home environment that welcomed everyone, from nervous new midshipmen,[32] to French officers on parole,[33] to destitute young women[34] and many more, though she was less enthusiastic about the exotic animals that her husband had a tendency to bring home from far-flung stations.

> I hope, dearest, that you will dispose of your <u>tiger</u> and your wild <u>beasts</u> by your return, for remember they are too expensive to keep had we room, a keeper and no fears, which I frankly confess I have.[35]

In their own different ways Susan Frowd and Philemon Pownoll both had a considerable impact on the development of Pellew's character, smoothing off some of the rougher edges and enabling his generous nature and his aptitude as a commander and a sea officer to flourish.

Pellew had only one command in the interwar years between 1783 and 1793, the 32-gun frigate *Winchelsea*, which he commanded between 1786 and 1789. In late 1792, as war with France appeared ever more likely, Pellew lost no time in requesting a ship, and he was appointed to the 36-gun frigate *Nymphe* in early January 1793. At the outbreak of the war the navy was desperately short of seamen, so although Pellew had a ship, he lacked a crew; however he famously overcame this problem through judicious use of the pressgang and by recruiting eighty Cornish tin miners. Despite setbacks, not least of which was the unsuitability of about half the miners, he succeeded in moulding his unpromising crew into a skilled and capable fighting unit. So much so, that when he encountered the French frigate *Cléopatre* in June 1793 he was able to force her to surrender after a brief but bloody engagement, and so took the honour of capturing the first French ship of the war.

---

[30] Smallwood, pp. 15–16.

[31] Taylor, pp. 168–9.

[32] Smyth Papers, D/CB/4/14/3, John Smyth to Rev. John Smyth, 14 May 1803.

[33] Exmouth Papers, Box 22, MSS/92/027, Bergeret to Pellew, 16 April 1798.

[34] Susan provided a home for a 'young derelict' named Jane Smith, who wrote fondly to Pellew while he served as Commander in Chief in the Mediterranean. Taylor, pp. 231–2.

[35] Exmouth Papers, Box 22, MSS/92/027, Susan to Pellew, 10 April 1814.

News of the victory spread rapidly and gave cause for great celebration. Pellew was feted by the press, presented to the King and awarded a knighthood for his services. The aftermath of the action also made a significant impression. After the *Cléopatre* had struck, Pellew had boarded the ship to confirm his victory and found her commander, Captain Mullon, dying on his quarterdeck. Pellew subsequently arranged for Mullon to be buried at Portsmouth and wrote to his widow, ensuring that her husband's personal property and what little money Pellew could afford were sent to her in France. This heady mixture of the brave and gallant sea officer and the compassionate victor was an inspiration not only to those reading the accounts in the press, but also to young gentlemen aspiring to become successful naval officers: young gentlemen like Midshipman Francis Beaufort, later Hydrographer to the Navy, who regarded Pellew's victory as the benchmark for naval glory. Writing to his father in June 1794 to bemoan his ship's lack of success in bringing a chase to heel, Beaufort exclaimed somewhat theatrically:

> What ardour was in every man's countenance? The studdingsails, tacks, sheets, clewlines, dunits, halyards etc. actually flew. What vexation and gloom ran throughout when we were necessarily obliged to give up the chase at 4. Oh Pellew, thy action would be forgot. Thy name sink into obscurity if that night Stopford and his noble, brave Aquillons had had their dearest and only wish.[36]

Following his victory in the *Nymphe*, Pellew was awarded a new ship in December 1793. She was the *Arethusa*, a powerful 38-gun fifth rate, part of a new detached squadron of fast heavy frigates commanded by Sir John Borlase Warren. Based in Falmouth with orders to harass and intercept French ships in the Channel, the Western Squadron provided Pellew with the perfect opportunity to exercise his skill as a partisan frigate commander. Warren's squadron was so successful that the Admiralty established a second squadron towards the end of the following year under Pellew's own command. Pellew's star was now very much in the ascendant, so when he wrote to Lord Chatham, First Lord of the Admiralty, in November 1794 requesting a new ship, the First Lord immediately acquiesced.[37] The ship which Pellew had set his heart on was HMS *Indefatigable*. Originally an obsolete 64-gun ship of the line, the *Indefatigable* had been cut down to make a 44-gun fifth rate frigate, but one that was much bigger, more powerful, and more heavily armed than other ships of her class.

By any measure, Pellew's command of the *Indefatigable* was spectacularly successful. With a detached squadron under his own command, a crew he had trained and nurtured, and with skilled officers

[36] Francis Beaufort to Augustus Beaufort, 25 October 1794, in Courtney, pp. 56–7.
[37] Chatham to Pellew, 27 November 1794, in Taylor, p. 82.

whom he trusted and in whom he placed great confidence, Pellew was enormously successful in engaging enemy ships and capturing prizes. In every sense of the word, he had become a real partisan, the leader of a light detached force whose flexibility made it a potent weapon against an enemy.

In addition to the famous *Droits de L'Homme* engagement, another notable victory was the *Indefatigable*'s capture of the new French frigate *Virginie* in 1796. Once again, Pellew proved to be a chivalrous victor when he and Susan invited the *Virginie*'s defeated Captain Bergeret to live at their home in Falmouth as their personal guest while he was a prisoner on parole. Bergeret remained with the Pellews until an abortive attempt to exchange him with Sir Sidney Smith, then a prisoner in Paris, resulted in him being incarcerated in Stapleton Prison in Bristol. It was, however, the start of a lifelong friendship between the two officers and subsequent generations of their families.

Adding further to Pellew's heroic reputation was his role in the rescue of hundreds of soldiers and civilians from the wreck of the *Dutton* East Indiaman, which ran aground while attempting to enter Plymouth harbour in a gale in January 1796. Pellew boarded the *Dutton*[38] and helped to oversee the safe evacuation of the ship by means of boats and cables rigged to the shore, thus saving many lives. In recognition of his 'laudable Humanity and Spirit', Pellew was awarded a baronetcy.[39]

With Pellew's growing reputation for heroism and valour, he had become the commander whom many young gentlemen aspired to serve with. Whether anxious widowed mothers like Mrs Pateshall, or influential politicians like Lord Spencer, it seemed that everyone with a young protégé to promote beat a path to Pellew's door.

Pellew's years aboard the *Indefatigable* from 1794 to 1799 were, in many ways, the happiest and most fulfilling of his naval service, and they were years he harked back to throughout his career. Later, while struggling to navigate the treacherous political waters of the East India command, Pellew was to write to Sir Evan Nepean, former Secretary to the Admiralty: 'I wish to God I was out of it. I would rather command a frigate with her bowsprit over the rocks of Ushant all my life than command here on such terms.'[40]

Despite Pellew's good fortune, he had been pushing the good will of the Admiralty rather too hard[41] and some of his demands to Lord Spencer,

---

[38] Pellew's earlier biographers, Osler and Parkinson, claimed he swam to the stricken ship; however Taylor states that Pellew told his youngest son George that he reached the ship by using a rope to pull himself across the wreckage of the *Dutton*'s mainmast rigging. Taylor, p. 93.

[39] Taylor, p. 95.

[40] Pellew to Nepean, 1 June 1806. Quoted in Parkinson, *Edward Pellew: Viscount Exmouth, Admiral of the Red*, p. 359.

[41] Taylor, pp. 131–9.

2 George John Spencer, 2nd Earl Spencer, by John Singleton Copley, *c.* 1800.
Spencer was First Lord of the Admiralty, 1794–1801.

though they had an element of chutzpah, must have been regarded as somewhat beyond the pale. Following the *Droits de L'Homme* engagement in 1797 he wrote to Spencer asking for the *Indefatigable* to be re-rated from a fifth to a fourth rate in order to reward the entire company with promotion without splitting up the crew:

> I cannot speak too highly of my officers and men. I beg of your lordship to give them all a step without our parting; it can be done by making the Indefatigable a fourth-rate as a mark of your approbation of their conduct.[42]

Although there is something rather admirable about the boldness of Pellew's request, such a move would have been both unprecedented and inconceivable at the time. While this particular request was politely rejected, other demands Pellew made as he grew over-confident of his power and reputation riled Lord Spencer sufficiently to cause him to reassert his authority. In February 1799 Pellew received an order out of the blue informing him that he had been promoted and was to leave the *Indefatigable* and take command of the *Impetueux*, a 74-gun third rate with a notoriously ill-disciplined and mutinous crew. Due to his seniority, Pellew's promotion from a frigate to a ship of the line was quite justified and long overdue; nevertheless the order caused real distress. Despite his rather minimal schooling, Pellew had the ability to write eloquently and emotively, and throughout his long career he made skilful use of language to benefit his own ends and those of his men. However, even by Pellew's own standards, his exchange of letters with Lord Spencer during February 1799 is exceptionally moving and shows a man who was genuinely hurt and grieving the loss of something very dear to his heart.[43]

In an extraordinary third-person letter, Pellew pleaded not to be parted from his ship and his men:

> Sir E.P. is deprived of a desirable and advantageous appointment, after constant employment without relaxation for six years; and sent to a Ship at Portsmouth, amidst entire strangers and without being permitted to take one Officer, one Man, or even one Domestic. It is fair then to presume Sir E.P. has no sensibility, no attachment, no feeling, that his heart must be adamant, that he can part from faithful, and attached Companions, grown from boys to manhood under him, without a sorrowful Countenance, or a Moistened Eye. He grants it may be thought so. But he begs to assert the Contrary. And he dares to say, to those who think thus of him, that language does not furnish words sufficiently strong to express his feelings upon

---

[42] Pellew to Spencer, January 1797, in Corbett, pp. 381–328.

[43] Exmouth Papers, Box 22, MSS/92/027, Pellew to Spencer, no date 1799; Spencer to Pellew, 21 February 1799; Pellew to Spencer, 24 February 1799; Spencer to Pellew, 26 February 1799; Pellew to Spencer, 28 February 1799.

such unmerited hard treatment; nor can time, however soothing on most other occasions, blot from his remembrance, Circumstances so debasing to the reputation of an Officer; to your Lordship he leaves the regret of having occasioned them.[44]

As well as pushing the boundaries of Spencer's personal tolerance, Pellew was fighting a tide of changing policy within the Admiralty. Rodger has noted that:

> this independence declined rapidly in the 1790's. The construction and maintenance of large private followings was coming to be seen less as a contribution to the Navy's manpower, more as a threat to the Admiralty's control of the service, and Pellew's treatment was more a personal privilege denied to less fortunate officers.[45]

In the end, Pellew had no choice but to bow to orders and he transferred to the *Impetueux*, taking with him only the younger midshipmen and master's mates, and a small core of petty officers and seamen. This was the end of an era not just for Pellew, but for this pattern of naval recruitment.

> Pellew was almost certainly the last Cornishman, if not the last officer of any origin, to build up so formidable a following from his own county. 'The ships company, who have been my faithful companions during the war', as he described them in 1796, were representative of a method of recruitment which was rapidly dying.[46]

The *Impetueux* continued to be an insubordinate ship after Pellew took command and when the expected mutiny came later that year, he dealt swiftly and harshly with those responsible. It is unfortunate that Pellew's severe rates of punishment aboard the *Impetueux* at this time have erroneously been taken as typical of his entire career, as reference to his captain's and masters' logs shows this is far from the case. Despite the unpromising start, the crew of the *Impetueux* soon settled down under their new captain and Pellew continued to command the ship until the Peace of Amiens briefly brought the war to an end in 1802.

Like many of his contemporaries, Pellew spent the short Peace of Amiens 'on the beach', during which time, encouraged by Lord St Vincent, he made his first and only foray into politics as Member of Parliament for Barnstaple. When war recommenced in 1803, Pellew was given command of the 84-gun *Tonnant* and stationed in the Channel where he patrolled off Ferrol.

In 1804 Pellew was promoted to Rear Admiral and appointed as Commander in Chief of the East India station. Many of his former officers and men, including a number of the *Indefatigable*'s former young

---

[44] Exmouth Papers, Box 22, MSS/92/027, Pellew to Spencer, no date.

[45] Rodger, in Duffy, *Parameters of Naval Power 1650–1850*, p. 90.

[46] *Ibid.*, p. 89.

gentlemen, followed Pellew to India and benefited from his patronage and the opportunities offered by the east. But none benefited more than Pellew's own two sons, Pownoll and Fleetwood, whom he promoted outrageously young and far beyond their abilities. Although Fleetwood initially showed some ability, though surely not enough to justify being promoted to post captain at the age of eighteen, his elder brother Pownoll struggled from the first and his naval career was brief and unremarkable. Despite Fleetwood's early promise and his father's assertion that he was 'the flower of my flock and the flower of my fleet',[47] his career suffered a terminal setback ten years later in 1814 when the crew of his frigate *Resistance* mutinied in protest at harsh treatment. Pellew later came to understand the damage he had done by promoting his sons too early and too rapidly, but at this time his only concern was securing what he saw as the best advantages for them.

Although the East India command brought Pellew enormous wealth and enabled him to indulge his personal ambitions for his sons, it was not a happy time in his life. Pellew was uneasy with the decadent culture of the Indies and he became angry and aggressive when, as a result of political machinations, Admiral Troubridge was sent out to take over the command. He was also homesick; a devoted father and an affectionate husband, Pellew longed for home and came to hate India. He confided his grievances to his oldest and closest friend, Alex Broughton, and it was undoubtedly a grave loss when Broughton died in 1808, a year before Pellew returned to England. As his most recent biographer, Taylor, has ably illustrated, Edward Pellew was not only a man who had a gift for friendship but also one who needed friends.

In a serendipitous turn of events, just as Pellew lost his closest confidant, he was able to draw strength from another long-term friendship: the fortunes of war had brought him together with Jacques Bergeret once more. As captain of the frigate *Psyche*, Bergeret had been sent to harass British merchant shipping in the eastern seas, and had considerable success doing so until he was captured by the 36-gun frigate *San Fiorenzo*, Captain Henry Lambert. Pellew personally petitioned Lord Wellesley, the Governor General of Calcutta, to ensure that Bergeret was released on parole, but not before they had a touching reunion aboard the *Culloden* in Trincomalee before Bergeret's cartel sailed for Mauritius. In a letter to Bergeret around this time, Pellew wrote candidly, as he had to Broughton, of his struggles with Admiral Troubridge and his longing for home.

> I have written you twice and if you have received them they will inform you of the situation I stand in and of the arrival of Sir Thomas Troubridge. I shall not permit myself to speak to you on these

---

[47] Exmouth Papers, Box 22, MSS/92/027, Pellew to Broughton, 1 June 1808.

subjects here. They must be reserved for our next meeting. I wish that may be in Europe with all my heart.[48]

This letter is all the more remarkable considering the Commander in Chief's friend and correspondent was an enemy officer, but in such circumstances Pellew refused to be ruled by convention. In one exchange of letters the two veterans rather poignantly expressed their longing for their countries to declare peace so that they might share the long voyage home and enjoy each other's company and conversation, with Pellew writing: 'my return to Europe is very likely to happen shortly and were it peace I should like to call for you as my passenger'.[49] Inevitably this was not to be, though the friendship between Pellew and Bergeret outlasted the war by many years.

In 1809, Pellew finally left the East Indies and sailed home in the *Culloden* to a wife and family he had not seen for four years. After a short spell in command of the North Sea fleet, Pellew was appointed to the Mediterranean command in 1811. Of all the British naval stations, the Mediterranean was arguably the most strategically significant and carried the heaviest burden of diplomatic service, which consequently placed considerable social and political demands on the Commander in Chief. The Admiralty archives from Pellew's Mediterranean command contain a significant volume of diplomatic correspondence and intelligence reports, not just from his predecessor Admiral Sir Charles Cotton, but stretching back to Admiral Lord Collingwood who held the command from 1805 to 1810. Pellew retained the Mediterranean command until the war ended in 1814, when, in recognition of his long service, he was made Lord Exmouth of Canonteign.

Pellew had one final opportunity for naval action in 1816, when he led a combined British and Dutch fleet in an assault on Algiers after the failure of diplomatic attempts to free Christian slaves and curtail the threat posed by Barbary corsairs. It was a daunting task that involved sailing a fleet into an enemy harbour heavily defended by shore batteries and protected by the crescent island of Algezeire, which together mounted almost 600 guns. Knowing that casualties would be high and that many, including himself, might not return, Pellew refused requests from many of his former officers to join the expedition. Of the former Indefatigables, he allowed only John Gaze and William Kempthorne to accompany him to Algiers.

As a result of Pellew's meticulous planning and exemplary gunnery, the combined British and Dutch attack on Algiers was a success, though, as predicted, casualties were high. Pellew escaped the bombardment with minor injuries and his usual good fortune, though correspondence between former Indefatigables Nicholas Pateshall and William Kempthorne reveals

---

[48] Bergeret Papers, 153 J1, Pellew to Bergeret, 1 January 1809.
[49] *Ibid.*

that his injuries were more severe than Pellew himself admitted and popular accounts implied.

Arriving back in Britain, Pellew was feted by press and public and became the object of media fascination once more, as he had previously been in his partisan days. He was the recipient of gifts, civic honours and awards, including the Freedom of the City of Oxford and an honorary degree of Doctor of Civil Law from the University.[50] Pellew appears to have enjoyed many of these occasions: the papers recorded Lord Exmouth's 'gracious response' on receiving the freedom of the city and quoted extensively from the speech he gave at the dinner held in his honour.[51] There was certainly a part of Pellew that revelled in this attention, the hero of the people and the doyen of the Admiralty, but there was also a part that appreciated the quieter pleasures of home and family life. In addition to public honours and galas, Pellew was also showered with private congratulatory messages and invitations. One such solicitation was from Lord Keith, who wrote to invite him to stay at his home on his way to the triumphs in London. Though in previous years Pellew might have regarded an invitation from Lord Keith as an opportunity to bolster his standing and career, in this instance he politely declined.

> My dear Lord
> A thousand thanks for your kind letter and friendly note of invitation, which I would cheerfully accept if I was at liberty to pass upon your road but my dear good wife has very affectionately waylaid me to our daughters, Lady Halsted, near Alton on my road to London, and I am in duty bound to take her up there.[52]

Pellew's response to Lord Keith, which is not what might be expected from a man who some historians have regarded as overly ambitious and rather above himself, gives the sense of a man who has fought his last battle and whose priorities have turned from the service to more domestic concerns.

A later reflection of this change may be seen in correspondence between Pellew and Frederick Michell, who had commanded the battering flotilla at Algiers[53] and subsequently published an account of the bombardment.[54] Michell wrote to his former commander in 1824 sending him the blue flag that had flown from the *Queen Charlotte*'s mainmast during the bombardment. The flag arrived in time for the anniversary of Algiers, but Pellew's reply, while affectionate and grateful, reveals that he had spent the

---

[50] Oxford University archive has records confirming the degree of DCL awarded to Pellew but the text of the oration about him does not survive.

[51] *University and City Herald*, 2 December 1816.

[52] Pellew to Keith, 7 October 1816, private collection.

[53] Marshall, *Royal Naval Biography*, vol. 3, part II, p. 124.

[54] Michell, *Personal recollections of the expedition to Algiers in August, 1816*.

anniversary quietly with family, as he found marking the occasion brought back too many painful memories.

> A thousand thanks for your very kind present of my old flag. I have often wondered what became of it and how it was I had not got it. You are a bad fellow to purloin your old admiral's flag ...

> I was not at home the 27th and you know well that I am not a lover of such display as people make on those occasions. I never could enjoy such scenes – they give me more pain than pleasure. Not from any real indifference, but it always awakens melancholy thoughts ...[55]

Pellew served for two more years as Commander in Chief at Plymouth before he finally retired from the service in 1822. After his retirement Pellew resided at Teignmouth where he and Susan presided over a large and growing family, which included numerous grandchildren. Writing to Lord Sidmouth in 1827, in response to his 'congratulations on a twenty second grandchild', Pellew complained: 'the branches are heavy on one old trunk but as we can not help it we must bear it as well as others'.[56]

Despite his rather tongue-in-cheek complaint to Lord Sidmouth, Pellew was very much involved in domestic life at West Cliff House and appears to have welcomed the opportunity to settle down into the role of husband, father and grandfather. While there were no more queues of aspiring midshipmen and junior lieutenants coming to be fed by Lady Pellew,[57] family hospitality at West Cliff House encompassed a wide circle of relatives, friends and former shipmates, including his former adversary and lifelong friend, Jacques Bergeret and his wife. The Bergerets and the Pellews had clearly strengthened their close bonds of friendship in the years after the end of the war. Writing to Pellew in 1831, Bergeret expressed his regrets that he would not be able to visit that year, but added that he had enjoyed several visits from Fleetwood Pellew and his family:

> pour me conseiller l'expression de mes sentiments du plus affection respect et aussi de mes régrets de n'avoir pui aller vous faire une visite cette annee ... je me trouve cependant beaucoup mieux je me voyage que je viens de faire en Bretagne ... J'ai plusieurs fois le trés grand plaisir de revoir vos cher enfant Fleetwood, sa femme et leur charmante fille ce qui m'a rendre fort hereux.[58]

---

[55] Exmouth Papers, Caird Library, MIC/1, Letters and Papers of Admiral T. H. Michell, Exmouth to Michell, 30 August 1824.

[56] Exmouth to Sidmouth, 2 October 1827.

[57] Southampton Archives, D/CB/4/14/3, John Smyth to Rev. John Smyth, 14 May 1803.

[58] Bergeret Papers, 154 J1, Bergeret to Pellew, 12 July 1831. '[in order] to give expression to my most affectionate feelings of respect and also my regrets at not having been able to visit you this year ... I have nevertheless felt better since the journey I made to Britain ... I have several times had the

This circle of hospitality at West Cliff House also included the wide extended family of officers and men to whom Pellew had been captain, patron, and mentor. John Thomson junior, son of the *Indefatigable*'s first lieutenant, married into the Pellew family in 1816, so drawing family, friends and former shipmates even closer together. Pellew also kept up a regular correspondence with many of his former officers, including *Indefatigable* midshipman Nicholas Pateshall, who retained copies of letters he had received from his captain at key points in his life.

It seems likely that the theological and social inspiration for this extended family life came, at least initially, from Susan Pellew; however there is no evidence that Pellew himself saw any conflict in being both a decorated Admiral and an open-handed grandfather, wryly reconciled to having his afternoon nap interrupted by thundering feet racing around in the rooms overhead. Having at length realised his grave error in the overambitious promotion of his elder sons, the mature Edward Pellew was consistent in providing an accepting and stable environment for all his large extended family. By adopting the role of paterfamilias, Pellew was very much conforming to an archetypal ideal of Georgian parenthood, which was the subject of many books and pamphlets on the family published at the time. In *Parenting in England 1760–1830: Emotion, Identity and Generation*, Joanne Bailey writes:

> Similarly the notion that being a parent fully humanised an individual and made him or her truly sensible permeated ideas about grandparents who were supposed to share deep feelings for their children's children. The result was a flexible, diverse pattern of care, which linked carers and children across residences, locations and social ranks.[59]

After almost sixteen years back on land, ten of which passed in mainly contented retirement, Pellew died in 1833, aged seventy-five. He was mourned quietly at a service which, at his own insistence, was largely a private event. However, many men who had served with him wrote moving condolence letters expressing their wish that they could be present and adding that they would mark the time that the service was taking place.[60] All the condolence letters that have survived were those sent to Fleetwood Pellew, and they came from a wide range of former officers, both commissioned and warrant. One came from two generations of the Jenney

---

very great pleasure of seeing your dear son Fleetwood, his wife and their charming daughter, which has made me extremely happy.'

[59] Bailey, p. 199.

[60] Alexander Lumsdale, Master Superintendent of Portsmouth Dockyard, wrote: 'Few can feel his loss more than I do, and it would have been to me a mournful satisfaction to have paid my last affectionate tribute by following his last earthly remains to his place of rest.' Exmouth Papers, Box 28, MSS/92/027, Lumsdale to Fleetwood Pellew, 27 January 1833.

family whose careers Pellew had nurtured, and several from those who served aboard the *Indefatigable* in 1797, including George Cadogan, John Gaze, William Kempthorne and Jeremiah Coghlan.[61] The common word that many of the condolence letters share, particularly from those who served under Pellew as junior officers and young gentlemen, is that they all praised Pellew's 'kindness'. This shared vocabulary appears to be more than simply a stock phrase in the spirit of *de mortuis nil nisi bonum*, as the letters are not merely formulaic. Nor are they confined to men from one era, rank or ship; for instance James Weymss, grandson of the 5th Earl of Weymss, who entered the service as a midshipman on the *Tonnant*, wrote of Pellew's 'confidential kindness' and described him as 'my father afloat',[62] and Alexander Lumsdale, a warrant officer, praised his 'excellent qualities as well as the numerous kindnesses I received from him'.[63] On the basis of Pellew's earlier biographers, 'kindness' is not a word commonly associated with him; however the eloquent testimony of his former officers suggests that this was one of his defining characteristics. Pellew was large and loud, he could be greedy, arrogant and sharp-tongued and he was certainly an over-partial father to his own sons. Yet he was also intelligent, heroic, chivalrous, generous and possessed of great sensitivity and, contrary to Parkinson's assertion, he was indeed a man who was deeply loved and who had earned the lasting devotion of his men.

---

[61] Exmouth Papers, Box 22, MSS/92/027.

[62] Exmouth Papers, Box 28, MSS/92/027, James Weymss to Fleetwood Pellew, 28 January 1833.

[63] Exmouth Papers, Box 28, MSS/92/027, Alexander Lumsdale to Fleetwood Pellew, 27 January 1833.

2

'My Dear *Indefatigable*'

HMS *Indefatigable*, the ship with which Pellew's name is most closely associated, was built by Master Shipbuilder Henry Adams at Bucklers Hard shipyard on the Beaulieu River in Hampshire in 1781. She was one of five Ardent class 64-gun third-class ships of the line ordered by the Royal Navy over a five-year period from 1777 to 1782.[1] The Ardent class had been designed by Sir Thomas Slade well over a decade earlier and was based on the lines of the French ship *Le Fougueux*, built at Brest in 1747 and captured and bought into the Royal Navy in 1748. Two Ardent class ships were built in Slade's own lifetime, HMS *Ardent*, in 1761, and HMS *Raisonnable*, in 1765. Although the *Raisonnable* had a long and successful history, and remained in service until 1810, the Ardent class was already becoming obsolete by the time the *Indefatigable* was completed and launched in 1784. Sixty-four-gun ships were increasingly regarded as too small to serve in the line of battle, where their place was being taken by larger, heavily armed 74s, and too slow and heavy to take on frigates, despite the fact that the French were building ever larger ships in this class. At a time when some notions of honourable conduct in battle still prevailed, it was regarded as somewhat disreputable for a ship to take on an opponent of a lesser class. The outcome of such an engagement might have been assured, but the victory would hardly have been regarded as gallant. Consequently the *Indefatigable* was never commissioned as a ship of the line and she remained for ten years at Portsmouth Dockyard, where she had been transferred for completion.

At the outbreak of the Revolutionary War in 1793 concerns were growing that the French possessed a number of large, heavily armed frigates that were superior to anything in the service of the Royal Navy. Some of these frigates, such as *Brutus*, were old, cut down, or raséed 74-gun ships of the line, and Gardiner has argued that the threat posed by these aged and unstable ships was more imaginary than real.[2] Others such as the *Pomone*, launched at Rochefort in 1785, and captured by Pellew in the *Arethusa*[3] in 1794, were frigates of conventional layout but increased

---

[1] The five Ardent class ships ordered were: *Agamemnon* (Bucklers Hard, 1777), *Belliqueux* (Blackwell Yard, 1778), *Stately* (Northam, 1778), *Indefatigable* (Bucklers Hard, 1780), *Nassau* (Hilhouse, 1782).

[2] Gardiner, *Frigates of the Napoleonic Wars*, p. 40.

[3] Pellew and the *Arethusa* were part of Sir John Borlase Warren's squadron at this time. On 23 February, the squadron, composed of *Flora*, 36, *Concorde*, 36, *Melampus*, 36, *Arethusa*, 38, and *Nymphe*, 36, engaged *Engageante*,

size, which carried an armament of twenty-six 24-pound guns.[4] In response to the very real threat posed by these 24-pounder frigates, the navy began work to convert three obsolete 64-gun ships of the line into rasée frigates. The ships chosen were two of the Intrepid class, *Magnanime* and *Anson*, and one Ardent class, *Indefatigable*. The process involved removing the original quarterdeck and forecastle; the middle section of the upper deck was cut away to create a new forecastle and long quarterdeck connected with gangways; the old lower deck then became the new partially covered single gun deck; and the mast and yards were also reduced in size. Initially it was intended that the rasées should carry their original twenty-six 24-pounders on their lower decks, plus an additional eight 12-pounders on the quarterdeck and four 12-pounders on the forecastle; however this armament was altered by Admiralty order as the work progressed, and an additional six 42-pound carronades were added to the upper works, resulting in the ships being rated as 44-gun fifth rates.

BUILD

Builder: Henry Adams, Bucklers Hard

Class: Ardent

Type: Ship of the line/rasée frigate

Rating: 64-gun third rate/44-gun fifth rate

Laid down: May 1781

Launched: July 1784

Commissioned: December 1794

Raséed at: Portsmouth Dockyard

Started: September 1794

Completed: November 1794

Sailed: 16 February 1795

DIMENSIONS

Length gundeck: 160 feet 1½ inches

Length keel: 131 feet 10½ inches

Beam: 44 feet 5 inches

Depth hold: 12 feet 3 inches

Burthen: 1384 tons

36, *Pomone*, 44, *Résolue*, 36, and *Babet*, 20. During the action the *Arethusa* took possession of the *Pomone*.

[4] Gardiner, *Frigates of the Napoleonic Wars*, pp. 40–3.

ARMAMENT

Gun deck: 26 × 24-pounder guns

Quarterdeck: 10 × 12-pounder guns
            4 × 42-pounder carronades

Forecastle: 4 × 12-pounder guns
            2 × 42-pounder carronades

Although Pellew had had considerable success in the *Arethusa*, by late 1794 he was on the lookout for a new frigate. The *Arethusa* had participated in several notable engagements with Sir John Borlase Warren's squadron and taken a good number of prizes but she was not a particularly fast or responsive sailer. Consequently, Pellew wrote to the First Lord of the Admiralty, Lord Chatham, to request that he be given the new rasée *Indefatigable*. Chatham, a long-standing supporter of Pellew, was only too happy to oblige, replying in November 1794:

> With respect to your wishes of going into the Indefatigable, I shall have great pleasure in meeting them, and this circumstance will occasion no change in your destination. I am sorry that the Arethusa has not answered in point of sailing, as I had expected her to have been among the best.[5]

As the alterations to the *Indefatigable* were still underway, Pellew had to wait two months to take command of his new ship. In the intervening period, the modifications to the *Anson* had already been completed and the ship had been given to another captain of Warren's squadron, Philip Durham. The *Anson* joined the squadron in Falmouth in January 1795 and Pellew lost no time in questioning Durham about her sailing qualities, 'her behaviour at sea, and her capacity in carrying her masts and sails'.[6] On hearing that the ship rolled heavily and that her officers feared she was undermasted, Pellew immediately wrote to the Admiralty requesting that the *Indefatigable* should retain her original masts and spars. Earlier in the month Pellew had already written to the Admiralty, where Lord Spencer had recently replaced Lord Chatham as First Lord, to request an alteration to the ship's armament, by transferring fourteen 32-pound carronades from the *Arethusa* to the *Indefatigable*. Although Spencer cautiously consented to allow Pellew the carronades, 'if it can be done without too much transgressing Rules',[7] the Navy Board was not inclined to be dictated to by a junior captain and neither request was granted, on the grounds that

---

[5] Chatham to Pellew, 27 November 1794, in Parkinson, *Edward Pellew: Viscount Exmouth, Admiral of the Red*, p. 116.

[6] Gardiner, *Frigates of the Napoleonic Wars*, p. 41.

[7] Spencer to Pellew, in Parkinson, *Edward Pellew: Viscount Exmouth, Admiral of the Red*, p. 119.

'We cannot in the present Urgent State of the Service comply with your request'.[8]

Pellew was not a man to give up easily however. He remained convinced that the *Indefatigable* was undermasted and would roll dangerously, so he bypassed the Navy Board and wrote directly to the Admiralty suggesting alternative alterations that he hoped would be 'deem'd worthy of my Lords Consideration as being the next preferable thing to her proper Masts'.[9]

Pellew's recommendations aimed to ameliorate the effect of the ship's undermasting by lifting her centre of gravity by reducing and raising the ship's ballast and carrying a larger number of 18-pound guns on the quarterdeck. The Admiralty referred Pellew's requests to the Navy Board who replied that 'notwithstanding it may be found proper to make an alteration in her Masts at a future opportunity, the present will not admit of any alteration further than lessening her quantity of Ballast'.[10] Although the Navy Board could not be moved, Pellew's request had not fallen on deaf ears, and a few days later he received a private response from Lord Spencer.

> Your statement respecting the two Ships is certainly very good reasoning & I wish I could have persuaded the Navy Board to listen to it, but they are absolutely determined to have a Trial of their own chusing, & till Experience has convinced them, it will be impossible for me to set up my Ignorance against their Wisdom. You will of course keep this letter to yourself.[11]

It did not take long for Pellew's concerns to be borne out. *Anson* continued to perform poorly, repeatedly carrying away her yards and springing her masts, and in one incident lost chain and futtock plates. The newly launched *Magnanime* also suffered and was damaged aloft on her first operational cruise with the Irish squadron. When the *Indefatigable* was eventually completed and ordered to join John Borlase Warren's squadron at Falmouth, she damaged her mainmast during the short cruise down the Channel.[12]

The Admiralty could not ignore such woeful underperformance, and finally in March 1796 all three rasées were recalled to have their original mast and yards replaced. The *Indefatigable*'s refit was completed by the end of the following month and Pellew reported her ready to put to sea

[8] Marshall, Hemslow and Marsh to Pellew, 2 February 1795, in Parkinson, *Edward Pellew: Viscount Exmouth, Admiral of the Red*, p. 121.

[9] Pellew to Admiralty, 6 February 1795, in Parkinson, *Edward Pellew: Viscount Exmouth, Admiral of the Red*, p. 123.

[10] Ibbetson to Pellew, 12 February 1795, in Parkinson, *Edward Pellew: Viscount Exmouth, Admiral of the Red*, p. 123.

[11] Spencer to Pellew, 16 February 1796, in Parkinson, *Edward Pellew: Viscount Exmouth, Admiral of the Red*, p. 124.

[12] Gardiner, *Frigates of the Napoleonic Wars*, p. 42.

under her new masts on 25 April. *Anson* and *Magnanime*'s alterations were completed later in the year, but even after the refit they continued to be unweatherly ships, particularly in heavy seas. When stationed off Brest in 1807, *Anson*'s last captain, Charles Lydiard, expressed his regret that she was appointed to such a station, as she was such a bad sea boat.[13] Lydiard's fears were far from unfounded and in December of that year *Anson* was wrecked in Mounts Bay off the southern tip of Cornwall, with the loss of sixty lives including her captain.

Most of Pellew's biographers have suggested that his detailed understanding of the technical challenges facing the *Indefatigable*, and his tenacity in arguing with both the Navy Board and the Admiralty to rectify them, were a direct result of the experience he gained under the command of John Schank building a flotilla of ships on Lake Champlain during the American War of Independence. Only Parkinson has argued otherwise, suggesting that Pellew's insight was simply common sense:

> Some have supposed that he benefited here by his early experience on Lake Champlain, and his friendship with Schanck which dated from that time. This theory has little to commend it. Schanck was a skilful shipwright and spent his ingenuity in designing centre-boards for frigates, and similar devices. But no such extraordinary skill was needed in this matter. No captain liked his ship's centre of gravity to be very low ... Little more than common sense was needed to detect the Board's mistake. And common sense was a quality in which Pellew excelled.[14]

It is somewhat disingenuous of Parkinson to dismiss the expertise Pellew gained from working with Schank, as in his later fictional biography of Horatio Hornblower he credits the *Indefatigable*'s alterations to Hornblower who had learned about Schank's ideas from a carpenter who had previously served under him.[15]

> *Hornblower:* With the masts and spars ordered there is a danger that her centre of gravity will be too low.

> *Pellew:* Just entered and you already know better than the Navy Board!

> *Hornblower:* I think, sir, that Captain Schank, were he here, would advise reducing the amount of ballast.

> *Pellew:* You are known to John Schank my old shipmate? Good God![16]

Of the three ships raséed in 1794 the *Indefatigable* was undoubtedly

[13] *Ibid.*, p. 43.

[14] Parkinson, *Edward Pellew: Viscount Exmouth, Admiral of the Red*, p. 121.

[15] Parkinson, *The Life and Times of Horatio Hornblower*, p. 42.

[16] *Ibid.*, p. 49.

the most successful, but even she had her faults. Parkinson claimed that, carrying her original masts and sail area, she was an exceptionally fast ship;[17] however, this is contested by Gardiner who notes that the best quoted speed for the *Indefatigable* was twelve and a half knots before the wind.[18] In addition, one of the *Indefatigable*'s subsequent, and very successful, captains, Sir Graham Moore, reportedly found her awkward to handle close to shore.[19] In view of these flaws, it is a remarkable testament to Pellew's exemplary skill as a sea officer that he went on to achieve such success with the ship. In the words of Gardiner: 'That Pellew did not complain is possibly a reflection on his superb seamanship, rather than any outstanding qualities in the ship.'[20] The *Indefatigable* may have had her flaws but as a large, powerful and heavily armed frigate she was well suited to Pellew's capabilities and he had every opportunity to take advantage of her potential.

In early 1794, in response to the threat posed by marauding French frigates in the Channel, the Admiralty had established a number of detached cruising squadrons. These independent squadrons were composed of fast, heavy frigates commanded by the most gifted young captains at the Admiralty's disposal, and supported by a number of smaller vessels, such as sloops, cutters and despatch luggers. Rather than being attached to a fleet and answerable to a Commander in Chief, these squadrons operated independently under direct Admiralty orders. This arrangement had a number of advantages, some tactical, some political, some financial. Detached squadrons were a powerful weapon that the Admiralty used to great effect in the early years of the war. They could be deployed at short notice, and could put to sea in considerably less time than it took to mobilise a fleet. In addition to harassing the enemy at sea and undertaking shore-based operations such as destroying signal stations and cutting out vessels, they also played an invaluable role in gathering intelligence, and undertaking strategic and tactical reconnaissance. The financial rewards from such commands could be lucrative, as cruising squadrons had the best possibility of taking prizes, and no Commander in Chief to take a cut of the prize money.

Pellew had been appointed to just such a squadron in 1794 when he was given command of the *Arethusa*. The Western Squadron was established by the Admiralty that same year under the command of Sir John Borlase Warren, a shipmate of Pellew's from the *Apollo*. The squadron was based at Falmouth and comprised five heavy frigates, each mounting no less than 36

---

[17] Parkinson, *Edward Pellew: Viscount Exmouth, Admiral of the Red*, p. 127.

[18] Gardiner, *Frigates of the Napoleonic Wars*, p. 43.

[19] Taylor, p. 122.

[20] Gardiner, *Frigates of the Napoleonic Wars*, p. 43.

guns.[21] Osler credits the original idea of establishing the Western Squadron to Pellew, claiming that he put the proposal to Warren and asked him to exert his influence with the Admiralty to apply for such a command. There is no evidence to support Osler's claim, but he is quite correct in stating that all the officers of the Western Squadron 'rose to high distinction, and a list of well-known flag-officers may be traced in connexion with them, such as, perhaps, was never formed by any other service'.[22]

Such was the success of the Western Squadron that the Admiralty split the force in early 1795 and established a second independent squadron, also based in Falmouth, under Pellew's own command. Pellew's squadron was composed of five powerful frigates, *Indefatigable*, 44, *Concorde*, 36, *Jason*, 38, *Revolutionnaire*, 36, and *Amazon*, 36, two of which, *Amazon* and *Revolutionnaire*, were captained by his close friends, Robert Carthew Reynolds and Frank Cole. Three chasse-marées, a cutter and the *Duke of York* hired armed lugger supported the squadron.

Command of the Western Squadron gave Pellew ample opportunity to exercise his undoubted talents as a partisan commander, but at the same time it also enabled him to consolidate his base in Falmouth, a town where his family had deep roots and increasing influence. Despite its distance from London, Falmouth was a port of considerable significance during the early years of the French Revolutionary and Napoleonic Wars. It was ideally located as the base for the Western Squadrons as, not only was it strategically placed at the mouth of the Channel and the edge of the Atlantic, it was the closest British port to Brest, and provided a large sheltered harbour that vessels as large as frigates could enter or leave, regardless of wind or tide. In addition, Falmouth was an important Post Office packet station, serving the West Indies, North and South America, the Mediterranean and the crucial allied port of Lisbon; and in the early years of the war, it also became a dedicated transhipment port for Admiralty despatches.[23] Since the late seventeenth century Falmouth had also been designated as a customs out port, with its own legal quays, customs house and customs officers.[24]

Falmouth may have been regarded by some as remote and provincial, but by the end of the eighteenth century it was a rich town and Pellew was a man of considerable influence and standing. In addition to having connections to the town through his grandfather, Pellew's elder brother

---

[21] In 1794 the Western Squadron was composed of *Flora*, 36, Captain Sir John Borlase Warren; *Melampus*, 36, Captain Thomas Wells; *Concorde*, 36, Captain Sir Richard Strachan; *Nymphe*, 38, Captain George Murray; and *Arethusa*, 38, Captain Sir Edward Pellew. They were later joined by *Diamond*, 38, Captain Sir Sidney Smith; *Artois*, 38, Captain Edmund Nagle; and *Galatea*, 32, Captain Richard Keats. Taylor, pp. 78–80.

[22] Osler, p. 88.

[23] Morriss, pp. 22–3.

[24] Pawlyn, p. 11.

Samuel had been appointed as Collector of Customs at Falmouth in 1784, a post he held for almost fifty years. After his marriage to Susan in 1784, Pellew and his new wife had set up home in Flushing, across the harbour from Falmouth, where they lived in a handsome terraced house on New Road, next door to packet captain William Kempthorne,[25] whose son later served as a midshipman aboard the *Indefatigable*. As the commodore of a naval squadron based at Falmouth, brother of the highest ranking civic official in the town and an increasingly wealthy individual in his own right, Sir Edward Pellew was a man of considerable status in Falmouth at the time, though his rapid elevation inevitably resulted in petty jealousies arising.[26] The life suited Pellew well; he was able to exercise his talents as an independent commander, free from the interference of a Commander in Chief, and he had ample opportunity to secure financial reward and progress the careers of the officers and men who looked to him for patronage. With his family settled in the squadron's home port, he was able to return regularly between cruises to spend time with his wife and their growing family.

The *Indefatigable* was a hugely successful command and, despite the notable achievements of her later commanders, it is Pellew's name that is still associated with the ship. In addition to the celebrated engagements with *Les Droits de L'Homme* and the *Virginie*, the *Indefatigable* also took numerous smaller prizes. It was not unknown for the frigate to capture three or four prizes in as many days, and in one ten-day period between 11 and 21 March 1796, Pellew's squadron captured a total of nine vessels.[27] With an independent squadron at his command, a tried and trusted crew and the blessing of the Admiralty, Pellew had ample opportunity to pursue both reward and glory. Without exception, all Pellew's biographers regard this period as the happiest and most fulfilling of his long naval service, and it is little wonder that Pellew was later to refer to the ship that finally enabled him to achieve the security and status he craved as 'my dear *Indefatigable*'.[28]

As the war dragged on and the threat of invasion from France increased, the Admiralty moved to a system of close inshore blockade. This shift in tactics brought both the Western Squadrons under the indirect command of Admiral Lord Bridport, Commander in Chief of the Channel fleet, although the Admiralty reserved the right to direct the deployment of the squadrons. As semi-autonomous commodores within his command,

[25] *Ibid.*, p. 42.

[26] Taylor, pp. 89, 126–7.

[27] ADM 51/1171, Captain's Log, His Majesty's Ship the Indefatigable, 1 March 1796–28 February 1797.

[28] Exmouth Papers, Box 22, Pellew to Spencer, 24 February 1799.

Bridport regarded Warren and Pellew with antipathy and distrust, feelings that both commodores reciprocated.[29]

From 1796 onwards the *Indefatigable* was to be found traversing the stormy seas of the Bay of Biscay, monitoring French ports from Ushant to Cape Finisterre, or patrolling the inner reaches of Brest roads, observing the movements of the French fleet and delivering intelligence back to Admiral John Colpoys whose fleet was stationed off Ushant. Blockade duty was difficult and dangerous, with ships stationed on the enemy's lee shore throughout the year, regardless of the weather. Blockade ships had to be powerful enough to resist being driven off station, fast enough to escape capture when necessary, and weatherly to avoid being wrecked.[30] It was a tedious and hazardous undertaking, but the *Indefatigable* was well matched to the task and Pellew executed his duties with diligence and zeal, though a certain terseness can be detected in his Admiralty despatches around this time. A 'Report of The State of the Enemies Fleet at Brest by Sir Edward Pellew Bart, Captain of His Majesty's Ship Indefatigable', dated 29 December 1798, reads simply: 'The Enemies Fleet appears to be exactly in the same state as when last reported on the 22nd inst. Both in number and situation.'[31]

Pellew appears to have taken personal responsibility for monitoring the state of the Brest fleet, spending many hours at the mast head each day. Osler quotes one of the *Indefatigable*'s older midshipmen as recalling

> that on being one day relieved to go down to my dinner, I was obliged to have some of the main-top-men to help me down the rigging, I was so benumbed with the intense cold: yet the captain was there six or seven hours at a time, without complaining, or taking any refreshment.[32]

The identity of the benumbed midshipman is sadly unknown; however his shipmate, John Gaze, added a note to the Pellew family's own copy of Osler confirming that 'Watching that fleet did Sir Edward as much credit as anything I know'.[33]

---

[29] When Bridport finally retired in 1799, Pellew famously wrote to his friend, Alex Broughton; 'You will have heard that we are to have a new Commander-in-Chief, heaven be praised. The old one is scarcely worth drowning, a more contemptible or more miserable animal does not exist. I believe there never was a Man so universally despised by the whole Service. A mixture of Ignorance, avarice and spleen.' Pellew to Broughton, December 1799. Parkinson, *Edward Pellew: Viscount Exmouth, Admiral of the Red*, p. 228.

[30] Gardiner, *Frigates of the Napoleonic Wars*, p. 163.

[31] ADM 1/108/767, Commander in Chief, Channel, documents, 29 December 1798.

[32] Osler, p. 137.

[33] Pinhey, p. 19.

Despite the grim tedium of blockade duty, appointment to a frigate was still the most sought-after station for ambitious young gentlemen of the fleet. In addition to learning their trade from arguably the most gifted and daring captains that the Admiralty had at their disposal, frigate service also provided ample opportunity to gain experience, promotion and prize money. In the words of N. A. M. Rodger:

> Many of the best captains for training youngsters were in frigates, and frigates, with continual cruising and activity were the best schools of service. Their officers and men were recognised (not least by themselves) as a professional elite, honed by independent cruising and frequent action.[34]

It is hardly surprising that many authors of naval adventure fiction have chosen to place their heroes aboard frigates during their formative years as midshipmen, and it is while serving aboard frigates, first as junior officers and later as fledgling captains, that many of them have their greatest adventures.

The opportunities of serving among the fleet's elite are vividly illustrated by the experiences of the *Indefatigable*'s most famous fictional midshipman, Horatio Hornblower. In *Mr. Midshipman Hornblower*, the sixth book in the series, written by C. S. Forester in 1950 to provide a backstory for his eponymous anti-hero, Hornblower begins his naval career aboard *Justinian*, a decaying ship of the line lying at anchor at Spithead, with a 'useless captain ... worn out first lieutenant and old midshipmen'.[35] When Hornblower receives the offer of a transfer to the *Indefatigable* at the outbreak of war, he initially refuses, due to a misplaced sense of loyalty to the elderly and ailing Captain Keene. Keene, however, makes it clear that he would be foolish to refuse such an opportunity.

> "I don't have to point out that any ambitious young officer would jump at the chance of serving in a frigate!"
>
> "A frigate!" said Hornblower.
>
> Everybody knew of Pellew's reputation and success. Distinction, promotion, prize money – an officer under Pellew's command could hope for all these. Competition for nomination to the *Indefatigable* must be intense and this was the chance of a lifetime.[36]

In the 1998 UK televised adaptation of the Hornblower novels, another of *Justinian*'s young gentlemen, Midshipman Archie Kennedy, breaks the news of their good fortune to his jubilant shipmates by paraphrasing the St Crispin's Day speech from Shakespeare's *Henry V*: 'A third of the crew are

---

[34] Rodger, *The Command of the Ocean: A Naval History of Britain 1649–1815*, p. 511.

[35] Forester, *Mr. Midshipman Hornblower*, p. 36.

[36] *Ibid.*, pp. 35–6.

to remain with Justinian. A third will go to Arethusa under Black Charlie Hammond, and we few – we fortunate few – Keene has recommended our transfer to ... Indefatigable!'[37] Hornblower and his shipmates were indeed fortunate to be joining the elite of the Royal Navy. Rodger has identified three types of midshipmen from this period: 'sophisticated and hard–swearing in ships of the line, slovenly and ill-bred in the little sloops and brigs, but an elite in the frigates, smart and proud of early danger and responsibility'.[38]

Hornblower, Kennedy and their historical counterparts had much to hope for: action, prize money and early promotion. But the young men starting out in a frigate like the *Indefatigable*, with a captain like Pellew, could also expect less tangible benefits, such as a degree of protection from the worst excesses of naval life.

On entering a new ship, all young gentlemen, whatever their rank or station in life, could expect some degree of ragging at the hands of their messmates. They might also be subjected to an 'Inquisition'[39] by the omnipotent figure of the senior midshipman of the mess. Such rites of passage were expected to be endured without complaint but, as always, there is a fine line between a bit of rough treatment and outright bullying and the potential existed for sport to turn into abuse, particularly on a ship where discipline was lax. In *Mr. Midshipman Hornblower* Forester chillingly illustrates the fear and misery that a vindictive senior messmate could inflict on his shipmates, where *Justinian*'s gunroom is ruled by Jack Simpson, a violent and malicious older midshipman. Simpson is a typical, if extreme, example of the kind of men described by Rodger as 'the disappointed midshipmen, embittered and often hard drinking men in their thirties or even forties who had hoped and failed to get a commission'.[40]

Simpson had apparently always been an ingenious tyrant, but now, embittered and humiliated by his failure to pass his examination for lieutenant, he was a worse tyrant and his ingenuity had multiplied

---

[37] *The Even Chance*, screenplay by Russell Lewis, for Meridian Broadcasting, 1998.

[38] Rodger, *The Command of the Ocean: A Naval History of Britain 1649–1815*, p. 508.

[39] Fictional representations of the 'Inquisition' appear in Forester's *Mr. Midshipman Hornblower*, p. 16, and also the televised adaptation of the book, *The Even Chance*. An early twentieth century account of a midshipman's 'Inquisition' appears in Lt-Commander Walker's *Young Gentlemen: The Story of Midshipmen from the 17th Century to the present day*, p. 68.

[40] Rodger, *The Command of the Ocean, A Naval History of Britain 1649–1815*, p. 507.

itself ... he was diabolically clever at making other people's lives a burden to them.[41]

The television adaptation of the novel, *The Even Chance*, depicts the arbitrary terror and intimidation that Forester describes, in the portrayal of the troubled Midshipman Kennedy.[42] His story, though not specific in detail, strongly suggests the bullying, humiliation and abuse which it was only too easy for older bitter midshipmen to inflict on their younger messmates, particularly on a disfunctional ship with an inadequate captain and inefficient first lieutenant. Thus Kennedy's joy at their impending transfer to the *Indefatigable* may well be motivated by more than glory and prize money; he is judging, rightly, that the chances of such persecution on a frigate, and one commanded by Pellew, are almost nil. While these were not matters likely to be aired in personal letters or recorded in official documentation, it is probably safe to presume that a captain who, as a midshipman himself, had been famous for using his considerable boxing skills to defend younger shipmates against bullies, would be no less tolerant of such behaviour as a commander. When one of the *Indefatigable*'s historical young gentlemen, Nicholas Pateshall, was involved in a brawl with a seaman, he did indeed earn Pellew's wrath, though his anger did not last long.

With a cohort of senior officers known and trusted by Pellew, young gentlemen joining the *Indefatigable* had little fear of suffering from the arbitrary punishments and petty revenges that incompetent and resentful officers could inflict on their subordinates, which in some cases could result in innocent young gentlemen being gratuitously court martialled. No less a man than Admiral Cuthbert Collingwood was charged, when a young lieutenant, on a vexatious complaint brought by a jealous commanding officer. Collingwood was acquitted of all charges but still had to endure a court martial. On a discontented or ill-disciplined ship small acts of insubordination and malicious behaviour could escalate rapidly, resulting in situations that inexperienced or incompetent officers could find difficult to manage. Two of the *Indefatigable*'s young gentlemen, George Cadogan and William Kempthorne, had very different but equally damaging experiences of this nature later in their careers.

On board a ship commanded by Pellew there was little to fear from harsh or unjustified punishment, though strict discipline was rigorously maintained. Taylor and Rae have shown that Pellew was far from the martinet that Parkinson has suggested. Following John D. Byrn's methodology of analysing punishment statistics on board ships, Taylor has used Pellew's masters' and captain's logs to show that Parkinson's

---

[41] Forester, *Mr. Midshipman Hornblower*, p. 15.

[42] Midshipman Kennedy appears only briefly in *Mr. Midshipman Hornblower*; however his character was significantly expanded and developed in the 1998 ITV television series.

characterisation of Pellew as a stern disciplinarian is inaccurate and not borne out by the evidence. In fact, Pellew did not in ordinary circumstances[43] order much punishment at all and normally on the *Indefatigable* he did not need to.

It is clear from contemporary correspondence that Pellew took his patriarchal responsibility to his young gentlemen seriously, and that he strove not only to be their surrogate father, but also their friend. During this period, the dual role of father and friend was considered to be a very positive model of parenting and patronage, as Joanne Bailey has ably illustrated in *Parenting in England 1760–1830: Emotion, Identity and Generation.* In addition to suggesting a degree of intimacy, the term 'friend' was often used to describe family members who embodied the role of guide, protector and mentor. In her 1824 publication, *Friendly Advice on the Management and Education of Children*, Louisa Hoare informed middle- and labouring-class parents: 'Happy will it be for your children, if by prudence and tenderness you can bring them not only to honor you as parents, but to be free and open with you as their best and kindest friends.'[44]

Pellew had himself described Philemon Pownoll as both father and friend and there was a conscious effort on his own part to live up to this ideal. This is in part a persona he chose to be identified with in later life, but it was far from being merely a superficial affectation. John Smyth, a midshipman on one of Pellew's later commands, the *Tonnant*, recalled his welcome aboard the ship

> I arrived safely aboard the *Tonnant* on Saturday morning, as soon as I came on deck I asked for the commanding officer, on which I was sent for into the Ward Room, where I was introduced to Mr Bell[45] the first lieutenant, the most pleasant gentlemanlike man I ever saw, very like Uncle George, he asked me whether I was come to join the ship to which I replied in the affirmative. He then conducted me to the Captain to whom I delivered your letter. He told me I should be supplied with what I want, he then sent me ashore to dine with Lady Pellew and spend the evening there, the next day we mustered and afterwards the Captain asked me to do him the honour of my company at dinner.[46]

To the young gentlemen of the *Indefatigable*, Pellew was both father and subsequently friend, and many of them were later to recall that they found in Edward and Susan Pellew parental love and encouragement

---

[43] The exception is the mutinous ship of the line *Impetueux*, where Pellew's rate of punishment shows a marked increase.

[44] Bailey, p. 85.

[45] George Bell was Acting Master of the *Indefatigable* in January 1797.

[46] Smyth Papers, D/CB/4/14/2, John Smyth to Rev. John Gee Smyth, 3 May 1803.

that were not lightly forgotten. This was particularly true of two of the 1797 cohort, William Kempthorne and Jeremiah Coghlan, who had both lost their fathers and who served almost their entire naval careers under Pellew's command. Of course it is not hard to make the link between the loss of Pellew's own father and the exceedingly high value he placed on family life. However it is clear that Pellew's and Susan's commitment to parental support went far beyond duty and mere good will, and extended to opening their home to young officers and providing them with financial and emotional support when circumstances required.

For the younger boys, in particular, Pellew effectively acted *in loco parentis.* The two most extensive surviving archives of correspondence from midshipmen who served under Pellew, Nicholas Pateshall and John Smyth, make it clear that he corresponded regularly with their parents. John Smyth refers to letters from Sir Edward to his father[47] and it is evident that Ann Pateshall also received letters from Pellew about her son. This aspect of their captain's care was not always so welcome to the boys concerned. Nicholas Pateshall wrote to his brother speaking highly of his captain's command skills but complaining that he controlled his allowance too tightly and made him account for everything too closely.[48]

The advantage derived from investing in the careers and well-being of young officers was of course mutual. While the young gentlemen who appear on the *Indefatigable*'s 1797 muster benefited from serving on a fine frigate with a daring and gifted commander, the ship's officers and company gained a cohort of competent and diligent midshipmen and volunteers, and the Admiralty acquired a cadre of promising future commanders. With one or two exceptions, the *Indefatigable*'s young officers grew into their roles in the service; in their subsequent naval careers they were hard-working and, on occasion, inspired sea officers, and in their peacetime occupations in later civilian life they were engaged and compassionate citizens. The concern and affection that are evidenced by the ongoing correspondence between many of these men in later life are testimony to the lifelong friendships cemented in the midshipmen's berth of the *Indefatigable* and suggest that this was a time of their lives that they continued to remember with some pride.

---

[47] Smyth Papers, D/CB/4/14/5; in a letter dated 'April 14, off Ferrol' John Smyth wrote 'I hope that Sir Edward Pellew gave such an account of my conduct that you will not think me undeserving of it.'

[48] Pateshall Papers, A95/EB/LD/1, Nicholas Pateshall to Edmund Pateshall, 20 January 1797.

NICHOLAS PATESHALL

As is so often the case, fictional adventures rarely outdo reality, and there is one of the young gentlemen of the *Indefatigable*'s 1797 muster, Nicholas Pateshall, whose early experiences of joining Pellew's crew mirror those of the fictional Horatio Hornblower. Nicholas wrote numerous letters to family and friends throughout his naval career, many of which survive in the family archive in Hereford. The young man's early letters give a rare first-hand account of what it meant to join the fleet's elite and become one of Pellew's Indefatigables.

Nicholas was sent to Plymouth in early 1794 to begin his naval career as a thirteen-year-old volunteer. The new rating of 'Boy first class or volunteer' had been introduced that year for 'young gentlemen intended for the sea service'.[49] Nicholas was from the sort of family that had long supplied sons to the navy; he was a younger son in a family of two daughters and six sons born to a country squire who died when Nicholas was nine and many of his siblings younger. Their future was naturally a concern to their widowed mother, as Nicholas was well aware when he wrote to his brother, Edmund, in November 1794: 'My dear brother, when we come to think within ourselves how many children she has to provide for we ought to take whatever she appoints for us.'[50] Despite his awareness of his responsibilities, Nicholas promptly abandoned his ship in Plymouth and returned home to his appalled mother. In a letter to Edmund, he attempted to explain that there was a good reason for his action:

> Dear brother, It was not that I took a dislike to the sea, it was because the ship would not sail this eight or ten months and the captain is so very ill. I don't think he will live to go to sea again. I therefore know it would be very dull for me to stop so long at Plymouth spending time to no advantage.[51]

Nicholas's experience here directly parallels Hornblower's, who initially found himself posted to a decaying ship of the line with a sick and worn out captain.

> Captain Keene ... was a sick man, of a melancholy disposition. He had not the fame which enabled some captains to fill ships with enthusiastic volunteers, and he was devoid of the personality which might have made enthusiasts out of the sullen pressed men.[52]

---

[49] Rodger, *The Command of the Ocean: A Naval History of Britain 1649–1815*, p. 508.

[50] Pateshall Papers, A95/EB/42/1, Nicholas Pateshall to Edmund Pateshall, 25 November 1794.

[51] *Ibid.*

[52] Forester, *Mr. Midshipman Hornblower*, p. 13.

However, like Hornblower, Pateshall's opportunity did come, though less immediately, truth being, if not always stranger, then certainly often slower than fiction. About a month earlier, Nicholas's mother, Ann, had written to Captain Charles Henry Lane, who had helped her to find a position for her son, commenting on his apparent aversion to a career in the navy: 'I have also hinted at the discredit that will follow if you find upon conversing with him that he really has so great an aversion as his letters seem to indicate (which are very melancholy indeed).'[53] Nicholas, however, spoke to his brother Edmund of a longing to be actively engaged with a life at sea and a cause that could bring both honour and a sense of achievement:

> I would with all my heart go with any ship that would sail immediately as I told Captain Chamberlaine ... I don't think there is any state in life more honourable or more pleasant than the sea fairing life ...[54]

Nicholas's family correspondence eloquently reveals what was a common trajectory for young men from minor aristocratic or county families, or those hovering on the further fringes of society like Pellew himself, son of a packet captain, or Collingwood, with a family in trade – young men, sometimes without a father to help them find their direction in life, and without 'interest' in the form of influential naval officers or powerful political allies to further their career. Ann Pateshall evidently did have some allies, but her first attempt at placing her son in the service seems to have resulted in disillusionment and misconduct, as a letter from Captain Lane reveals when he asked Mrs Pateshall: 'Whether he is sensible of his misconduct and whether he has made any resolutions in consequences of it.'[55]

Whether or not Nicholas was sensible of his misconduct, his troubles continued: correspondence between his mother and Captain Lane throughout the autumn of 1794 makes continued reference to his poor behaviour and disaffection. Perhaps because of her son's failure to take to the navy, Ann Pateshall next turned to the East India service. Several letters from the early part of 1795 indicate that she was attempting to secure a berth for her son aboard the *Rodney*; however, by April of that year it was clear her best efforts had failed.[56]

[53] Pateshall Papers, BD30/9/1-50, Ann Pateshall to Charles Henry Lane, 27 October 1794.

[54] Pateshall Papers, A95/EB/41/1, Nicholas Pateshall to Edmund Pateshall, 25 November 1794.

[55] Pateshall Papers, BD30/9/1-50, Captain Charles Henry Lane to Ann Pateshall, 2 January 1795.

[56] Pateshall Papers, BD30/9/1-50, Exchange of letters between Captain Evans, Ann Pateshall and John Davies concerning Davies and Captain Caruthers of the East India Company attempting to get Pateshall taken on as a midshipman in the *Rodney*, owned by a William Cameron, February–April 1795.

Unfortunately there is a gap in the surviving correspondence at this critical juncture in Nicholas's life, and there is no indication how his troubled career took a turn from failure and disaffection to something altogether brighter. At some point between April and October 1795 something occurred that had a decisive impact on Pateshall's life, as the next letter he writes to his mother is from the *Indefatigable*.

Indefatigable, Monday 5th 1795

Dear Mama

I write with a great deal of pleasure to enquire after your health and with as much pleasure to inform you that we are going to sail this evening with the *Revolutionnaire* and two more frigates who are cruising off the harbour whose names we know not.

By a packet arrived from Lisbon said that there was 4 frigates, a cutter and a sloop of war cruising off Lisbon therefore the Admiralty has ordered we brave fellows there where we may hope to give a good account of them by next Sunday ...

PS I hope you will forgive this horrid scrawl but I am so overjoyed I know not what to do. We fear not while we have this brave commander Sir Edward.[57]

The transformation here is undeniable and Nicholas's naïve excitement is engagingly endearing. But he was not merely star-struck by the glamour of Sir Edward and the reputation of the ship; by the time he wrote his next letter a few days later, he had already had a chance to see Pellew and his crew in action, not in battle but in another honourable cause, that of duty to fellow seafarers in trouble. This letter very much epitomises what it meant to be one of Pellew's Indefatigables at this point in time.

Indefatigable at Scilly, October 12th 1795

My dear Mama

I write to inform you that we sailed from Falmouth on Wednesday the 7th October ... but by stress of weather we were put in here and in our passage we met with a large merchant ship which sailed from the West Indies about a month ago. She had her three masts carried away in a gale of wind. The owner was aboard her. She was all but going to the bottom when we met her for it was very heavy weather. All her men, her captain, her mate were in their hammocks and had been for three weeks and so had the ship been drifting. All but the poor owner, who has a wife and eight children. We immediately sent a boat aboard her where they found them in the above sorry state the owner crying

---

and working at the pump leaving the ship to the mercy of the waves, thinking the ship was going to the bottom every minute.

We immediately sent a number of men aboard and made a rope fast to her and towed her in to the harbour. It was a pitiful sight to see that man (the owner of the ship) it was like a man who had the rope about his neck and then reprieved, we thought he would have dyed but thank God he and his ship are both well. We are going to sail tomorrow to look for the other frigates and to add something to this wonderful year, but all with great joy. I am become a great favourite of the Captain's and am made signal officer and his *aide du langue* which is a famous berth.[58]

Nicholas had previously expressed his longing for action, enjoyment and honourable service, and here, in this eloquent letter, he gives testimony to having found all that and more with the *Indefatigable*. His words already reveal a sense of belonging: 'we immediately sent a boat', 'we immediately sent a number of men aboard'. It is no longer 'I', it is 'we'; he is an Indefatigable. For the first time Nicholas had witnessed not only the perils of the sea and a ship in distress, but also the swift humanitarian actions of the frigate's officers and men. His account of the rescue is all the more vivid because of the terseness overlaid by genuine awed wonder at the immensity of emotion that overwhelmed the rescued ship owner.[59] Evidently Nicholas had already learned much from his captain and could appreciate the courage and skill shown by his shipmates during the rescue. He could identify many of his aspirations embodied in the *Indefatigable*'s crew and he appears transformed into a young man with a purpose he was proud to own. He had also seen in the person of Edward Pellew some of the traits that he, and many others, would come to value as they served as midshipmen under his command. Implicit in every line of this letter is the sense that here at last was a life worth living, a captain to inspire and an example to follow. So the discontented and wayward youngster whose naval career had begun so unpromisingly could now write 'in great joy' of 'this wonderful year'. It was not to be all fair winds for Nicholas Pateshall; there were a few further episodes of difficult behaviour and on several occasions he found himself at odds with his mentor, but he was now established on a ship with a group of comrades who would remain part of his life for the rest of his days.

[58] Pateshall Papers, BD30/9/1-50, Nicholas Pateshall to Ann Pateshall, 12 October 1795.

[59] ADM 51/1171, Captain's Log of His Majesty's Ship the Indefatigable. A certain economy in retelling heroic events appears to have been the prevailing mode of correspondence aboard the *Indefatigable*; the following year, Pellew described the rescue of around 700 people from the wreck of the stricken Indiaman *Dutton* with the log entry 'Sent two boats to the aid of a stricken ship'.

The seventeen young men present in the midshipmen's berth on the *Indefatigable* in 1797 arrived there by various routes: taken on at the request of powerful patrons, or out of loyalty or affection for family and friends; offered a hand up from the ranks of the warrant officers; or recruited from the merchant service under Pellew's patronage because he saw in them good officers and skilled seamen in the making. Whatever their route to the larboard berth, their experiences, chronicled not only by Nicholas Pateshall but by letters to one another in later life and their tributes to their former captain after his death, show that Pellew was both a father and a friend to his young protégés and a figure that many of his officers and young gentlemen sought to emulate. Offered a chance of joining the frigate *Indefatigable* at a crucial point in their seafaring lives, most, though not all, embraced the opportunity with enthusiasm. They were well aware that they were, in the quasi-Shakespearean words of the fictional Midshipman Kennedy, the 'fortunate few'. And as Shakespeare's Henry predicted of his men at Agincourt, the veterans of the *Indefatigable* who saw old age did indeed rouse themselves in remembrance of the night of the *Droits de L'Homme* engagement.[60]

---

[60] Cf. Shakespeare, *Henry V*, act IV, scene III.

3

The Fortunate Few

A WIDE range of original source materials have been used to identify the young gentlemen present aboard His Majesty's Ship *Indefatigable* on the night of the *Droits de L'Homme* engagement and to trace their naval careers, civilian lives and ongoing personal relationships. These sources include the *Indefatigable*'s muster[1] and pay books,[2] which have been cross-referenced with captains' and masters' logs. Musters and pay books generally contain much the same information, but on occasion one will record a detail that is missing from the other, while captains' and masters' logs can be used to broaden the picture. For example, entries in the muster which record that crew members despatched in a prize ship have been captured, can be cross-referenced with logs of the appropriate date to reveal the name and provenance of the prize. Lieutenants' passing certificates[3] also provide a useful overview of young officers' early careers; however, these particular documents should be treated with caution as some of the data they contain, particularly age and years of service, often appears to have been falsified.[4] Additional invaluable source materials include Admiralty service records, personal correspondence from serving officers and published service biographies such as Marshall's *Naval Biography*.

Where available, non-naval sources have also been used to provide an accurate picture of the lives of the *Indefatigable*'s young gentlemen outwith the service. These can be broadly divided into two categories: genealogical sources, including birth, marriage and death records, wills, tax records and property deeds; and publications and manuscripts, including articles from local and national newspapers and contemporary journals and manuscript letters from a variety of public archives and private collections.

The primary source used to identify this distinct cohort of young gentlemen is the *Indefatigable*'s muster book for January–February

---

[1] ADM 36/13144, Muster Table of His Majesty's Ship the Indefatigable, November 1796 to October 1797.

[2] Eighteenth- and nineteenth-century Royal Navy muster books are held at the UK National Archives, Class ADM 36 and 37; pay books are Class ADM 35.

[3] ADM 6, ADM 107, Lieutenants' Passing Certificates.

[4] Cavell has shown that around 19 per cent of midshipmen who passed the examination for lieutenant in 1791 were underage, and 24 per cent in 1801. Cavell, pp. 84, 218.

1797.[5] Ships' musters normally cover two-month periods, with occasional variations, for instance when a ship is paid off. Although the information contained in the double-page entries of muster books appears sparse on first sight, these bald facts provide a solid basis for investigating the lives and careers of individual officers and men. Most of the relevant details appear on the verso page of the muster in columns recording date of first joining, age on joining ship, birthplace, name, rating and discharge. The columns of the recto page, which concern payments for tobacco, clothing etc., are less likely to be filled in consistently.

The January to February 1797 muster roll of the *Indefatigable* is representative of a ship operating as part of a squadron with a stable and established crew; the first 250 names in the muster are all marked as being from the *Arethusa*'s pay books and supernumerary list. This pattern is typical of Pellew's commands at this period. Taylor has noted that despite the 'impetuous, improvident and short-lived' nature of seamen, 133 out of the *Nymphe*'s full complement of 236 had previously transferred into the *Arethusa* with Pellew.[6]

However, the 1797 muster also captures the fluid patterns of service that would have been a common feature of the lives of young gentlemen serving in a squadron of this kind. Midshipmen, warrant and commissioned officers are often listed as being transferred into other ships in the squadron on temporary promotions, presumably to cover for losses resulting from promotions, prize crews, illness or death. This practice is a significant feature of Pellew's management of aspiring officers and his command of the squadron as a whole. Temporary transfers and promotions provided young officers with the opportunity to assume greater responsibility and to develop their skills in new contexts, while at the same time ensuring that the entire squadron was efficiently manned.

Temporary promotions were one way that the *Indefatigable*'s young gentlemen were afforded the opportunity to test their skills; another was selection for prize crews. Taking and crewing prizes was a highly significant aspect of service aboard detached frigates. While the entire crew stood to gain proportionally from taking prizes, crewing prize vessels often brought significant challenges, particularly when it was not unknown for the *Indefatigable* to capture three or four prizes in as many days. Decisions had to be taken as to which home port to send the prize to, the size of crew required, how many men the squadron could afford to lose and which officers and ratings had the requisite skills to crew the prize safely home. Clearly it was unwise to allow prize crews to deplete the company of the ship to the point where she was too undermanned to fight her guns.

---

[5] ADM 36/13144, Muster Table of His Majesty's Ship the Indefatigable, November 1796 to October 1797.

[6] Taylor, pp. 87, 317. Taylor also notes that the muster of the *Arethusa* is unusually detailed in recording the comings and goings of the crew.

A captain such as Pellew had to balance the requirements of his own ship and squadron as a whole, with those of the prizes, and to select his prize crews accordingly.

In a comprehensive study of the prize system, *The Prizes of War: The Naval Prize System in the Napoleonic Wars*, Richard Hill explores the impact of the system on morale, manning and individual careers.[7] Regardless of who commanded a prize vessel, it was the captain of the capturing ship who bore the responsibility for what happened between taking the prize and the final judgment in the High Court of Admiralty. The captain also bore the full brunt of the financial risk if the prize was adjudged to be returned or some other failure meant there was a cost to be borne.

> It might be thought a little hard to saddle the captain or master of a capturing ship with the responsibility for the shortcomings of his prize master. Yet it could scarcely be otherwise. Picking the right subordinate to do a job is one of the principal functions of command; training juniors to do jobs that may fall to them is another. If a captain failed in either of these functions, the responsibility had to be his.[8]

The musters of the ships Pellew commanded, from the *Nymphe* to the *Impetueux*, reveal that most of his young gentlemen had opportunities to command prizes at this early stage of their career. Accounts in the *Indefatigable*'s log of prizes captured and 'sent to England' do not routinely record the names of the prize crews, unless they were unfortunate enough to have been captured. More evidence exists for prizes re-taken by the enemy, as once the capture became known, the unlucky crew were recorded in the muster as having been discharged with a note, 'captured in a prize by the enemy'.[9] This unfortunate fate befell several of the *Indefatigable*'s 1797 midshipmen. One of Nicholas Pateshall's letters home to his brother Edmund describes how one prize crew had the bad luck to lose their prize a mere five miles from Falmouth.

> All I wish is our captain had the command of the English fleet instead of the person who had it when the French fleet were out. The most valuable of our prizes which I mentioned in my last was retaken by a French privateer within 5 miles of Falmouth in which I lost a worthy messmate and two other midshipmen.[10]

---

[7] Hill, p. 133.

[8] *Ibid.*

[9] For instance Alex McVicar, George Tippett and others' entries are annotated in this way in the January/February 1797 muster. When reunited with their ship a few months later, they duly appear as supernumeraries, before being reintegrated into the ship's company.

[10] Pateshall Papers, A95/EB/40/1, Nicholas Pateshall to Edmund Pateshall, 20 January 1797. The three men Pateshall refers to are George Tippett,

The challenges of selecting the right men to take charge of prizes and of ensuring that young officers were sufficiently well trained to assume responsibility were part of the daily routine of a frigate captain, but they were also training and maturing opportunities essential to the successful career development of the young gentlemen. As a midshipman on Lake Champlain, Pellew himself had experienced command devolving on him in an instant and he knew first-hand the value of preparing even the most junior of his young officers for the responsibility of command.

The experience of losing a prize is one that Forester puts Hornblower through during his time as midshipman aboard the *Indefatigable*, in the adventurous tale of the brig *Marie Gallante* and the privateer *Pique*. Though Hornblower berates himself for the loss of his prize, the fictional Pellew is neither angry nor inclined to blame him, as despite the loss of the brig, the French have been deprived of a valuable cargo.[11] In the aftermath of the loss of the prize lamented by Nicholas Pateshall, Pellew seems to have regarded Alex McVicar, the senior midshipman and prizemaster, in a similarly positive and tolerant light. Shortly after the prize crew returned to the *Indefatigable* via a cartel, Pellew promoted McVicar to acting lieutenant.[12]

The opportunities presented by serving aboard a successful frigate, with an active and diligent captain like Pellew, clearly illustrate why the *Indefatigable*'s young gentlemen were indeed among the fleet's fortunate few.

The seventeen young gentlemen chosen for this study are those that are either identified as midshipman on the January/February 1797 muster, or who were among the ship's company on the night of the *Droits de L'Homme* engagement and were subsequently promoted to the rank of midshipman or master's mate, albeit temporarily in some cases. Midshipmen who are named on earlier or later musters are not included in this study.[13] Pellew's two sons, Fleetwood and Pownoll, are also not included; although they are named on the muster, it is likely that their names were 'carried on the books' and that they were not actually present on the ship.

In many respects these seventeen young men are both typical and representative of the junior commissioned officers serving in the Royal Navy at this time. Their ages, in January 1797, ranged from thirteen to twenty-eight. Five first appear on the books of Pellew's ship *Nymphe*, four came aboard the *Arethusa* and eight began their naval service on the

Alex McVicar and James Bray.

[11] Forester, *Mr. Midshipman Hornblower*, p. 79.

[12] ADM 36/13144, Muster Table of His Majesty's Ship the Indefatigable, November 1796 to October 1797.

[13] Those who are named on the January/February 1797 muster but who were discharged from the ship's company before 13 January are similarly excluded.

Indefatigable. In terms of their backgrounds, three were Scottish, one was Irish, and another descended from Irish stock, five were from their captain's home county of Cornwall, one was born outside the UK, in the British community in Lisbon, and the remainder hailed from other parts of England. Six were the sons of the captain's friends and acquaintances, and one was related to his wife.

Regarding social class, one was an 'Honourable', the son of an earl, and another the son of a baronet. Four were the sons of merchant seamen and men who worked for the packet service and two were the sons of serving naval officers. Two, like Horatio Hornblower, were the sons of doctors. In *Mr. Midshipman Hornblower*, Captain Keene of *Justinian*, in his first interview with Hornblower, remarks to the young man: 'A doctor's son – you should have chosen a lord for your father if you wanted to make a career for your self.'[14] In actual fact the *Indefatigable*'s titled young gentlemen did not have markedly more successful careers than their non-aristocratic shipmates.

On joining the Royal Navy, seven already had some experience of the merchant service and the East India Company. Later in their careers, one of the seventeen left the service voluntarily; two were court martialled and dismissed the service, though one was later reinstated with full honours. Only four of the cohort died in service, one of wounds sustained in action, one of fever, one of exposure at sea, and one as a result of shipwreck. Of those who survived, two went on to become warrant officers, ten made post captain, six became admirals in retirement and seven lived long enough to apply for the Naval General Service Medal in 1847.

What follows is an introduction to each of these young officers in order of their seniority once aboard the *Indefatigable*.

The most senior of the *Indefatigable*'s young gentlemen, in terms of naval experience, was George Chace. Although Chace's place and date of birth have been difficult to pinpoint with accuracy, he appears to have been born in or around London between 1771 and 1775, suggesting he was in his late twenties when he joined the *Indefatigable*. According to his muster entries, Chace had previously served with Pellew on both the *Nymphe* and the *Arethusa*,[15] making him the most senior midshipman aboard the *Indefatigable* in the early months of 1797. Indeed later that year he was ready to move on, and in July 1797 he was the first of the group to gain promotion, being appointed to the 28-gun *Enterprise*, as gunner. This was the beginning of a long career for George Chace as a master gunner.

Chace was one of two of this group who were to follow the warrant officer path; the other was John Gaze. Gaze's date and place of birth are unclear; however he may have been born in Hickling, a small village in

---

[14] Forester, *Mr. Midshipman Hornblower*, p. 13.

[15] Pellew commanded the *Nymphe* from 1793 to 1794, and the *Arethusa* from 1794 to 1795.

north Norfolk, in the late 1770s. Although he was only around eighteen when he joined the *Indefatigable*, Gaze was another veteran of Pellew's previous two commands, making him the next most senior to Chace in terms of experience. Gaze was eventually promoted to the rank of master and served many years in this capacity until further promotion came his way. During a long and distinguished career, much of it served under Pellew's command, Gaze rose to the rank of First Master to the Commander in Chief and served as Master of the Fleet at Algiers.

The names of two more of the *Indefatigable*'s young gentlemen, Robert Carthew Reynolds and William Warden, also appear on the muster of the *Nymphe*, as captain's servants.[16] On paper this makes them next in seniority; however it is almost certain that neither of them actually served aboard the *Nymphe*. It is more likely that their names were carried on the books to reduce the period of active service required before they could sit their lieutenants' examinations. Though sometimes regarded as an abuse of power, so-called 'false muster' was common practice at the time, and many captains carried the names of sons of influential patrons or family friends on their muster books.

Robert Carthew Reynolds was the son of Pellew's fellow Cornishman and captain of the *Amazon*, Robert Carthew Reynolds senior. The Reynolds family were friends of the Pellews and it is more than likely that Pellew was willing to carry Reynolds junior's name on his books for a number of years. William Warden's family may also have had links to the Pellews. He came from a family that had been part of the British Factory, or trading community, in Lisbon for three generations, and his great-great-grandfather, also William Warden, had been a shipbuilder to the Royal Court of Portugal.

A third boy, also listed on the *Nymphe*'s muster as a captain's servant, was Pownoll Bastard Pellew, Pellew's eldest son; however he would only have been around six years old in 1793. Pownoll's name also appears on the muster of the *Arethusa*, and later the *Indefatigable*, but there is evidence from a letter that Pellew wrote to his close friend, Alex Broughton, that Pownoll was in fact at school ashore at that time. Pownoll did not actually go to sea until he joined his father aboard the ship of the line *Impetueux* in 1799, and for this reason Pownoll is not included in this study.

Identifying the start of Reynolds's and Warden's careers afloat raises a common problem: unless there is corroborating evidence in the form of letters or family correspondence, it is difficult, if not impossible, to ascertain when individuals carried on ships' books actually went to sea. Both Reynolds and Warden were born in 1782[17] and would have been eleven

---

[16] Pellew's eldest son, Pownoll Bastard Pellew, also appears on the muster of the *Nymphe* as Captain's Servant, but he was not aboard the ship at the time.

[17] LDS 104589-9, record of baptism, St Clement, Cornwall, 30 December 1782, Robert Carthew, son of Robert Carthew Reynolds and Jennifer

at the time of the *Nymphe* musters. It was certainly not unheard of for boys as young as eleven to go to sea; however the balance of probability suggests that both Reynolds and Warden were carried on the *Nymphe*'s books and did not join the ship's company until Pellew took command of the *Arethusa* the following year.

In terms of seniority, the next subset of this cohort are those who joined the crew of the *Arethusa* and transferred with Pellew from there to the *Indefatigable*. The most senior of this group is John Thomson, born in Leith in 1774 into a family with merchant shipping connections.[18] Thomson's father, also John Thomson, served as Pellew's second, then first lieutenant on the *Indefatigable* and had previously served on the *Nymphe* and the *Arethusa*. Thomson, who is identified in the ship's books as John Thomson (2), joined the *Arethusa* in December, making him one of the first of the new crew to be mustered. Later in life Thomson went on to marry into the Pellew family.

Two others joining at this stage had similar backgrounds in the merchant service. John McKerlie, another Scot, born in Galloway in 1775,[19] joined the *Arethusa* in April 1794. His entry records that he came via the *Royal William* guard ship as a volunteer from the merchant service. Thomas Groube, born in Falmouth in 1774,[20] came from a family of merchants who owned a ship that served the India trade. He joined the *Arethusa* from the *Leviathan*, which had been his first posting.

Philip Frowd had no previous background with the sea service but he does appear to have had a tangential connection to the Pellew family. Born in 1779 in Market Lavington,[21] a village in Wiltshire, Philip Frowd was almost certainly a relation of Pellew's wife, Susan Frowd. The connection

---

(Jane) née Vivian. LDS C88000-1, record of baptism, the British Factory Chaplaincy, Lisbon, Portugal, 2 March 1782, William son of George Warden and Elizabeth, née Barclay.

[18] Scotland's People, OPR Birth 692/01 0030 0276, Leith North, Record of baptism, North Leith Parish Church, 6 September 1774, John son of John Thomson and Jean, née Redpath.

[19] Scotland's People, OPR Birth 894/00 0010 0104, Record of baptism, Glenluce Parish Church, Galloway, 12 August 1775, John McCarlie (sic) son of John and Agnes Wallace, Old Luce.

[20] LDS P00172-1, record of baptism, King Charles the Martyr, Falmouth, 11 January 1775, Thomas, son of Samuel Groube and Catherine, née Boulderson.

[21] LDS C05849-1, record of baptism, St Mary of the Assumption, Market Lavington, Wiltshire, 30 May 1779, Philip, son of William Frowd and Elizabeth. LDS C15321-1, record of baptism, St Michael, Brixton Deverill, 20 August 1779, Philip, son of William and Elizabeth. It is possible that the second entry was merely a copy of the original baptism, as Brixton Deverill was the location of the manor house that had been in the family for several generations.

may be relatively distant as families seeking to secure careers for their sons frequently took advantage of any influential connections they had access to, never mind how tenuous. There is some discrepancy in the records relating to Frowd; although he does not appear in the *Nymphe*'s muster,[22] he is described in the *Arethusa*'s muster[23] as 'from *Nymphe*'. Frowd was fourteen or fifteen in 1794 when he appears to have joined the *Arethusa*, so it is possible that he had already served several years at sea, though the evidence is contradictory.

The last *Arethusa* entrant to be found in the Volunteers/Boys section of the muster was born in Falmouth, in 1781.[24] William Kempthorne was the son of a packet captain whose family lived next door to the Pellews on New Road in Falmouth. Later correspondence of Pellew's[25] suggests that Kempthorne may have gone to sea with his mentor before 1794, but his name does not appear on the muster of the *Nymphe*. Initially Kempthorne had a successful career, but he was dismissed the service following a questionable court martial. Pellew immediately took him back aboard his flagship and helped him to be reinstated to the service with his rank restored.

The final group of young gentlemen are those who joined the *Indefatigable* either as new recruits or by transferring directly from the merchant service, and they provide a good illustration of the wide differences in experience and background among the ranks of midshipmen and volunteers. Two youngsters who came aboard the *Indefatigable* in 1795 are a case in point. Nicholas Pateshall and George Cadogan joined the *Indefatigable* in August and September of 1795 respectively, both were younger sons of large families and neither had much in the way of prior sea-going experience. Pateshall, born in 1781[26] in landlocked Herefordshire, was the fourth son of a family of relatively modest county squires, and his widowed mother was desperate to secure a position for him following an earlier failed attempt to place him on another ship in 1794. Cadogan, born in 1783 in Westminster, was the eighth son of the wealthy

---

[22] ADM 36/13161, Muster Table of his Majesty's Ship the Nymphe, 1793. ADM 35/1177, Pay Book of His Majesty's Ship the Nymphe, October 1787–June 1794.

[23] ADM 36/11471, Muster Table of his Majesty's Ship the Arethusa, September 1793–February 1795.

[24] LDS 103101-6, record of baptism, St Gluvias, Flushing, Cornwall, 25 July 1781, William, son of William Kempthorne and Elizabeth, née Goodridge.

[25] In 1805 Pellew wrote in defence of Kempthorne that he had taken him up since he had been eleven years old, but this may be poetic licence. Pellew also referred to him as being the only son of his parents, when in fact he had a younger brother, Renatus.

[26] LDS C13105-1, record of baptism, St Andrew's, Allensmore, Hereford, 14 October 1781, Nicholas Lechmere, son of Edmund Pateshall and Ann, née Burnham.

1st Earl Cadogan,[27] and had spent his formative years at school in London. As the son of an earl, Cadogan could command considerable interest and it was his father's friend, Lord Spencer, then First Lord of the Admiralty, who penned an elegant missive to Pellew requesting that he accept the boy 'among the young gentlemen aboard the *Indefatigable*'.[28]

Two further recruits joined the *Indefatigable* in 1795 and, being Cornish born, they are perhaps more typical of the men and boys who joined Pellew's crews at this stage of his career. James Bray, who entered in the autumn of 1795, was born in Falmouth in 1778.[29] At seventeen, he was relatively old to be joining the service, though it is possible that he had previous naval experience that has yet to be discovered. Unusually for the service at this time, Bray's family had distinguished Irish Roman Catholic roots and he had an uncle who was Archbishop of Cashel and Emly.[30] John Harry, born in Bodmin in 1781,[31] was the final newcomer that year; he joined the *Indefatigable* aged seventeen, again with no evidence of previous sea service. He served as a Volunteer, First Class from September 1795 to August 1797, at which point he left at his own request. Harry is unique among this group in that he left the service voluntarily and forged an illustrious career outside the navy. Nevertheless, fifty years later in 1847, John Harry joined his surviving shipmates to apply for the Naval General Service Medal.[32]

The next year, 1796, saw another influx of promising new recruits to the midshipmen's berth. Alexander McVicar, another experienced merchant sailor from Scotland, joined on 18 February. Like Thomson, McVicar was born in Leith in 1768, the son of a merchant seaman, and at twenty-eight was the oldest of the midshipmen on joining.[33] McVicar already had considerable experience of both the merchant and naval service before joining the *Indefatigable* and Pellew pressed hard for him to be promoted to lieutenant.[34]

---

[27] LDS c13540-3, record of baptism, St James, Westminster, 17 May 1783, George, son of Charles Sloan, 1st Earl Cadogan and Mary, née Churchill.

[28] Exmouth Papers, Box 22, MSS/92/027, Spencer to Pellew, 28 September 1795.

[29] Records of baptisms, King Charles the Martyr, Falmouth, Cornwall, 17 June 1778, James, son of James and Margaret, née Fullerton.

[30] O'Donnell.

[31] LDS P00275-1, records of baptism, St Petroc, Bodmin, Cornwall, 19 December 1781, John, son of John Harry and Elizabeth, née Deacon.

[32] ADM 171/2, Naval General Service Medal Roll. George Cadogan, John Gaze, Thomas Groube, Henry Hart, John McKerlie and Nicholas Pateshall all survived to apply for the Naval General Service Medal.

[33] Scotland's People, OPR Birth 692/02 0060/0271, records of baptism, South Leith Parish Church, 1 November 1768, Alexander, son of William McVicar and Majory 'May', née Berry.

[34] Exmouth Papers, Box 22, MSS/92/027, Spencer to Pellew, 18 September 1797; Spencer to Pellew, 1 October 1797.

About a month later, Henry Hart came aboard. His first entry on the *Indefatigable*'s muster records that he was a volunteer from the East India Company who had been paid £2 10s 0d, half the bounty money available for joining up. Hart was born in 1781 in Sussex to a 'county' family. Like many of his shipmates, he was a younger child, being the eighth son of Richard Hart of Uckfield, and his wife Sarah.[35]

Easily the most dramatic entrant to the *Indefatigable*'s company was Jeremiah Coghlan, who came aboard in July 1796. Like Hart, the muster records Coghlan as being an East India Company volunteer, who was paid the same joining bounty of £2 10s 0d. Born around 1775 in the remote coastal village of Crookhaven in West Cork, Coghlan was one of at least three brothers. Coghlan achieved considerable fame in his own lifetime as a result of his naval exploits, and consequently there are numerous versions of his first meeting with Pellew and the decisive turn in his career that led him to the larboard berth of the *Indefatigable*; most, however, agree that Coghlan was a mate of a merchant vessel that assisted in the rescue of six hundred or more souls from the stricken East Indiaman, *Dutton*, in January 1796. Pellew, who oversaw the rescue, was said to have been so impressed with Coghlan's conduct that he offered him a berth on the *Indefatigable* and promised to assist him to become a commissioned officer.[36]

The final name to appear on the books, and to be included in this cohort, is that of Richard Delves Broughton, a relation of Alexander Broughton, Pellew's oldest and closest friend and former fellow midshipman. Born in Broughton Hall, Staffordshire in January 1784,[37] Delves Broughton was the youngest child of the Reverend Sir Timothy Broughton, Baronet. Although Broughton had a number of relatives in the navy, including a brother-in-law who was captain of a ship of the line, his family no doubt hoped for greater things by placing him with Sir Edward Pellew. This was not to be the case. Broughton had a turbulent naval career and was eventually court martialled and dismissed the service.

In light of Pellew's character and reputation as being both a mentor and father figure to his young officers, it is perhaps noteworthy that six of the seventeen young gentlemen included in this study, Bray, Coghlan, Harry, Kempthorne, Pateshall and Warden, had all lost their fathers by the time they joined Pellew's company. In addition, Broughton had been bereaved of his mother and Cadogan had witnessed his parents' acrimonious divorce and his mother's subsequent disgrace. In letters written by these young gentlemen throughout their lives it is clear that during their formative

---

[35] Ferguson, pp. 17–23.

[36] This incident is recorded in numerous books, journals and press reports, e.g. Marshall, *Royal Naval Biography Supplement*, part III, 1828, pp. 298–305.

[37] LDS C01336-7, record of baptism, All Saints, Eccleshall, 28 March 1784, Richard Delves, son of Thomas Broughton and Mary, née Wicker.

years afloat, they identified Pellew as being a caring and respected father figure, though many of them were later to also call him their friend.

Of all the young gentlemen listed in the *Indefatigable*'s 1797 muster, only one appears to have left the service voluntarily and had no further naval career. John Harry's naval service began and ended on the *Indefatigable*. He is listed in the muster as having joined the ship in September 1795 as a Boy, First Class, and was discharged in August 1797. The muster entry for his discharge simply reads that he was discharged 'at own request' and there is no indication that he was discharged to another ship. No one by the name of John Harry appears in the lieutenants' lists for the succeeding years, and there is no one by that name in the officers' records of this period. On the basis of this evidence it appears that John Harry simply left the navy after a short but eventful career during which he was present at the engagements with both the *Virginie* and the *Droits de L'Homme*.

However a John Harry does appear in one other naval record. The Naval General Service Medal roll shows that an individual of that name applied for, and was awarded, the General Service Medal with two clasps for the *Virginie* and *Droits de L'Homme* engagements in 1847, over fifty years after the events they commemorated.

The Naval General Service Medal was awarded retrospectively in 1847 to every surviving seaman, regardless of rank, who had seen action in various battles and engagements from 1793 to 1815. Two hundred and thirty-one qualifying battles and engagements were identified by the government, and each medal was accompanied by a clasp bearing the name of every action the claimant had participated in. In order to receive the medal, individuals had to apply in person; no posthumous awards were made to the families of deceased seamen. Eligibility was determined by referring to ships' books to check that the claimant was present during the week that the action in question took place, and was not marked as having 'run'.

By 1847 the surviving members of the *Indefatigable*'s crew who were awarded the Naval General Service Medal were inevitably few in number. Those that were still living had mostly been volunteers, midshipmen or master's mates, aged between thirteen and twenty-seven, at the time of the engagement with the *Droits de L'Homme*; so even the youngest of the surviving claimants was in his sixties when the medal was awarded.

Harry was one of only six men who were awarded the clasp for the capture of the frigate *Virginie* on 29 April 1796.[38] The others were all members of the *Indefatigable* cohort: George Cadogan, Thomas Groube, John McKerlie and Nicholas Pateshall, along with able seaman John Jones. All except Jones also applied for the *Droits de L'Homme* clasp, together with surgeon's mate Richard Williams, John Gaze and Henry Hart, who joined the *Indefatigable* subsequent to the *Virginie* engagement.

---

[38] ADM 171/8, Naval General Service Medal Roll, 29 April 1796, pp. 60–1.

Of all those that survived to apply for the Naval General Service Medal, John Harry is the only one whose naval career did not progress beyond the rank of volunteer. So what happened to Harry between his discharge from the *Indefatigable* in 1797 and his appearance on the General Service Medal roll fifty years later?

The muster and pay books of the *Indefatigable* consistently record Harry's place of birth as Bodmin, Cornwall and his age on joining the service in 1795 as seventeen. Parish records indicate that a John Harry was born in 1781 and baptised in Bodmin parish church. In fact he is the only boy of that name born anywhere in Cornwall around that time to appear in the digitised parish registers, which cover almost the entire county. The boy born to that family had two brothers, William, born in 1779, and James, born in 1783.

Further research has identified an archive at Queen's University, Ontario, of a Dr John Harry, born in Bodmin at this time, who became a physician to several royal courts in Russia and Europe. Dr Harry travelled widely in China and Europe and his archive contains a fascinating series of letters in multiple languages addressed to many politicians, influential people and members of royal households. Although it is difficult to establish his identity conclusively, on the basis of the evidence from the Cornish parish registers, it seems highly likely that Dr John Harry is one and the same as Mr John Harry, Volunteer, First Class, of HMS *Indefatigable*.

The Canadian archive includes a medical dissertation on the subject of dysentery from the University of Leyden written by a John Harry in 1778, which initially appeared to call this hypothesis into question. However it appears that this dissertation is the work of John Harry senior, father of the young naval recruit. Harry senior qualified as a doctor in 1778,[39] aged around twenty-five; he married the following year and fathered three children. Dr John Harry senior died in Bodmin in 1786 aged only thirty-three.[40] If Dr Harry senior was indeed the father of the *Indefatigable*'s young volunteer, then a familiar pattern emerges of a boy losing his father while still a young child, and a mother, possibly in reduced circumstances, left with three sons to care for. The sale of Dr Harry's books two years after his death further suggests that his widow and young family may have struggled to make ends meet. In October 1788 *The Bath Chronicle and Weekly Gazette* announced the sale of

Many strange and uncommon books

The libraries of two late eminent physicians, Dr John Harry and Dr Dunning, are now to be sold, a catalogue of which is just printed and the reasonable prices (ready money) therein marked to each book.

---

[39] *The Medical Register for the Year 1783*, p. 56. The Medical Register records that Physician J. Harry M.D. graduated from Leyden in 1778.

[40] *Bath Chronicle and Weekly Gazette*, 26 October 1786.

By S Woolmer, bookseller, Exeter.[41]

The younger John Harry was not the eldest son of the family and it is impossible to know whether he originally intended to follow his father's profession but lacked the opportunity, or whether his inclinations initially lay elsewhere. Whatever the reason, like many Cornish boys at the time, he turned to the navy to attempt to forge a career.

Other than the Leyden dissertation, the earliest of the documents in the Queen's University archive appears to date from 1803, and, as Harry left the *Indefatigable* in August 1797, this is entirely consistent with him going to university in the autumn of that year and beginning a period of study that culminated in the award of certificates in 1803 at the age of about twenty-four. These certificates, from doctors teaching at St Thomas' and Guy's Hospitals,[42] qualify Harry in surgery, prescribing, the practice of medicine, and midwifery.

John Harry's will,[43] written in 1852, made bequests to his niece and nephews, including one Philip Harry, who had emigrated to Washington DC during Dr Harry's lifetime. Other members of the family followed Philip Harry to the United States and later moved to Canada, taking Dr Harry's papers with them. These papers were subsequently presented to Queen's University, Ontario in 1967.[44]

Dr Harry's will reveals tangible evidence that he enjoyed a successful and high-flying career. Among his bequests are diamond-set gold snuffboxes, gold watches, seals and many more similar items,[45] though sadly there is no mention of his Naval General Service Medal. However the very fact that Dr Harry applied for this medal so long after the events it commemorated, and after such a short naval career, says a great deal about the enduring significance of those two eventful years. Despite his eminent medical career, John Harry, like all the others, never forgot the night of the thirteenth of January 1797.

The seventeen young gentlemen mustered on the *Indefatigable* in early 1797 are unique by virtue of their involvement in the famous *Droits de L'Homme* engagement; however, in most other respects they are broadly typical of the thousands of junior officers who served in the Royal Navy in the late eighteenth and early nineteenth centuries. Most had moderately successful naval and civilian careers, though few achieved fame in their own lifetimes. However in-depth analysis of the full range of archival

---

[41] *Bath Chronicle and Weekly Gazette*, 2 October 1788.

[42] John Harry Papers, Queen's University, Ontario, Series 1, Numbers 1–6.

[43] PCC Wills PROB 11/2149, Will of Dr John Harry of Paignton, probated London, 27 March 1854.

[44] The archive was donated to Queen's University, Ontario by a Mrs R. V. Cook of Saskatoon, who is described as a descendant of Dr John Harry.

[45] PCC Wills PROB 11/2149, Will of Dr John Harry of Paignton, probated London, 27 March 1854.

evidence, above and beyond the Admiralty archives, reveals a detailed picture of each individual that shows they all had lives of note and each was remarkable in his own way. Although their names are not to be found in the canon of the great and the good, detailed study of their individual careers through the more obscure pages of the Admiralty archives is not without reward. Although they may not have left their mark on history on the grand scale, their resourcefulness, adaptability and skill made a significant contribution not only to the Royal Navy, but also to civic life and technological innovation, and their legacy should not be overlooked.

4

'Never Was Such an Action Known'

PELLEW'S engagement with the *Cléopatre* in June 1793, at the very outbreak of the war, had already brought him public honours and huge popular acclaim; he was knighted for his services, awarded an annuity from the Privy Purse to cover the expenditure associated with his new title, and feted by the King, George III, the First Lord of the Admiralty, Lord Chatham, and the Prime Minister, William Pitt the Younger. However it is the engagement with the French 74, *Les Droits de L'Homme*, five years later, that has gone down in history as the most iconic frigate action of the French Revolutionary and Napoleonic Wars, and which sealed Pellew's reputation as the quintessential frigate captain.

Les Droits de L'Homme was one of the remnants of the ill-fated expedition to Ireland, a joint military and naval endeavour that proved to be a resounding disaster for the French, and an embarrassment for the British. The Admiralty had been monitoring the build-up of the French fleet at Brest for months, and although they had sufficient intelligence to know that an expedition of considerable force was imminent, they had no knowledge of the destination. Ireland, Portugal, Gibraltar and England itself were all speculative targets. In order to counteract the threat of invasion, the Admiralty instigated a system of close blockade under the command of Admiral Lord Bridport, Commander in Chief of the Channel Fleet. The main complement of the fleet was based at Spithead under the command of Bridport himself, while a squadron of fifteen sail of the line under Admiral Colpoys was stationed off Ushant. An additional inshore squadron of detached frigates commanded by Pellew in the *Indefatigable* patrolled the inner reaches of Brest, often peering right into the roads to watch the activity of the fleet at anchor.

The destination of the planned expedition was Ireland, the seeds having been planted in Basel the previous year when Lord Edward Fitzgerald and Arthur O'Conor of the banned republican Society of United Irishmen met with General Hoche to discuss support for their cause.[1] The following spring of 1796, another of the leaders of the United Irishmen, the Protestant lawyer Theobald Wolfe Tone, travelled from exile in Philadelphia to Paris to personally lobby the Directory to support their intention to sever Ireland's connection with England. As the supremely sarcastic nineteenth-century historian Fitchett wryly commented, 'Irish

---

[1] Gardiner, *Fleet Battle and Blockade*, p. 138.

facts, when planted in French imaginations, are naturally of tropical growth'.[2]

Tone's representation met with support, and the revolutionary government agreed to despatch a force of approximately 15,000 troops under the command of General Hoche, together with the French Atlantic Fleet under Admiral Villaret de Joyeuse. Progress in mustering troops, supplies, munitions and ships was slow, with Hoche publicly blaming the navy for the delays.

> God keep me from having anything to do with the navy. What an extravagant compound. A great body whose parts are disunited and incoherent; contradictions of all kinds; indiscipline organised into a military body. Add to that haughty ignorance and foolish vanity, and you have the picture filled out.[3]

The force was originally intended to sail before the end of October; however Hoche preferred to wait for the arrival of additional forces from Rochefort under the command of Admiral Richery. It was 11 November before Richery put in to Brest, where his arrival with five sail of the line and three frigates was observed by the ever-vigilant Pellew. When the *Indefatigable* was chased from her customary station the following morning by four French frigates, Pellew suspected that the fleet was preparing to get underway and immediately despatched the *Amazon* to England and the *Phoebe* to Ushant, to report the intelligence to Admiral Colpoys. Finally on 16 December Pellew's suspicions were confirmed, and a French fleet comprising forty-four sail in total, including seventeen sail of the line and thirteen frigates, sailed through the Goulet into Camaret Bay late in the afternoon. As Pellew had received no response either from England or from Colpoys, he despatched the *Revolutionnaire* to search for the admiral, leaving the *Indefatigable*, along with the *Duke of York* armed lugger, to watch the entire expeditionary fleet.

Believing Colpoys's fleet to be close at hand, de Galles, who had embarked with Hoche aboard the frigate *Fraternité*, sought to conceal the fleet's departure by ordering the ships to proceed to open sea through the narrow and treacherous Passage du Raz. Although the light was fading, the wind was initially favourable from the east; however, as the winter night grew darker, the wind became variable and increased in strength. Judging the Passage du Raz to be too risky, de Galles changed his orders and signalled to the fleet with guns and blue lights to proceed through the wider Iroise channel. With the night growing thick, only a few ships observed the signal and the majority of the fleet proceeded through the Bec du Raz with the wind rising. The confusion amongst the fleet was exacerbated

---

[2] Fitchett, *How England Saved Europe: The Story of the Great War (1793–1815), Volume I, From the Low Countries to Egypt*, p. 165.

[3] Mahan, p. 850.

by distress signals fired from the *Seduissant*, which had grounded on the Grand Stevenet rock, and guns and rockets from the *Indefatigable*, which Pellew had manœuvred ahead of the French fleet as they made their way out to sea. In the resulting chaos, almost 700 men were lost from the grounded *Seduissant*, two ships ran foul of one another and the fleet was scattered and dispersed.

The following morning, still having heard nothing from the British fleet, Pellew despatched the *Duke of York* for Falmouth and set of for Ushant in search of Colpoys; instead he found the *Revolutionnaire*, which had seen no sign of the admiral or his squadron. Initially Pellew intended to set a course for Lisbon, as he believed the French fleet to be sailing for the southwest; however, the wind being against him, he instead set sail for Falmouth, arriving close on the heels of his own lugger and telegraphing his report to the Admiralty.

Finally, on 20 December, Admiralty Secretary Evan Nepean was able to communicate Pellew's intelligence to Admiral Lord Bridport at Spithead that the French fleet had put to sea four days previously and escaped Colpoys's squadron. The Admiralty ordered Bridport to use every means in his power to put to sea the moment his ships were ready.[4] Bridport replied that he would use every exertion to sail at the shortest possible notice; however, adverse weather conditions detained him and it was 3 January before the Channel Fleet put to sea. The delay allowed time for the fleet to be joined by the missing Colpoys who had arrived back at Spithead on 31 December.

In the intervening period the North Atlantic weather had succeeded in frustrating French and Irish hopes where the British Navy had failed. The French fleet arrived off the west coast of Ireland, always a treacherous coastline, in the teeth of one of the worst winter storms in living memory. The fleet had been scattered in passage and, critically, there was no sign of the frigate *Fraternité* carrying the expedition commanders. Of those ships that did arrive at their appointed station in Bantry Bay, some foundered or were wrecked on the coast, others were driven far out to sea by the ferocious storm, and one or two were picked off by the small squadron of frigates in Bantry Bay. Not a single ship managed to disembark troops. Finally, after riding out the storm for several weeks, the battered remnants of the fleet left the Irish coast to struggle back to France on 3 January, the very day Admiral Lord Bridport and the Channel Fleet set sail to hunt them down. The expedition to Ireland, and the hopes of the United Irishmen, had been beaten by the winter storms of the Atlantic northwest. The cost to the French was significant: a quarter of the fleet was lost, mostly through grounding and foundering. When the last of the ships returned to France, on 13 January, they had been at sea for almost a month, and during that

---

[4] Morriss, p. 168.

time, with the exception of Pellew's inshore squadron, the Channel Fleet had failed to sight a single French ship.

The narrow failure of the expedition to Ireland and the Royal Navy's inability to intercept the French fleet caused considerable political and public consternation, and commentators and historians have been scathing about the performance of the Channel Fleet and Admiral Lord Bridport ever since. James notes the 'extraordinary circumstance' that in the course of three to four weeks traversing the English and Irish Channels in every direction, neither of the two British fleets appointed to the task succeeded in capturing a single ship.[5] In Fitchett's rarely lofty estimation, 'never was an expedition more favoured – at its start, at least – alike by fortune and by the stupidity of its enemies'.[6] For good measure, Fitchett also accuses Bridport of 'loitering indolence'. Rodger is rather more measured in his criticism, though hardly less damning, pointing out that Bridport and Colpoys knew nothing of the French threat until it was all over, 'defeated by bad weather and French incompetence and almost no help from the Royal Navy'.[7]

One of the last French ships to leave the coast of Ireland was the new 74-gun ship of the line, *Les Droits de L'Homme. Les Droits de L'Homme* was the flagship of Rear Admiral Bouvet; however, as he had embarked in the frigate *Immortalitie*, the ship was commanded by Commodore Raymond de Lacrosse, an experienced naval officer of the *ancien regime*, who followed his orders to the letter. The ship cruised off the coast for eight days and on 5 January encountered the British letter of marque, *Cumberland*, Captain Peter Inglis, which it seized as a prize. Lacrosse removed the *Cumberland*'s crew and passengers to his own ship, and despatched the prize to France. Among the prisoners was infantry officer Lieutenant Elias Pipon of the 63rd Regiment, who later wrote a vivid and harrowing account of the fate of the French ship. After Lacrosse made one last reconnaissance of Bantry Bay, *Les Droits de L'Homme* finally set sail for France on 9 January.[8]

Unlike his Commander in Chief, Pellew had wasted little time in putting back to sea after he returned to Falmouth. On 21 December he sailed for Ushant hoping to intercept the French; however by this time they had already reached the coast of Ireland and it was three weeks later before the *Indefatigable* finally encountered one of the scattered remnants of the Brest Fleet.

[5] W. James, *The Naval History of Great Britain from Declaration of War by France in 1793 to the Accession of George IV*, vol. 1, p. 20.

[6] Fitchett, *How England Saved Europe: The Story of the Great War (1793–1815), Volume I From the Low Countries to Egypt*, p. 166.

[7] Rodger, *The Command of the Ocean: A Naval History of Britain 1649–1815*, p. 438.

[8] W. James, *The Naval History of Great Britain from Declaration of War by France in 1793 to the Accession of George IV*, vol. 2, pp. 10–11.

The furious gales that had battered the western seaboard, and which Pellew described as 'a continued gale of wind ... such as I have never met with',[9] had moderated somewhat when on 13 January, in latitude 47, 30 N. Ushant bearing N.E. 50 leagues, a large ship was sighted on the *Indefatigable*'s northwest quarter. *Les Droits de L'Homme* had arrived off the coast of France earlier on the thirteenth but, the weather being thick and hazy and the wind blowing hard from the west, Lacrosse kept well clear of the coast and stood to the south with the freshening wind on her starboard beam.[10] Initially identifying her only as a 'large ship', Pellew made the signal to the *Amazon* for a 'General Chace' and immediately followed this with the signal that the 'Chace was an Enemy'. On sighting the two frigates, *Les Droits de L'Homme* immediately made sail to escape. While Lacrosse's ability and bravery as a sea officer are beyond doubt, there has been continued speculation as to why the French 74, with its superior weight of broadside and large number of troops, fled from two frigates which, in normal circumstances, would not have represented a serious challenge.

In his recent biography of Pellew, Taylor has suggested that as the ship was handicapped by her heavy load of troops, horses and military hardware and was restricted by the weather from opening her lower ports, Lacrosse opted to run for home.[11] Henderson has also speculated that the presence of an important general and a valuable battalion of soldiers on board discouraged Lacrosse from risking an engagement.[12] French sources, however, simply state that the ship ran, not to refuse to fight, but to allow time to clear for action.[13]

Whatever the reason, by 4.00 p.m. the *Indefatigable* had gained sufficiently on the chase for Pellew to distinguish that she had two tiers of guns, but that her lower deck ports were shut. At a quarter to five, with the wind 'blowing very hard and a great sea', the chase was observed to have carried away her fore and main topmast. At the same instant, while travelling at ten to twelve knots, the *Indefatigable* lost her steering sail booms. Rapidly assessing the enemy's situation and tactics, Pellew judged in his own words that

> ... the escape of the Enemy under her lower masts only in a stormy night of 14 hours continuance, should her defence prove obstinate was very possible and I believed as a ship of large force that she would be induced to persevere in her resistance from the expectation that

[9] Taylor, p. 117.

[10] W. James, *The Naval History of Great Britain from Declaration of War by France in 1793 to the Accession of George IV*, vol. 2, p. 11.

[11] Taylor, p. 118.

[12] Henderson, p. 37.

[13] Mullié, p. 128.

we should be apprehensive of entangling ourselves upon a Lee shore with the wind dead upon it.[14]

Undeterred, the *Indefatigable* reduced sail to close reefed topsails and, with the *Amazon* still eight miles astern, at quarter to six brought the enemy to close action. Although *Les Droits de L'Homme* carried a significantly heavier weight of broadside than the *Indefatigable*, the 74 was hampered by the high sea and the rolling of the ship resulting from the loss of her stabilising topmasts, which meant that Lacrosse was unable to open his lower gun ports to bring his heavy 32-pound lower deck battery to bear. Elias Pipon, the infantry lieutenant seized from the *Cumberland*, recalled how the English prisoners were ordered down into the cable tier as *Les Droits de L'Homme* cleared for action. The lower deck ports were opened as the engagement commenced, but were quickly closed again 'on account of the great sea, which occasioned the water to rush in to that degree that we felt it running in the cables'.[15] Pipon also noted that the French ship had been built to a new design and her lower deck ports were two and a half feet lower than usual.

Unable to bring her thirty-six heavy guns to bear, *Les Droits de L'Homme* instead attempted to ram and board the *Indefatigable*. In an annotation to the Pellew family's personal copy of Edward Osler's biography of Admiral Lord Exmouth, John Gaze, Assistant Master of the *Indefatigable* during the engagement, noted:

> ... we constantly ran ahead of her and at such time we fired at her bows until she approached very near to us when we used to bear up. On one occasion, not wearing quite so soon as usual, her bowsprit came close over our stern and we were very nearly run down.[16]

The initial exchange of well-supported fire continued on both sides for close on an hour before the *Indefatigable* shot ahead, only to be replaced by the *Amazon* which came up under a press of sail to engage the French ship before she too shot ahead.

After the *Indefatigable* had replaced some necessary rigging, the *Amazon* had reduced her sail, and *Les Droits de L'Homme* had cleared her decks of the debris of her fallen masts, the action recommenced with the frigates placing themselves on either quarter of the harried 74 to deliver repeated raking broadsides. Throughout the engagement the troops aboard the French ship kept up a heavy fire of musketry, 'with great vivacity altho' she frequently defended both sides of the ship at once'.[17] The attack, Pellew noted, 'often within pistol shot was by both ships unremitted for about

[14] Corbett, p. 383.

[15] Pipon, p. 207.

[16] Pinhey, p. 19.

[17] Corbett, p. 383.

five hours'[18] until both frigates sheered off to secure their masts. The engagement then resumed with unrelenting fury until after 4.00 a.m. In his eloquent official account of the action, Pellew vividly described the scene on board the *Indefatigable*.

> ... every creature was too earnestly and too hardly at work to attend exactly to the run of the ship, and I believe 10 hours of more severe fatigue was scarcely ever experienced, the sea was high, the people on the main deck were up to their middles in water; some guns broke their breechings four times over and some drew the ring bolts from the sides and many of them were repeatedly drawn immediately after loading; all our masts were much wounded; the main topmast completely unrigg'd and saved only by uncommon alacrity.[19]

Conditions were similar on the *Amazon* where the men 'fought half way up their legs in water, cheering and inspiring courage to all around by their own animated gallant example'.[20]

Aboard *Les Droits de L'Homme*, conditions were scarcely less appalling. The ship's mizzen mast had been shot away and her bowsprit badly damaged; many of the gun crews had been killed at their guns, but wherever a man fell, 'ten sprang up to take his place'.[21] Having expended all his shot, Lacrosse ordered the gun crews to start firing shells.[22] Despite the carnage, the officers of *Les Droits de L'Homme* had escaped relatively unscathed until just after 1.00 a.m. when Commander Lacrosse was struck in the knee by a ricocheting bullet. Despite his injury, Lacrosse refused to leave the deck until his second-in-command vowed that he would sink the ship rather than strike. Crying through the raging storm and the thunder of the guns he called to his crew, 'Equipage des Droits de L'Homme, jurez-moi de ne point amener le pavillon français! Vaincre ou mourir!', to which the crew responded, 'Nous le jurons! Vive la République!'[23]

The ferocity of the battle continued for ten hours through the night and the storm, with the French ship running straight before the wind and never

---

[18] *Ibid.*, p. 384.

[19] *Ibid.*

[20] ADM 1/5341, Amazon Court Martial. Reynolds, 25 September 1797, testimony to court martial.

[21] Mullié, p. 129.

[22] Gaze has disputed that the French ship fired shells during the engagement, noting 'Shells would have been utterly useless, the distance being unknown & changing & one in 500 would have struck the ship fired at. No shells were fired.' Pinhey, p. 20. However French sources consistently maintain that the 74 fired shells when round shot was expended.

[23] 'Crew of the Droits de L'Homme, swear not to strike the French flag! Victory or death!' 'We swear! Long live the Republic.' Mullié, p. 129.

once altering her course[24] while the two frigates hounded her on either quarter. One broadside from the 74 nearly proved fatal to the *Indefatigable* with seven shot striking the hull and damaging the lower masts and one cutting the main topmast shrouds right through by the seizing. The loss of the main topmast in such conditions would inevitably have led to the loss of the ship; however Master's Mate John Gaze, who commanded the guns under the poop, immediately went aloft with the captain of the maintop to cut away the topgallant yard, while John Thomson, the acting master, clinched the end of a hawser around the mast head, saving the topmast and preventing the mainmast itself from springing.[25]

By this time the *Amazon* had suffered even greater damage than the *Indefatigable*. Her mizzen topmasts, gib, spanker boom and mizzen topsailyard were entirely shot away; the mainmast and foremast and fore main yards damaged in several places by large shot, some of which Reynolds judged to be of 36 pounds. In addition, many of the *Amazon*'s shrouds, stays and backstays had been shot through, her cordage had all been expended in renewing running rigging and she had three feet of water in her hold.[26]

At last, at about 4.20 a.m., the moon broke through the clouds and the *Indefatigable*'s Lieutenant George Bell, who commanded the forecastle guns, caught a glimpse of land. John Gaze later noted that as Bell had 'previously acted as master, his attention therefore was particularly drawn to the navigation of the ship'.[27] No sooner had Bell's report reached the quarterdeck than Pellew himself saw the breakers. Immediately realising the peril of their position, he made the night signal for danger and the *Indefatigable* wore to the southward while the *Amazon* wore to the north. In his report of the engagement, Pellew acknowledged that at this point it was only the prompt execution of his orders by the crew that saved the ship: '... here it is with heartfelt pleasure I acknowledge the full value of my officers and ship's company, who with incredible alacrity hauled the tacks on-hoard, and made sail to the southward'.[28] However, Gaze suggested that some credit for saving the *Indefatigable* belonged to the ship's pilot: 'It was first intended to haul to the northward, but the old French Chouan Pilot we had on board cried out "non, non, mon Capitaine, the oder way".'[29]

Although the land was not clearly visible, Pellew believed it to be Ushant and therefore had little fear for the safety of the ship, despite her crippled state. However another gap in the clouds showed breakers again on the *Indefatigable*'s lee bow and Pellew realised that the land they had

[24] Gaze in Pinhey, p. 20.

[25] Osler, pp. 145–6; Gaze in Pinhey, p. 20.

[26] ADM 1/5341, Amazon Court Martial.

[27] Gaze in Pinhey, p. 20.

[28] Corbett, p. 385.

[29] *Ibid.*

seen could not have been Ushant. The ship wore again to the northward and an anxious watch was kept until day broke at about 6.30 a.m. and revealed land close ahead. Shortly after, at 7.10 a.m., they discovered 'the enemy, who had so bravely defended herself, lying on her broadside, and a tremendous surf beating over her'.[30] Pellew was sensible to the unfortunate fate of the French crew and also the danger that they would share their fate. 'The miserable fate of her brave but unhappy crew was perhaps the more sincerely lamented by us, from the apprehension of suffering a similar misfortune.'[31] However, with four feet of water in the hold, a huge sea running, and the wind dead on the shore, the *Indefatigable* was powerless to help, for Pellew was now sure beyond doubt that they were embayed on the lee shore of Hodierne Bay and that their survival depended on weathering the Penmark Rocks to the south.

From the wreck of *Les Droits de L'Homme* the dreadful scene was watched by Lieutenant Elias Pipon. Along with the other English prisoners, Pipon had been brought on deck at about 4.30 a.m., just at the point that the moon broke through the cloud revealing the land dead ahead and *Les Droits de L'Homme* lost her foremast over the side. Roused from their terror by French cries of 'Pauvres Anglais! Pauvrais Anglais! Montes bien vite, nous sommes tous perdus',[32] the prisoners 'rather flew than climbed' to the upper deck, where Pipon observed the terrible sight of the dead and wounded covering the decks; not a mast was standing and the sea was breaking all around. On the starboard quarter Pipon could see the *Indefatigable* standing off from the Penmark Rocks in a tremendous sea, which threatened her with instant destruction. Even then the frigate was still perceived to be a threat, and in his subsequent account Pipon gave thanks to

> the great humanity of her commander, those few persons who survived the shipwreck were indebted for their lives; for had another broadside been fired, the commanding situation of the Indefatigable must have swept off at least a thousand men.[33]

On the *Indefatigable* the guns were now silent and every exertion was made to save the ship. Exhausted as they were, the crew set every inch of canvas that could be carried and after four hours of exertion the *Indefatigable* clawed her way out of Hodierne Bay, to the palpable relief of her captain and all on board: '... at eleven A. M. we made the breakers, and, by the blessing of God, weather'd the Penmark Rocks about half a mile'.[34]

---

[30] *Ibid.*

[31] *Ibid.*

[32] Pipon, p. 208. 'Poor Englishmen! Poor Englishmen! Come on deck as fast as you can, we are all lost!'

[33] Pipon, p. 209.

[34] Corbett, pp. 385–6.

Although Pellew had witnessed the awful wreck of *Les Droits de L'Homme* he initially believed the *Amazon* had escaped such a fate. In his official account, written immediately after the engagement, Pellew stated:

> The Amazon had haul'd her Wind to the Northward, when we did to the Southward, her condition I think was better than ours, I knew that her activity & exertions were fully equal to them, the judgement with which she was managed during too long an Action, & the Gallantry of her Attacks could not but warm the bosom of every spectator, & to the heart of a Friend it was particularly delightful.[35]

Despite her activity and exertions, the *Amazon* did not escape Hodierne Bay. Half an hour after the *Indefatigable* had made the night signal for danger and the *Amazon* wore to the northward she struck ground on *Les Droits de L'Homme*'s starboard quarter. Reynolds's crew immediately set about making rafts and the entire ship's company was ferried safely to the shore, excepting six men who, defying orders, stole the cutter and were drowned. On reaching the shore, the crew were apprehended by a company of French soldiers who took them to the nearby town of Audierne. From there, the warrant officers and men were marched to the prison depot of Pontanezan and the commissioned officers to Quimper.

When Pellew did eventually hear of the fate of Reynolds and his crew he wasted no time in attempting to obtain their earliest release and immediately suggested to the Admiralty that Reynolds should be exchanged for Jacques Bergeret, captain of the *Virginie*. Since the capture of his ship by the *Indefatigable* in April 1796, Bergeret had been paroled and was living with Pellew's family at Plymouth. Much to the disappointment of all concerned, the Admiralty refused to exchange Bergeret for Reynolds. Meanwhile, on the other side of the Channel, Lacrosse was also attempting to secure Reynolds's release. In his letter to Pellew dated 10th Messidor, Lacrosse assured his former adversary:

> I am going to write to my friend the minister of the marine for him to send back (on his word of honour) our dear and worthy Captain Reynolds, that he may have the happiness of embracing his family and friends who will make him forget the sorrowful accident which followed his honourable engagement.[36]

Despite their earlier disappointment, the officers, captain and crew of the *Amazon* did not have to wait long for their release: Reynolds was

---

[35] *Ibid.*, p. 286.

[36] Exmouth Papers, Box 22, MSS/92/027, Lacrosse to Pellew, 10th Messidor in the 5th year of the Republic.

pleased to inform their Lords Commissioners of the Admiralty of his return from captivity in early September.[37]

On their return, Reynolds and his officers were required, by Admiralty policy and convention, to face a court martial for the loss of their ship. The court martial took place at Hamoaze on 25 September, and found

> the loss of the Amazon to be the result of a Noble Pursuit of an Enemy on her own Coasts; and with respect to it do consequently acquit Captain Reynolds his Officers & Crew with every sentiment of its highest approbation.[38]

The crew of *Les Droits de L'Homme* were much less fortunate than their British adversaries. Their terrible fate was recorded by Lieutenant Elias Pipon who, on his eventual return to England, wrote a harrowing account of the shipwreck, which is corroborated by contemporary French reports.[39] Despite having struck so close to the shore, all attempts to reach the stricken ship were defeated by the rising storm, and the ship quickly started to break up. Many of those aboard were swept into the sea and drowned immediately and panic broke out among the troops. The second day after the ship grounded, Pipon related how, under the direction of an English captain, the English prisoners were able to reach land by means of a small boat; this encouraged the French to strike out for shore in rafts and boats, but all were drowned.[40] On the third day, the ship's largest boat was got over the side with the intention of bringing the women and the injured to safety. However, in defiance of orders, over a hundred men crowded into the boat, which was swamped by a huge wave, drowning all aboard. By the third night, those left aboard were suffering terribly from exposure and were dreadfully weakened from hunger and thirst as all the ship's supplies had been washed away and her water casks stoved in. Eventually, on the fourth day, 18 January, the brig *Arrogante* and cutter *Aiguille* reached the wreck and took off the remaining survivors. Captain De Lacrosse, General Humbert, Lieutenant Pipon and two English officers were the last to leave the wreck of *Les Droits de L'Homme*.

As there is no definitive figure for the number of troops carried aboard *Les Droits de L'Homme*, it is not clear how many men perished during the engagement and the subsequent shipwreck. Considering the length and ferocity of the engagement, which continued for twelve hours at close quarters, and the terrible conditions in which it was fought, casualties were inconceivably light aboard the two frigates. Not a single man was lost aboard the *Indefatigable*, and only nineteen were injured, mostly

---

[37] ADM 1/2400, Captains' Letters R, letter 142, Reynolds to Nepean, 6 September 1797.

[38] ADM 1/5341, Amazon Court Martial.

[39] Pipon, pp. 206–10.

[40] Pipon, p. 209.

with minor contusions from splinters. Among the injured was Pellew's 'brave and worthy' First Lieutenant John Thomson who received a severe contusion on his breast and shoulder. Casualties were somewhat higher on the *Amazon*, which had three killed and fifteen badly wounded during the engagement, in addition to the six lost while evacuating the ship. Estimates of the number of sailors and troops aboard *Les Droits de L'Homme* vary widely: Pellew estimated that the ship had 'not less than 6 or 700 men';[41] Pipon claimed that 600 seamen and 900 troops were aboard;[42] while French historian Troude claimed the total figure was 1,280, including 580[43] troops, of which 103 were killed and 157 wounded during the engagement, a figure with which James agrees.[44] It is even less clear how many perished during the subsequent wreck. Pipon claimed that almost half those on board had perished by the third day after the shipwreck; however James believes this figure is exaggerated; and Troude places the figure as low as 217. The true extent of the loss of life aboard *Les Droits de L'Homme* remains unknown.

On returning to Falmouth three days later on 17 January, Pellew immediately dashed off his official despatches, one a formal account of the engagement addressed to the Admiralty, the other a covering letter addressed directly to the First Lord. In the latter he entreated His Lordship to indulge any errors in his reports as he had 'never experienced such severe fatigue' and had 'run over a night of severe difficulties'.[45]

At this stage Pellew still had no knowledge of the fate of the *Amazon* and his concern is palpable. Indeed this letter to Spencer begins with a candid and heartfelt expression of concern.

> I am laboring under some difficulty in communicating with your lordship from my want of certain knowledge of my invaluable friend, Captain Reynolds. We have been very long brothers in affection and my grief would never cease should any misfortune on this occasion happen to him.[46]

In both despatches Pellew carefully refrains from identifying his adversary as a ship of the line, though he noted privately to Spencer: 'All those about me believe her a ship-of-the-line.'[47] Such a claim, had it proved false, would have been extravagant and potentially damaging. Instead Pellew described the enemy as a large ship with two tiers of guns

---

[41] Corbett, p. 380.

[42] Pipon, p. 206.

[43] Troude, p. 59.

[44] W. James, *The Naval History of Great Britain from Declaration of War by France in 1793 to the Accession of George IV*, vol. 2, p. 15.

[45] Corbett, pp. 381–2.

[46] *Ibid.*, pp. 379–80.

[47] *Ibid.*, p. 380.

and no poop, and speculated that she was a French ship *en razee*. Perhaps anticipating censure rather than praise, Pellew also appears to have been keen to deflect any criticism that might have arisen from such a risky action, with two frigates taking on a ship of such superior force in a night engagement on the enemy's very coast.

> Night actions should not be inconsiderately engaged in, but in this instance everything was to be hazarded or the escape of the enemy was absolutely certain, and altho' she was running for her own ports, yet the confidence I felt in my own knowledge of the coast of France forbade me to listen for a moment to any suggestions of danger therefrom. I placed also some considerable reliance that her commander would not voluntarily sacrifice his ship and his crew by running her for a dangerous part of the coast, and I promised myself to see the day before we should have run down our distance.[48]

To Spencer, Pellew was even more eloquent:

> I fear your lordship will think me rather imprudent on this occasion, but what can be done if an enemy's coast is always to frighten us and give them protection as safely as their ports? If Lord Hawke had no fears from a lee shore with a large fleet under his charge, could I for a moment think of two inconsiderable frigates?[49]

Typically, in his official despatch, Pellew was unstinting in his praise for his officers and men. He singled out Thomson, the master, Lieutenants Thomson, Norway and Bell, and Lieutenants O'Connor and Wilson of the Marines, but also commended 'every inferior officer in the ship'.[50] However, it was in this letter to Spencer that Pellew took the extraordinary step of requesting that the First Lord promote the entire crew by re-rating the *Indefatigable* to a fourth rate. To press home his request, Pellew reminded His Lordship that none of the crew had received promotion as a result of taking the *Virginie*.[51] Despite the brilliance and success of the engagement, Spencer did not fulfil Pellew's audacious request.

While cautiously welcoming news of the engagement, the response from Admiralty Secretary Evan Nepean was typically restrained. He noted the particulars of the engagement, remarked on the fact the Pellew had been unable to prevent his opponent running on shore and acquainted him that their Lordships were 'satisfied' with the gallantry and good conduct of both captains and crews.[52]

---

[48] *Ibid.*, p. 384.

[49] *Ibid.*, p. 380.

[50] *Ibid.*, p. 386.

[51] *Ibid.*, pp. 381–2.

[52] ADM1/2314, Captains' Letters 1797, Surname P, nos. 1–150. Enclosed with document 145.

'Satisfied' may seem like rather faint praise, and indeed several more effusive approbations have been crossed out in the draft of Nepean's reply, including 'their Lordship's command to acquaint you that they applaud very highly ...' and 'their Lordship's command to acquaint you that they Highly approve of your gallant and judicious conduct on that occasion'. However the reply also brought Pellew the undoubtedly welcome news that their Lordships were pleased to promote Lieutenant Thomson to the rank of commander.

Writing directly to Pellew on 25 January, Lord Spencer was rather more forthright in his praise and wasted no time identifying the French ship:

> I think it will turn out as I conjectured about the French ship & that she will prove to be Les Droits de L'Homme, & if so, you have the credit of having beaten an 80 gun ship with two frigates, an exploit which has not I believe ever before graced our naval Annals.[53]

While Pellew had been writing his official despatches in the great cabin of the *Indefatigable*, another account of events was being penned in the midshipmen's berth by fifteen-year-old Midshipman Nicholas Pateshall. As a previously unpublished first-hand account of this iconic engagement, Pateshall's letter to his mother bears quoting in its entirety.

Indefatigable, January 17, 1796[54]

I have not been to the post office

Dear Mama

It is with pleasure I inform you of the safe return of our ship into the land of the living. When we sailed from Falmouth we shaped our course for the coast of Spain but after a heavy gale of wind we there arrived and the same day captured a large Spanish ship and a brig, the latter is a very valuable prize for two frigates. As we were but two the next day we stood close to in shore and sent our boats in chace of 2 vessels close under the land, when they returned they brought with them one brigg and a large boat. The former one not being worth much we put what prisoners we had in her and let them go to Spain.

3 days afterwards we fell in with another Spanish brigg which we captured. We then left the Spanish coast and was returning home when on the 13th we saw a large ship shaping her course for France. The weather being very foggy we were close to her before we saw one another. We immediately prepared for action we got alongside of her by 4 o clock in the afternoon when we plainly saw her French colours. The Amazon the only ship in company was out of sight so that we had it to ourselves. The action upon both sides was extraordinary high till

---

[53] Exmouth Papers, Box 22, MSS/92/027, Spencer to Pellew, 25 January 1797.

[54] Pateshall has clearly mistaken the year.

5 o clock when the Amazon came up and then we sheered off to repair our rigging. We then saw much to our astonishment saw her to be a line of battle which of course surprised us but as we had begun then we must go through with it. We ran alongside her a second time and for 5 hours we kept up a continual fire as did she. We then dismasted her which bothered her much but we was obliged to sheer off for to repair our rigging as did the Amazon. We then went at her again like bull dogs and after an action of over 11 hours we found ourselves amongst the rocks. We then was obliged to make all sail away. The next morning we had the great pleasure to see the Frenchman go to pieces and we make no doubt but every soul must have perished as we are sure her boats must be shot to pieces. We suppose her to be one of the line of battle ships which I gave you an account of before that went with troops from Brest for the continual fire she kept up with small arms makes us believe she had a thousand men on board.

She must have had great slaughter on board her for Sir Edward himself says never was a ship fought better than we and the Amazon did. We had not one man killed which is the most surprise ... *(paper torn)* ... known but we had more than 50 men wounded ... *(paper torn)* ... I can assure you I did not at all ... *(paper torn)* ... fire so thick over my head. Sir Edward thinks that never was such an action known or even heard of. Now is the time for my asking to come home as the ship will take a long time to repair. I hope the moment you receive this that I shall hear from you.

> My duty to all.
> I remain your dutiful son.
> Nicholas Pateshall

If we had fought much longer we should have had no more powder or shot. Our first lieutenant was unfortunately wounded.[55]

Young Pateshall's letter corroborates his captain's account of the engagement almost to the letter; however it is notable that his reaction to the event differs. In his official despatch Pellew wrote that the Indefatigables 'sincerely lamented' the 'miserable fate' of the 'brave but unhappy crew'; however, while Pateshall is clearly delighted with their hard-won victory, his attitude to the 'great slaughter' and loss of life aboard *Les Droits de L'Homme* is somewhat blasé. It seems likely that although Pellew's noble assertion represented the views of the more experienced officers and men who had seen enough action to appreciate the loss, the attitude of the young gentlemen was rather more casual.

Three days later, Pateshall wrote another letter to his brother in which he related the aftermath of the engagement.

---

[55] Pateshall Papers, A95/Box 37, A95/AP/7, Nicholas Pateshall to Ann Pateshall, 17 January 1796.

20th January 1797

Dear Brother

It is with pleasure that I write to inform you that our ship is now in Hamoaze / Plymouth unrigged and will go into Dock in two days time it is astonishing the no of shot stuck in the ships side but I have the satisfaction to give you an account of the Amazon. She was so much damaged in our noble action that it was impossible for her to be saved so she ran herself on shore for to save her crew which are made prisoners of and are held in Brest Castle. Sir Edward has obtained leave to send the Captain of the Virginie in exchange for the captain of the Amazon which will be put in hand as soon as possible. The number of men killed on board the Amazon are not known in England likewise by the same report which brought the account of the Amazon that by the French account the vessel we fought and afterwards ran ashore is a 74 gun ship full of troops. Here was most of them lost after they got on shore – the number killed in the action is not yet known.

It is with concern I add that the French fleet that attacked Ireland is all got safe in Brest all save 2 which are yet missing.

All I wish is that our captain had command of the English fleet instead of the person who had it when the French fleet were out.

The most valuable of our prizes which I mentioned in my last was retaken by a French privateer within 5 miles of Falmouth in which I lost a worthy messmate and two other midshipmen.

The day I arrived I received a letter from Captain Lane concerning my coming home. He leaves it entirely to my wish but it is not at all my wish I Can assure you for it is the expectation that we shall have leave to cruise upon the Spanish coast where we please for the next cruise as our brave action is so much liked by the admiralty and the great people that they have made our worthy first lieutenant a captain and enquired if any of the Midshipmen had served their time if any of them had to send them to London immediately to pass.

Like wise ... *(illegible)* ... that the Amazons crew should be all saved as they thought by Sir Edwards letter that it was impossible for her to be saved and that they would lose no time in sending an equal number of Frenchmen to exchange for them if they would – and if they would not ... *(illegible)* ... Bravo!

...

Remember me to all

I remain your sincere NL Pateshall[56]

Pateshall's pride in his captain and in their achievement is clear, and it was no youthful boast that their brave action was 'so much liked by the

---

[56] Pateshall Papers, A95/EP/10/1, Nicholas Pateshall to Edmund Pateshall, 20 January 1797.

admiralty and the great people'. Among the tributes and commendations Pellew received was a letter from the Dowager Lady Spencer, the influential mother of the First Lord of the Admiralty, who shared 'with the nation the wish ... that your humanity and intrepidity had been crowned with the success they deserved by bringing your Prize into Port'.[57]

Word of the engagement had first reached the nation on 21 January when the London *Gazette* published a copy of Pellew's despatch only four days after it was written.[58] News of the gallant victory spread quickly as the story was picked up by other newspapers. The heroic engagement could not have come at a better time for the Admiralty as it went some way to deflecting attention from their disastrous handling of the expedition to Ireland. The public had been rightly and justifiably alarmed when it became clear that England had narrowly escaped a French invasion via Ireland and that it was the weather rather than the Royal Navy that they had to thank for their deliverance. A victorious engagement between two frigates and a ship of the line would have caught the public's imagination at any time, but the action appeared all the more heroic as it stood in stark contrast to the dismal performance of the rest of the Channel Fleet.

Accounts of the engagement in the French press were both muted and questionable. The *Gazette Nationale ou Le Moniteur Universal* reported the action on 25 January in a brief report under the heading Ministere de la Marine.[59] The report stated that *Les Droits de L'Homme* forced the *Amazon* frigate to throw herself on the coast in the Bay of Audierne, and while pursuing the rasée *Indefatigable*, the ship was attacked by an English division which made it necessary to fall on shore in the same bay.

Within months, the dashing victory of the brave frigates *Indefatigable* and *Amazon* was being celebrated across England in a popular play and broadside ballads, such as the rousing 'Amazon Frigate', which concludes with the verse:

So now the *Indefatigable* is bound for England's shore
To let our suffering country know the *Amazon*'s no more.
Still, we'll drink to George our King, we'll convince him all the same,
That British tars forever more rule lords of the main.[60]

---

[57] Taylor, p. 125.

[58] Pellew, *The Gazette*, p. 53.

[59] The full text of the brief report runs as follows: 'Le vaisseau *les Droits de l'homme*, capitaine Lacrosse, ayant recontré, aux atteráges de Brest, le vaisseau rasé anglais *l'Indefatigable* et la frégate *l'Amazone*, de 40 canons de 18, leur a livre un combat tres-vif, et la forcé la frégate, à se jeter sur la cote, dans la baie d'Audierne. Tandis, qu'il poursuivait le vausseau rasé, il a été attaqué lui-même, par a division anglaise, et il s'est trouvé dans la necéssité de s'échouer dans la même baie.' *Gazette Nationale ou Le Moniteur Universal*, p. 1.

[60] Firth, pp. 276-7.

The heroic engagement and the subsequent wreck of *Les Droits de L'Homme* also proved to be a popular and dramatic subject for contemporary marine artists, including Pocock, Brydon and Luny, and numerous representations of the action were reproduced and sold as etchings and aquatints. Thomas Luny, the Cornish artist and near neighbour of the Pellews, produced two particularly spirited and realistic paintings of the chase and the engagement, which graced the walls at Canonteign.[61] Not all painters were as concerned with authenticity as Luny, and some employed considerable artistic licence to portray an engagement that took place in pitch darkness. The *Droits de L'Homme* engagement continued to be a popular marine subject throughout the nineteenth and twentieth centuries, inspiring Victorian artists Colls and Lynn, and modern painters such as Gardiner and Hunt.

The *Droits de L'Homme* action has rightly taken its place in the annals of eighteenth-century naval history. Almost every scholarly and popular naval history of the period, from James[62] to Rodger,[63] includes a narrative of the engagement. James's lengthy account, which appeared in his influential *Naval History of Great Britain*, was published in 1837, well within the lifetime of veterans of the engagement.

The engagement also proved to be fertile ground for authors of naval adventure fiction. A highly elaborated version of the action appears in Captain Marryat's *The King's Own*, first published in 1830, although Marryat has transposed the three-way fight into a spirited duel between the *Aspasia* and her French opponent.[64] The story of *Les Droits de L'Homme* also features in Armstrong's *The Naval Lieutenant: A Nautical Romance*, published in 1865. Indeed Armstrong's account of the engagement is lifted almost word for word from Pellew's despatch, although the heroic lieutenant takes the place not of Pellew himself, but of the captured Lieutenant Elias Pipon aboard the doomed French ship.[65] On *The Naval Lieutenant*'s publication, *The Ladies' Cabinet of Fashion, Music and Romance* described the novel as 'an interesting and stirring story of the sea' and praised the fact that 'the incidents of this engagement which are taken from "James Naval History" are very graphically described'.

C. S. Forester's handling of the engagement is considerably less graphic, and his chronology is famously slippery due to the lack of dates in the text and the order in which the Hornblower novels were written. There is no mention of the engagement in *Mr. Midshipman Hornblower*, which

[61] Devonshire Association for the Advancement of Science, Literature and Art, p. 114.

[62] W. James, *The Naval History of Great Britain from Declaration of War by France in 1793 to the Accession of George IV*, vol. 2, 1837.

[63] Rodger, *The Command of the Ocean: A Naval History of Britain 1649–1815*.

[64] Marryat, p. 7.

[65] Armstrong, pp. 67–94.

covers the approximate period 1794 to 1798; instead Acting Lieutenant Hornblower leaves the *Indefatigable* in the prize ship *La Reve* which is subsequently recaptured by the Spanish, resulting in Hornblower spending an indeterminate period of time as a prisoner of war at Ferrol, thus missing the *Indefatigable*'s most famous engagement altogether.[66] However, later in the chronology (though earlier in the written sequence of the novels), Hornblower recalls the engagement several times. In *The Happy Return*, while the *Lydia* sails south for Cape Horn following the destruction of the *Natividad*, Hornblower entertains Lady Barbara Wellesley with tales of 'how Pellew took his frigates into the very surf to sing the *Droits-de-l'homme* with two thousand men on board'.[67] Later, in *A Ship of the Line*, while accompanying a convoy of Indiamen off Ushant, Hornblower reminisces to himself how 'As a lieutenant under Pellew in the *Indefatigable* ... It was in these very waters that the *Indefatigable* and the *Amazon* had driven the *Droits de l'Homme* into the breakers, and a thousand men to their deaths.'[68] Two years later, as commodore of a squadron off the coast of Swedish Pomerania, Hornblower again recalls 'as a midshipman in Pellew's *Indefatigable* being at the lead that wild night when they went in and destroyed the *Droits de l'homme* in the Biscay surf'.[69] Hornblower's recollection of his rank may be unreliable but his memory of the event is faultless: 'The details of that wild fight thirteen years ago were as distinct in his memory as those of the battle with the *Natividad* only nine months back.'[70] In typically self-deprecating fashion, Hornblower regards such vivid recall as a symptom of approaching old age. He was wrong of course. As the memorials and obituaries of his fellow midshipmen clearly reveal, the *Droits de L'Homme* engagement had a lasting impact on the lives and memories of all those men who survived that ferocious twelve-hour engagement in the dark and the storm on a winter night off Hodierne Bay.

[66] Forester, *Mr. Midshipman Hornblower*, pp. 210–54.

[67] Forester, *The Happy Return*, p. 217.

[68] Forester, *A Ship of the Line*, p. 60.

[69] Forester, *The Commodore*, p. 78.

[70] Forester, *A Ship of the Line*, p. 60.

5

The Nature of Patronage

THE young gentlemen who served under Pellew's command aboard HMS *Indefatigable* in 1797 are in many ways indicative of the countless men and boys who benefited from his patronage throughout his long career. Three individuals, George Cadogan, the son of an earl, Jeremiah Coghlan, a brave and capable merchant seaman, and William Kempthorne, the son of a Falmouth packet captain, are particularly illustrative of the breadth of Pellew's patronage and the wide range of young officers whose careers he nurtured and promoted. Irrespective of their widely varying family backgrounds and social standing, all benefited from Pellew's support, particularly during their formative years in the service. These young gentlemen highlight the nature of Pellew's patronage, his enduring friendship and the ongoing, sometimes dogged, support he provided to those who ran foul of the vicissitudes of naval service.

The Honourable George Cadogan is unique among the young gentlemen of HMS *Indefatigable* in that he was the only one of the seventeen who came to the ship bearing his own aristocratic title. On the evidence of contemporary naval biographies, Cadogan's naval career bears all the hallmarks of privilege and patronage. The eighth son of Earl Cadogan joined the navy at the age of twelve, following a recommendation from the First Lord of the Admiralty, he made lieutenant at nineteen, commander at twenty-one, post captain at twenty-four, achieved the rank of Admiral of the Red in retirement and served as naval *aide-de-camp* to two monarchs.

While Cadogan's achievements appear respectable by any measure, archival evidence reveals a troubling picture of a man who had a turbulent naval career and an unsettled family life. By the time he retired from active service, George Cadogan had survived two mutinies, lost one ship, served time as a prisoner of war, been investigated by two courts of inquiry following accusations of cruelty and brutality, and been court martialled on charges relating to the death of a young midshipman. Though honourably acquitted of all charges, accusations of tyranny and brutality dogged George Cadogan throughout his career. Cadogan's personal life was also marred by a series of scandals. His parents and his sister were involved in acrimonious and very public divorce cases, which resulted in Cadogan fighting a duel in an attempt to restore the family's honour.

Although George Cadogan appears to be a deeply contradictory individual, the picture that emerges from a close examination of the archives is much more complex than the polarised images of the privileged aristocrat with the gilded career and the brutal, tyrannical martinet would suggest.

Among the *Indefatigable*'s young officers, Jeremiah Coghlan stands out not only for his devotion to Pellew and his singularly heroic entry into the Royal Navy, but also for the fame he achieved during his lifetime as a result of his naval exploits. From first to last, his life is the stuff of naval adventure and romance, and indeed Pellew's most recent biographer describes Coghlan as Pellew's 'young Hornblower'.[1] Feted by the press and the public, and honoured by the Admiralty, Coghlan was the subject of numerous reports and despatches in the contemporary press, which awarded him the epithet 'Intrepid Jerry'.[2] Coghlan's first meeting with Pellew, on the storm-tossed deck of the shipwrecked *Dutton*, is the stuff of legend, but like all legends, mythology has a tendency to obscure the facts which, in the case of Coghlan's early life, are few and far between.

Of all the Indefatigables, William Kempthorne is the one whose early life and background most closely resemble Pellew's own. The son of a Cornish packet commander, young William's life changed abruptly when he lost his father at the age of thirteen and became responsible for supporting his mother and younger siblings. The following year, Kempthorne joined the navy as a volunteer and spent his formative years as a midshipman under Pellew's command. During his time aboard the *Indefatigable* and the *Impetueux*, he was involved in a number of dramatic engagements; he was captured in a prize by the French, only to escape and return to his own ship several months later.[3] Kempthorne received his lieutenant's commission in 1800, but was court martialled for disorderly and improper conduct and dismissed the service only a year later. Though this would have been the end of most officers' careers, Pellew continued to support the young man, immediately accepting him back aboard his ship and doggedly pursuing his case for six years until Kempthorne was finally restored to the service. His subsequent career was meritorious, culminating in his service at Algiers where he commanded the *Beelzebub* bomb vessel and was appointed as captain of Pellew's flagship on their triumphant return to Britain.

Like George Cadogan, Kempthorne's naval career was far from easy; however, when he died in 1835, only two years after his mentor, he was remembered as a good and gifted sea officer.

---

[1] Taylor, p. 160.

[2] *London Literary Gazette and Journal of Belles Lettres, Arts, Sciences, Etc*, p. 834.

[3] Marshall, *Royal Naval Biography Supplement*, part IV, pp. 114–16.

THE HONOURABLE GEORGE CADOGAN, 1783–1864

GEORGE Cadogan was born in Westminster on 5 May 1783, the second son of Charles, 1st Earl Cadogan and Mary Churchill. He had six older half-brothers through his father's first marriage to Frances Bromley, who died fifteen years before George's birth. One of these elder brothers, Thomas Cadogan, was captain of HMS *Licorne* in 1779 when Edward Pellew joined her crew as a newly commissioned lieutenant bound for the Newfoundland station. Captain Cadogan was later lost on the same station with his ship *Glorieaux* and her entire crew during a terrible hurricane in the autumn of 1782.

Young George spent most of his childhood among his brothers and sisters at Downham Hall, Suffolk, until 1784 when, at the age of eleven, he was sent to Newcombe's School in Hackney. Newcombe's, a fashionable school with a notable tradition of staging highly regarded dramatic productions, was a popular choice for the sons of prominent Whigs. Around the same time that George left for school, his mother's affair with a family friend, Reverend William Cooper, came to light. The Earl sued Cooper for criminal conversation and Lord and Lady Cadogan separated publicly and acrimoniously.[4] The following year, after spending only one year at school, George was sent to join the navy. There is no surviving correspondence to suggest whether he went to sea as a willing volunteer, so one can only speculate as to the impact these upheavals had on the boy. Whether he went willingly or not, young Cadogan certainly had the best possible entry into the service, with a letter of recommendation from the First Lord of the Admiralty himself. On 25 September 1795 Earl Spencer wrote to Captain Sir Edward Pellew, requesting that he accept young George as a volunteer aboard HMS *Indefatigable*.

> A son of Lord Cadogan a very old friend of mine is destined to the sea service ... I have undertaken to recommend him to you. He is, I understand, between 12 and 13 years of age ... I have told his father that he can be no better placed for this purpose than with you.[5]

George Cadogan joined the navy in December 1795 and was entered on the *Indefatigable*'s muster book as a Volunteer, First Class.[6] He remained under Pellew's command for the next six years and during his time on the *Indefatigable* he participated in several notable frigate actions, including the famous engagements with the *Virginie* and *Les Droits de L'Homme*. In his report to the Admiralty following the *Droits de L'Homme* engagement,

---

[4] Pearman, pp. 27–8.

[5] Exmouth Papers, Box 22, MSS/92/027, Spencer to Pellew, 25 September 1795.

[6] ADM 36/13144, Muster Table of His Majesty's Ship the Indefatigable, November 1796–October 1797.

3 George Cadogan, 3rd Earl Cadogan, 1830.
The Earl is shown with his dog, Fen, who was a gift from Sir Walter Scott.

Pellew was careful to include a commendation of the First Lord's young protégé.

> Little Cadogan is a most delightful boy, I think he promises to be everything the heart can wish. He is stationed on the quarterdeck, where I assure you my Lord, he was my friend. He stood the night out in his shirt and kept himself warm by his exertions. I can not say too much in his praise.[7]

When Pellew's captaincy of the *Indefatigable* came to an abrupt end in 1799, Cadogan was among the thirty men and boys who transferred with him to the ship of the line *Impetueux*. Like his fellow Indefatigables, Cadogan was initially rated able seaman on entering the *Impetueux* and restored to his previous rank of midshipman several weeks later. The *Impetueux* already had a reputation for insubordination before Pellew joined her and, only months after taking command, mutiny broke out while the ship was stationed in Bantry Bay. There is no indication whether Cadogan witnessed the captain defending his quarterdeck from the mutineers; he was certainly aboard the ship at the time, though unlike his fellow *Indefatigable* midshipman, Henry Hart, he did not testify at the subsequent court martial, which handed down capital sentences to three of the mutineers, and ordered five others to be flogged round the fleet.

Cadogan and Pellew parted company in December 1801 during the Peace of Amiens when Pellew took up a seat in parliament and Cadogan transferred first to the *Narcissus* and then to the *Leda*, passing his examination for lieutenant in January 1802.

Lord Spencer had not forgotten his young protégé and in May 1804 when writing to Pellew to congratulate him on his appointment as Commander in Chief of the East India station, he requested that Pellew take his former midshipman with him.

> ... if you could take George Cadogan out, you will confer an obligation both on his father and on myself which would be sensibly acknowledged, and in pushing him forward, I think you know enough of him to be convinced that he would never discredit your patronage.[8]

For whatever reason, Pellew did not take Cadogan out to India with him in 1804, and instead he was sent to the Leeward Islands station where he received his first command, the 18-gun brig-sloop *Cyane*. Cadogan initially had some success with the *Cyane*, capturing a number of prizes before his own ship was taken by the French 40-gun frigates *L'Hortense* and *L'Hermione*. Captain and crew were taken to Martinique where they were held as prisoners for eight weeks before being exchanged and returned

---

[7] Exmouth Papers, Box 22, MSS/92/027, Pellew to Spencer, 17 January 1797.

[8] Pellew of Canonteign Collection, Devon Records Office, Spencer to Pellew, 22 May 1804.

to Barbados. Although their incarceration was short-lived, Cadogan was outraged by their treatment at the hands of *L'Hortense*'s Captain Le Melliere, and wrote a strongly worded letter to the Commander in Chief of the West Indies station, Vice Admiral Alexander Cochrane, complaining of Le Melliere's 'infamous conduct' and treatment that would 'disgrace the most barbarous'.[9] On being returned to Barbados, Cadogan faced a routine court martial[10] for the loss of his ship. Although the outcome of the court martial may appear to be a foregone conclusion, as there was no question of an 18-gun brig taking on two 40-gun frigates, one has only to consider Hornblower's anxiety following the loss of the *Sutherland* to glimpse how the threat of an impending court martial could affect the spirits of a man already demoralised by defeat and captivity.[11] In the event of the court martial, like Hornblower, Cadogan and his crew were honourably and unanimously acquitted of all charges.

Following the court martial, Cadogan returned to England where, six months later in March 1806, he was appointed to his next command, the new 18-gun brig-sloop *Ferret*, and ordered to sail for the Jamaica station. As a newly commissioned vessel, fresh off the stocks at Dartmouth, the *Ferret* required a new crew, and the muster reveals that many came from the *Salvador del Mundo* receiving ship at Hamoaze.[12] Receiving ships were hulks that housed seamen between cruises, newly pressed or recruited men, prisoners awaiting trial and some already convicted of offences. Forming such a mixed group into a competent and disciplined crew required considerable strength of character and ability to command, which it appears Cadogan lacked. The captain's log of the *Ferret* has not survived, but the master's log records numerous floggings, suggesting that Cadogan struggled to command his new crew.[13] Over a six-month period, discipline aboard the *Ferret* deteriorated and punishments increased until, on 26 September 1806, the crew mutinied, attempting to seize the sloop and carry her to the enemy in La Guaira or Porto Cabello. Cadogan may have lacked the ability to command, but he did not lack courage; roused from his cabin at midnight, he faced down the armed mutineers, regained control of the ship and returned to Port Royal, where eleven of the mutineers, including the boatswain, who was identified as the ringleader, were court martialled and condemned to hang.[14]

---

[9] ADM 12/117, Digest 79:31, Cadogan to Cochrane, 8 July 1805.

[10] ADM 1/5370, Cyane Court Martial 1805. The court martial took place on 11 July 1805, aboard HMS *Unicorn*, Carlisle Bay, Barbados.

[11] Forester, *Flying Colours*, p. 19.

[12] ADM 37/1605–1606, Muster Table of His Majesty's Sloop the Ferret, 1805–1806.

[13] ADM 52/2757, Master's Log of His Majesty's Sloop the Ferret, 12 May 1806.

[14] ADM 1/5373, Ferret Court Martial, 1806.

Prior to the court martial it appears that a court of inquiry was called to investigate the mutineers' complaints of tyranny and oppression against Cadogan. Although no record of the investigation survives, Cadogan stated in a letter to his father that he received a 'most flattering acquittal'.[15]

As a result of the *Ferret* mutiny, several authors have sought to compare Cadogan to Hugh Pigot, the notoriously brutal captain of HMS *Hermione*. In *Mutiny: In the British and Commonwealth Forces, 1797–1956*, James describes Cadogan as 'a pitiless officer whose remorseless use of the lash made Pigot appear gentle'.[16] While the master's log of the *Ferret* reveals that the rate and severity of punishments were indeed harsh,[17] comparison to Byrn's meticulous analysis of the disciplinary record of seventy-three ships stationed in the Lesser Antilles between 1784 and 1812 shows that it was by no means excessive for the Leeward Islands station at this time.[18]

The mutiny and court martial had a profound impact on Cadogan, and on the eve of the mutineers' execution, he wrote a despairing letter to his father.

> My mind is really in so agitated and wretched a state ... To add to my late misfortunes what to you think of my ship almost being all but carried in to a Spanish port by the most mutinous lot of rascals that ever existed?[19]

Cadogan provided his father with a brief account of the mutiny before lamenting the fate of the mutineers.

> Have since tried all unfortunate deluded wretches who are all doomed to suffer here tomorrow morning. I have not the words to express my feelings upon the occasion – and am only upheld by the conscious rectitude of the cause for which they suffer, and of having done justice to my country, and having acquitted myself, I trust, with personal credit. They are all thank God sensible of their guilt and in

---

[15] Huntington Library, ST6 Correspondence Box 137(29), Cadogan to Earl Cadogan, 13 October 1806.

[16] James, *Mutiny: In the British and Commonwealth Forces*, p. 71; Gutteridge, p. 84.

[17] ADM 52/2757, Master's Log of His Majesty's Sloop the Ferret, 12 May 1806. The master's log records forty-two separate punishment incidents in the period between 7 June 1806 and the mutiny on 26 September. These ranged from twelve to forty-eight lashes, mostly for insolence, drunkenness, disobedience of orders and neglect of duty. The log does not record the names of all those punished; however six of the mutineers' names do appear, including one who received ninety lashes for drunkenness.

[18] Byrn, Appendix B, pp. 211–20.

[19] Huntington Library, ST6 Correspondence Box 137(29), Cadogan to Earl Cadogan, 13 October 1806.

their last moments acknowledged their ingratitude to me and their treachery to their country – I have hardly spirit to proceed here further ...

I am very low, & unwell, & only hope somebody will say something for me for I really have neither health nor strength to go through much more here ... God send this may find you in better spirits and health than it leaves your unfortunate and wretched son.[20]

The contrast between the anguished tone of this extraordinary personal letter and the stiff formality of Cadogan's Admiralty correspondence is marked and gives a rare insight into the impact that the rigours of the service could have on a young man. The Earl was sufficiently moved to forward his son's letter to his former patron, Lord Spencer, writing:

I here enclose a most melancholy letter from Poor George I rec'd this day, & shall make no other observations on it except that I flatter myself as he has been honourably acquitted of the charges bro't against him, & has bro't his ships Crew to condign punishment that no obstacle can now be brought forward to his preferment on that score. What I most fear for is his health in that cursed climate.[21]

Spencer had not forgotten the young boy he had recommended to Pellew eleven years before and wrote a characteristically dry letter to Thomas Grenville, First Lord of the Admiralty, enclosing the correspondence from both Cadogan and his father.

I sent you a letter I have received from poor old L'd Cadogan inclosing one from his Son, and I really hope that it may melt your hard heart & that you will send him out a commission for the Pomona or some other frigate on the station. Though from the tenor of this letter, I really would not be surprised to hear that he had died of the yellow fever which always seizes people when they are in low spirits.[22]

Despite his wretched spirits, Cadogan confounded Spencer's expectations; although his health clearly suffered, he did not succumb. He finally made post captain on 27 March 1807 and three months later was discharged, 'Invalided', from the *Ferret* and the West Indies station.[23]

Cadogan appears to have rallied once he returned home and in October 1807 he was appointed to his next command, the sixth rate HMS *Crocodile*, and ordered to the Cape of Good Hope with despatches for his former captain, Sir Edward Pellew, then serving as Commander in Chief of the

[20] *Ibid.*

[21] Huntington Library, ST6 Correspondence Box 137(28), Earl Cadogan to Spencer, 27 November 1806.

[22] Huntington Library, ST6 Correspondence Box 163(73), Spencer to Grenville, 29 November 1806.

[23] ADM 35/2806, Ferret Pay Book, 1806–1810.

East Indies station. The *Crocodile* proved to be another troublesome command; returning from the Cape, trouble flared, centring around one Midshipman William Richard Badcock. Badcock was cautioned, reprimanded and punished repeatedly, but to little effect. By the time they returned to Portsmouth, Badcock had been disrated to landsman and he was discharged in June 1808 without the usual certificate of good conduct. Following his discharge, Badcock issued a formal complaint to the Admiralty about the conduct of Captain Cadogan and his first lieutenant, Barnet Devon. A court of inquiry investigated the charges, agreed there was a case to answer and ordered Cadogan to be court martialled and Badcock to provide evidence. Before he could leave the Nore, however, Badcock fell ill; his condition deteriorated rapidly and, despite being moved first to the hospital ship *Sussex,* and then to the house of his grandfather and guardian, Richard Cumberland, he died of fever and disease of the bowel in the '17th year of his age and the 6th of his service in the Navy'.[24]

Cumberland was a well-known critic and dramatist who, unfortunately for Cadogan, also happened to be famously litigious and protective of the family name. Barely a fortnight after his grandson's death, Cumberland submitted a lengthy memorial to the Admiralty accusing Cadogan and Devon of illegal, arbitrary, tyrannical and unjust punishment of Badcock which very materially contributed to his death.[25] The Admiralty summoned Cadogan for court martial on the charges brought by Cumberland, and in early April 1809, he was tried for cruelty, tyranny and oppression, exercised on Midshipman Badcock. However, all the evidence presented for both the prosecution and defence suggested that if there was fault to be found, it lay not with Cadogan but with Badcock. Witness after witness testified that he was insolent, insubordinate and ungovernable, that he continually left the deck during his watch, was repeatedly contemptuous to the officers and, most tellingly, that he had been disrated by the ship's previous captain. In the face of overwhelming evidence of Badcock's unruly and insubordinate conduct, the court martial found that the charges against Cadogan had not been proved, that many of Cumberland's allegations were unfounded and that Badcock's death could not in the most remote degree be ascribed to the punishment he received aboard the *Crocodile*. Consequently Cadogan was acquitted of all charges. Despite his acquittal, the court martial once again took its toll on Cadogan, and a fortnight later he wrote to the Admiralty, requesting two months' leave, explaining that 'The state of my health being so bad as to render me incapable to carry on my duty for the present.' The Admiralty agreed to Cadogan's request and he was allowed leave of absence before being discharged from command of HMS *Crocodile* in June 1809.

---

[24] ADM 1/5395, Cumberland Memorial in Cadogan Court Martial, 1809.
[25] *Ibid.*

Cadogan's family life was scarcely less turbulent than his naval career at this time. In 1808 his sister Charlotte left her husband Henry Wellesley, and eloped with the dashing cavalry commander Lord Paget, who abandoned his wife and eight children.[26] The affair caused a public scandal; with much of the opprobrium being heaped on Charlotte and the family name being dragged through the mud, Cadogan called Paget out in May 1809, barely a month after the *Crocodile* court martial. The duel took place on Wimbledon Common, and though both fired, neither party was injured and they agreed to leave the field.[27] In *The Hornblower Companion*, C. S. Forester described the elopement as 'one of the most resounding scandals of a scandal-ridden age' and credited the incident with providing the inspiration for the character of Lady Barbara Wellesley and her affair with Hornblower.[28]

Cadogan returned to sea in 1809 as captain of the 32-gun frigate *Pallas*, and joined the fleet sent to the Scheldt to evacuate the army following the disastrous Walcheren campaign, a service for which he was highly commended. The following year, in 1810, Cadogan obtained a short leave of absence to marry Honoria Blake, the sister of an Irish peer, and the couple later went on to have four sons and two daughters. Cadogan returned to the Channel Fleet after his marriage and in June 1811 was appointed to command the new 42-gun heavy frigate *Havannah*. The following year the *Havannah* was sent to join the Mediterranean Fleet, commanded by Cadogan's former mentor Sir Edward Pellew. The *Havannah* was despatched first to Toulon and then to join the Adriatic squadron where Cadogan had great success destroying shore batteries and seizing a total of fifty-eight armed vessels and merchant ships around the Illyrian Provinces. As the Adriatic campaign reached its conclusion with the fall of Trieste, Cadogan's successful command culminated with the Battle of Zara where he commanded the naval forces at the reduction of the heavily defended fortress after a sustained cannonade lasting thirteen days.[29] Once again, Cadogan was commended by his commodore, Vice Admiral Fremantle, for his 'judgement, perseverance and ability'. He was awarded the Knight's Cross of the Military Order of Maria Theresa by the Emperor of Austria in recognition of his 'outstanding distinction in the face of the enemy',[30] and in 1815 he was made Companion of the Order of the Bath. Zara marked the end of Cadogan's naval career afloat; however he went on to serve as naval *aide-de-camp* first to King William IV and later to Queen Victoria.

Despite being only eighth in line to inherit his father's title and estate, all seven of Cadogan's brothers pre-deceased him and in 1832 he became

---

[26] Pearman, pp. 104–6.

[27] *The Sporting Magazine*, vol. 34, 1809.

[28] Forester, *The Hornblower Companion*, pp. 83, 86.

[29] Marshall, *Royal Naval Biography Supplement*, part I, pp. 196–7.

[30] Pearman, p. 145.

3rd Earl Cadogan, having already been created Baron Oakley of Caversham the previous year. Cadogan took his seat in the House of Lords in 1831 and voted against a number of causes that threatened to impact on the rights of landowners and rural constituents, including the repeal of the Corn Laws and the Extension of the Great Western Railway Bill. Like several of his surviving *Indefatigable* shipmates, Cadogan supported a number of naval charities including the Royal Navy Club, the Shipwrecked Fishermen and Mariners Benevolent Society and the Royal Naval Benevolent Society.

It seems, however, that Cadogan's real passion lay with cultural activities. An enthusiastic collector and antiquarian, he was a trustee and member of both the Society of Antiquaries and the British Museum. He was also an accomplished amateur musician and friend of the author Sir Walter Scott. Cadogan's aesthetic and naval interests came together when he was elected to the Nelson Memorial Committee, which raised funds by public subscription for a national monument to commemorate the fallen hero of Trafalgar. When a design competition for the monument was launched, Cadogan was a member of the sub-committee chaired by the Duke of Wellington that selected the winning entry by William Railton.

In the upper echelons of society, it appears that Cadogan was held in high regard as the archetype of the cultured, aristocratic naval officer. In *The Idler in France*, the writer and socialite, Marguerite Gardiner, Countess of Blessington, described Captain Cadogan as 'frank high-spirited and well bred – the very *beau ideal* of a son of the sea, possessing all the attributes of that generous race, joined to all those said to be peculiar to the high-born and well educated'.[31]

In retirement Cadogan rose to the rank of Admiral of the Red and in 1837 he was one of only four Indefatigables who lived long enough to receive the Naval General Service Medal with clasps for both the *Virginie* and *Droits de L'Homme* engagements. Cadogan was widowed in 1845 and spent his final years at his home in Piccadilly, cared for by his two daughters. When he died in 1864 at the age of eighty-one, George, 3rd Earl Cadogan, was one of the very last survivors of the crew of the *Indefatigable* who had taken on *Les Droits de L'Homme* almost seventy years before.

Over the course of his naval career George Cadogan experienced the best and the worst of the sea service and his few surviving letters provide a glimpse of the personal cost of these events. Cadogan may never have ascended to the heights of his early mentor, Captain Sir Edward Pellew, but neither did he sink to the depths of the brutal Captain Hugh Pigot, as some have suggested. His letters suggest a man of some sensibility who was moved and affected by the events that he experienced and who is ultimately revealed as a deeply human individual.

---

[31] Blessington, p. 252.

4 Captain Jeremiah Coghlan, RN.
Silhouette by unknown artist.

JEREMIAH COGHLAN, *c.* 1778–1844

LITTLE of certainty is known about Jeremiah Coghlan's early life; his date of birth is unknown but it appears likely that he was born in the late 1770s. The *Indefatigable*'s muster book[32] records that he came from Crookhaven in southwest Cork and this is supported by his will, which refers to family and property in Crookhaven.[33]

Several accounts of Coghlan's life claim that he was a friendless orphan; however, one colourful report of his early years, by the celebrated dandy, Captain Gronow, alleges that he left home owing to the 'cruel conduct of his mother'.[34] Gronow relates that Coghlan went to sea as a cabin boy of a merchant sloop, but owing to the brutality of the captain, he deserted the ship in Neath, where he was caught and brought before the magistrate. On hearing Coghlan's plea of ill-treatment, the magistrate allowed him to leave the sloop and take up employment as a bricklayer's lad. Coghlan soon left this employment and joined a ship bound for Plymouth where he arrived just in time to witness the *Dutton* East Indiaman running aground in a storm. Though stirring, Gronow's account is highly suspect as he concludes his tale by stating that 'Poor Coghlan' died young 'owing to the wounds he had received in the service'.[35] In actual fact, Coghlan lived well into his late sixties.

Though details of his childhood are obscure, all accounts of Coghlan's life agree that he first encountered Pellew at the wreck of the *Dutton* East Indiaman, which ran aground below the citadel at Plymouth during a tremendous storm on 26 January 1796. But here the consensus ends and even the circumstances of this celebrated event are in dispute. In the myriad accounts of the disaster, sixteen-year-old Coghlan is variously described as the mate of a collier, a merchant vessel, a transport brig, an East Indiaman, and the *Dutton* itself. Some reports place Coghlan on shore at the time, relating how he swam out to the wreck carrying a line, which was then used to ferry passengers ashore.[36] Others have Coghlan stepping forward when Pellew asks if any man has heart enough to swim out to the ship with him carrying a line.[37] In some accounts, Coghlan takes a boat from the Barbican and rescues 'not less than fifty men from a watery grave'.[38] In other accounts, Coghlan is aboard a merchant vessel lying at

---

[32] ADM 36/13144, Muster Table of His Majesty's Ship the Indefatigable, November 1796–October 1797.

[33] Collyer, pp. 248–53.

[34] Gronow, p. 46.

[35] *Ibid.*, pp. 46–9.

[36] Marshall, *Royal Naval Biography Supplement*, part II, p. 298.

[37] *Westmorland Gazette*, Saturday 5 June 1824.

[38] Marshall, *Royal Naval Biography Supplement*, part II, p. 298.

Plymouth[39] and takes a boat manned by four volunteers, saving 'a hundred frightened wretches'[40] from the stricken East Indiaman. One fanciful version of events had Coghlan coming alongside in a boat, only to be chastised by Pellew for tying a lubberly bowline knot and told that he would be afraid to serve on board his ship. Coghlan responded that he would tie a knot with Pellew and was not afraid of any service, whereupon Pellew invited him to join the *Indefatigable* as midshipman.[41]

The majority of accounts relating Coghlan's heroic part in the *Dutton* rescue were published following Pellew's death in 1833 and Coghlan's own death in 1844, over forty years after the events being described. The reports that appeared in the immediate aftermath of the disaster make no mention of Coghlan, and the first press report that places him with Pellew at the wreck was published in 1801,[42] by which time Coghlan's name was already well known owing to his heroic command of the *Viper* cutter the previous year. Although the more credible contemporary accounts of the *Dutton* rescue do not mention Coghlan by name, several describe two open boats going to the assistance of the stricken vessel, and it is possible that Coghlan was present in one or other of these boats. An eyewitness account by the brother of the painter James Northcote, written two days after the disaster, describes how Pellew boarded the *Dutton* and, after helping to restore order, 'became active in getting out the women and the sick, who were with difficulty got into the open boats'.[43] Some years later, in a private letter to his friend and secretary, Edward Hawke Locker, Pellew recalled:

> I felt more pleasure in giving to his mother's arms a dear little infant safe than I ever felt in my life. The struggle she had to entrust me with the bantling was a scene I can not describe.[44]

If Coghlan was indeed aboard one of the open boats used to evacuate women, children and invalids from the wreck, it may account for the significant impression he appears to have made on Pellew.

The only man who could provide an authoritative account of the *Dutton* rescue, Coghlan himself, has left only tantalising glimpses of the event. In a letter written by Coghlan in 1836 to Pellew's third son George, regarding his plan to write a biography of his father to refute Osler's work, Coghlan denounces Osler's biography as 'catchpenny trash' before going on to state: 'The Dutton history I can put together in half an hour at any time and refute many of Mr Osler's statements which are entirely at variance with facts.'[45]

---

[39] Brenton, p. 100.

[40] *The Morning Post*, Monday 28 January 1833.

[41] *The Elgin Courant and Morayshire Advertiser*, Friday 29 March 1844.

[42] *The Morning Chronicle*, 14 August 1801.

[43] Northcote and Hazlitt, pp. 280–4.

[44] Pellew to Locker, 13 July 1811, quoted in Taylor, p. 94.

[45] Exmouth Papers, Box 22, MSS/92/027, Coghlan to Pellew, 22 August 1836.

If Coghlan did ever take half an hour to write the history of the *Dutton*, sadly his account has not come to light. However he did recall the event in a deeply moving condolence letter written to Fleetwood Pellew in 1833 following Pellew's death.

> It is thirty seven years this day since I first beheld that beloved man on the gangway of the Dutton. Great God! How strongly is his presence on that eventful day before my imagination at this moment, when totally regardless of the universal danger that surrounded him, he braved them all for the preservation of his fellow creatures, who under Providence, he rescued from inevitable destruction. His great master-mind directing and his noble example urging them to exertions never surpassed if ever equalled.

Whatever Coghlan's role in events, all accounts of the *Dutton* rescue conclude with Pellew offering him a place on his quarterdeck. While the terms of Pellew's offer may be a little fanciful, Coghlan did indeed join the *Indefatigable* later that year; the muster records that he came aboard in Falmouth on 20 July 1786, as a volunteer from an East Indiaman, and that he was paid five pounds bounty on joining.

On entering the *Indefatigable* Coghlan was initially rated able before being promoted to master's mate in January 1797. He was rated midshipman between June and October that same year, before being restored to master's mate, a rank he retained for the rest of his service aboard the frigate. This pattern of re-rating is typical of Pellew's deployment of experienced merchant seamen to supplement or replace officers who were temporarily seconded to other ships of the squadron, a practice clearly illustrated by the case of Coghlan's shipmate Alex McVicar.

When Pellew was forced to leave the *Indefatigable* in 1799, Coghlan accompanied him to the *Impetueux*, and it was during this stage of his career that he made a name for himself as 'Intrepid Jerry'. In 1800, in recognition of his gallantry during boat actions off Belleisle, Coghlan was appointed to command the 12-gun cutter *Viper* as acting lieutenant.[46] While stationed off Port Louis, south of Lorient, Coghlan requested a cutter with twelve volunteers from the *Impetueux*, in order to board one of the gunboats stationed at the entrance of the harbour. On the night of 29 July, Coghlan took the *Impetueux*'s boat with twenty men and, accompanied by two boats from the *Viper* and the frigate *Amethyst*, the former commanded by his *Indefatigable* shipmate Nicholas Pateshall,[47] they set out to board the *Cerbère* gun brig. The brig, which was anchored below three batteries, less than a mile from a flagship and two frigates, was armed with three 24-pound long guns and four 6-pounders. In a despatch

[46] Marshall, *Royal Naval Biography Supplement*, part II, p. 299.

[47] Pateshall was one of only four surviving veterans to be awarded the Naval General Service Medal clasp for the 29 July 1800 boat action.

to Lord St Vincent, Commander in Chief of the Channel Fleet, Pellew presented a stirring account of the engagement:

> Undismayed by such formidable appearances, the early discovery of the approach (for they were at quarters) and the lost aid of the two other boats, he bravely determined to attack alone and boarded her on the quarter; but unhappily in the dark jumping into a trawl net he was pierced through the thigh by a pike and several of his men hurt and all knocked back into the boat.
>
> Unchecked in ardour, they hauled the boat further ahead and again boarded and maintained against 87 men, 16 of whom were soldiers, an obstinate conflict, killing six and wounding twenty, among whom was every officer belonging to her. His own loss was one killed and eight wounded; himself in two places; Mr Paddon in six.[48]

Pellew concluded his glowing report of the action by professing his admiration for the courage and skill of the 'handful of brave fellows'.[49]

St Vincent was equally impressed and wrote immediately to the Admiralty expressing his pride and admiration and urging their Lords Commissioners to grant Coghlan promotion despite 'the circumstance of his not having completed his time in his Majesty's Navy'.[50] Lord Spencer was more than happy to take up Coghlan's cause and on 9 August wrote to Pellew informing him that he had submitted a humble request that His Majesty should be pleased to authorise an Order in Council dispensing with the regulations in respect to time in service and to approve Coghlan's promotion to lieutenant immediately.[51]

Writing to Pellew, St Vincent was even more unstinting in his praise: 'Sir – No language can convey the highest sense I entertain of the service performed by acting Lieutenant Coghlan, Mr Paddon, and the other brave fellows under his command.'[52] The Earl professed himself 'transported by the noble exploit performed by your friend Coghlan', adding that he had ordered a gold sword to the value of one hundred guineas to be made and presented to Coghlan.[53]

The Admiralty Office lost no time in publishing Pellew and St Vincent's despatches in the London *Gazette*[54] and the account of the *Viper*'s action was widely circulated in service journals and the popular press, sealing

---

[48] Marshall, *Royal Naval Biography Supplement*, part II, pp. 299–300.

[49] *Ibid.*, p. 300.

[50] *The Naval Chronicle*, vol. 4, pp. 153–4.

[51] Pellew of Canonteign Collection, Devon Records Office, Spencer to Pellew, 9 August 1800.

[52] Marshall, *Royal Naval Biography Supplement*, part II, p. 301.

[53] Coghlan's sabre survives and was sold at auction in 2010.

[54] *The Gazette*, from Tuesday 5 August to Saturday 9 August 1800, pp. 897–8.

Coghlan's reputation as a dashing naval hero. Owing to his injuries, Coghlan was unable to bring home his prize, the *Cerbère*, so the honour fell to his friend and former shipmate Nicholas Pateshall.[55]

On his return to England, Coghlan's lieutenant's commission was confirmed despite having served just over four years in the navy. Coghlan remained in command of the *Viper* for another year and had considerable success taking further prizes, which were sold through his agent, Samuel Pellew, brother of Sir Edward. Pellew himself continued to promote Coghlan at every opportunity and kept the Admiralty and the Commander in Chief informed of his successes.

The *Viper* was decommissioned in October 1801 and Coghlan remained on the beach until April 1802 when he was appointed to command the *Nimble* cutter and ordered to cruise off the west coast of Ireland to suppress smuggling, an activity for which he was publicly honoured by the city of Cork.

Like many of his contemporaries, Coghlan disappears from Admiralty records during the Peace of Amiens; however it appears that around this time he married Isabella Hay, daughter of Charles Hay of Jamaica. The couple had one son, William Marcus Coghlan,[56] who was born in 1803, and one daughter, named after Pellew's wife, Susan Pellew Coghlan.

In late 1804, Coghlan returned to active service when he was promoted to the rank of commander and appointed to the 18-gun ship-sloop *Renard* on the West Indies station. Over the next two years the *Renard* was involved in a number of notable engagements including one with the French privateer *Le Général Ernouf*, an 18-gun corvette, off Santa Domingo. At the commencement of the action the captain of the privateer is reported to have ordered Coghlan to strike, to which he is reputed to have responded 'Aye! I'll strike, and damned hard too, my lad, directly.'[57] Coghlan was as good as his word and after a short but severe action the privateer caught fire and blew up. Coghlan immediately ordered his only undamaged boat to be launched to rescue the 'brave but unfortunate survivors' and succeeded in saving all those that had survived the explosion.

In April 1807 Coghlan transferred to the 16-gun brig-sloop *Elk* and was placed in command of a small light squadron stationed in the Bahamas. It was a successful command, which he retained for four years. By the end of his six-year tour of duty in the West Indies Coghlan had received numerous letters of thanks from dignitaries, including the mayor of Kingston and the governor of Nassau, for his efforts in protecting the welfare and commercial interests of the colonies.

[55] O'Byrne, p. 871.

[56] Sir William Marcus Coghlan served in the Bombay Artillery and rose to the rank of Brigadier Colonel. He was knighted for diplomatic services in Aden.

[57] Marshall, *Royal Naval Biography Supplement*, part II, p. 304.

Jeremiah Coghlan finally made post captain in November 1810 and in September 1812 was appointed as flag captain of Admiral Sir Edward Pellew's 120-gun flagship *Caledonia*, in the Mediterranean. When Coghlan left England to join his old mentor, he carried with him a letter for Pellew from their former *Indefatigable* shipmate George Bell.

> I could not allow Coghlan to leave England for the Mediterranean without my most hearty wishes for your health and success ... I rejoice at your going to have Coghlan near you, for in him you will find a sincere Friend and a brave honourable Man.[58]

Even as flag captain, Coghlan continued his heroics, and in August 1813, he led a detachment of marines during an assault on five batteries defending the port of Cassis. For much of the period from 1812 to 1814 the *Caledonia* was engaged in blockading the French fleet in the port of Toulon. While Pellew's blockade successfully contained the fleet, he was unable to bring them to action. However, in February 1814 six of the French fleet put to sea and were pursued by fifteen of Pellew's ships. Although the *Caledonia* exchanged broadsides with the French Rear Admiral's 130-gun ship *Wagram*, a shift in the wind prevented a close engagement and the French were able to retreat under the protection of the shore batteries.

Towards the end of 1814, Coghlan transferred from the flagship to the 38-gun frigate *Alcmene*. He continued to serve in the Mediterranean and in the summer of 1815 was stationed in the Bay of Naples where he was instrumental in maintaining order following Murat's withdrawal from the city. In recognition of these services, Coghlan was created Commander of the Bath in June 1815.

After the end of the war, Coghlan, like many of his contemporaries, found himself beached on half pay, though he appears to have received occasional minor commissions. In May 1824 he was briefly appointed to the *Dartmouth*, a frigate in ordinary at Hamoaze being fitted out for the Jamaica station.

In March 1826 Coghlan received a final naval commission when he was placed in command of the *Forte* frigate and despatched to Brazil, where he became senior officer at the port of Rio. A series of letters from early 1828 between Coghlan, Sir Robert Gordon, Minister Plenipotentiary to Brazil, and Admiral Sir Robert Otway, Commander in Chief of the South American station, reveal a tense situation. British seamen were being induced by crimps to desert and join the Brazilian navy, and officers and men going ashore were harassed by men alleged to be in the pay of the Brazilian government. Coghlan reported these incidents to Gordon requesting that he make formal representation to the Brazilian

---

[58] Exmouth Papers, Box 4, Bell to Pellew, 29 July 1812, quoted in Taylor, p. 223.

government[59] to 'make immediate reparation for this unprecedented outrage'.[60] Gordon agreed to privately represent the case to the Brazilian minister but pointed out that the affair should not be treated officially between the governments. Outraged by Gordon's failure to act, Coghlan escalated his complaints to Admiral Otway who wrote to Gordon requesting that he call on the Brazilian government to 'remedy these acts of so great injury to the King's service and of injustice to the British seamen'.[61] Although it is unclear whether or how these incidents were resolved, Coghlan exacted a petty revenge on Gordon by refusing his request to transport a Mr Garcia to Montevideo, responding rather acidly:

> I beg to inform you that as it does not appear that Mr Garcia's intended visit to Monte Video is connected with His Britannic Majesty's service, I regret that it is not in my power to comply with your request ... it being contrary to positive orders.[62]

After spending four years in South America, Coghlan's final naval command came to an end and he retired from active service in July 1830. Few records have survived from Coghlan's later civilian years, though his name occasionally appears in press reports of social engagements and public events. In 1840 Coghlan was awarded an Admiralty pension of £150 per annum, and two years later, he was offered a position as commissioner of Greenwich Hospital, an appointment he declined.

When Coghlan died at his home on the Isle of Wight in 1844 at the age of sixty-nine, he was a man of considerable wealth and his will bequeaths significant sums to his family. However his relationship with his wife appears to have broken down irreparably, as his will also includes an extraordinary indictment of her.

> To the wretched woman I am obliged to call my wife Mrs Isabella Coghlan I will and bequeath one thousand pounds of the aforesaid sum which in addition to the pension she will receive in case of my death and which she has forfeited a thousand times by her abandoned and profligate conduct is infinitely more than she deserves.[63]

Although there is no indication as to what caused Jeremiah and Isabella's marital problems, they appear to have been living apart since the early

---

[59] British Library, MS 43214: 1826–1828, Aberdeen Papers, vol. 176, Coghlan to Gordon, 8 February 1828.

[60] British Library, MS 43214: 1826–1828, Aberdeen Papers, vol. 176, Coghlan to Gordon, 12 February 1828, *Forte*, Rio de Janeiro.

[61] British Library, MS 43214: 1826–1828, Aberdeen Papers, vol. 176, Otway to Gordon, 1 April 1828, *Ganges*, Rio de Janeiro.

[62] British Library, MS 43214: 1826–1828, Aberdeen Papers, vol. 176, Coghlan to Gordon, 25 February 1828, *Forte*, Rio de Janeiro.

[63] PROB 11/2910, Will of Jeremiah Coghlan.

1840s at least, and quite likely much earlier. At the time of the 1841 census, Coghlan was still living on the Isle of Wight, while Isabella was presiding over a large household in Blackheath consisting of her daughter and her four children, some of her son's children, four servants and a governess. The presence of children and grandchildren in Isabella's household suggests that her estrangement from her husband had not resulted in any separation from her family, and it appears that she provided a home base for her son and son-in-law when they returned from service in India. Isabella outlived her husband by many years and died in 1875 in Ramsgate, Kent, aged eighty-seven.

When Coghlan's death was announced, it was widely reported in the press along with many florid accounts of his funeral.

> His obsequies were those of a sailor. Six seamen, sons of the ocean, like himself, bore him to his place of final rest. Emblematic of the heart it shrouded – now cold indeed – but which once glowed with irrepressible energy and indomitable courage, his coffin was of English oak – and instead of the melancholy pall, it was covered with the flag beneath which he had fought his way through danger and death, to victory and fame, which was his glory in life, and now honoured in death.[64]

Countless memorials extolled Coghlan's virtues as a 'most excellent and meritorious officer'[65] and, without exception, every obituary lauded his distinguished bravery, 'intrepidity, firmness and humanity'.[66] Many also recalled his gallant service at the wreck of the *Dutton* and his relationship with Pellew. Of all the veterans of the *Indefatigable*, Coghlan is the only one whose obituaries fail to mention the *Droits de L'Homme* engagement; such was the mythology that surrounded Intrepid Jerry that his heroic exploits surpassed even this iconic engagement.

WILLIAM KEMPTHORNE, 1781–1835

William Kempthorne was born in 1781, the eldest of six children born to packet commander William Kempthorne, and his wife Elizabeth, herself a packet captain's daughter. The family lived in Flushing, the village across the Fal estuary from Falmouth where many naval officers and packet captains lived in fine houses overlooking the harbour.

When William was about two years old, a newly married couple, Edward and Susan Pellew, moved into the house immediately adjacent to the Kempthornes on the elegant terrace of New Road. The Pellew's first child, Emma, was born in 1785, the same year as William's sister Belinda, and the

---

[64] *The Hampshire Advertiser*, Saturday 30 March 1844.

[65] *The Freeman's Journal*, Dublin, 11 March 1844.

[66] *Bury and Norwich Post, and East Anglian*, 20 March 1844.

next four children of both families were born and grew up together between 1786 and 1793.[67] The two households became very close, and a connecting door is said to have been knocked between the two houses to allow the families to come and go.[68]

In 1794 William Kempthorne senior died of yellow fever when his packet *Antelope* was captured by a squadron of French frigates en route to North America. This left his son, still only thirteen, with a family of five younger siblings to support. The following year, in 1795, Pellew took young Kempthorne on board the *Indefatigable* as a second class volunteer, and the muster books show his standard progression through the ranks from second to first class volunteer, to able seaman, midshipman and a short period as master's mate.

Like many of the *Indefatigable*'s midshipmen, Kempthorne was given an opportunity to develop his command skills and test his seamanship when he was selected in the autumn of 1797 to join a prize crew commanded by his senior messmate and fellow Falmouth boy, Thomas Groube. In addition to the two midshipmen, the prize crew consisted of ten seamen, suggesting that the prize was a large vessel or had a considerable number of prisoners aboard.[69] Marshall's *Royal Naval Biography* takes up the account:

> At the age of sixteen years he was taken by the republicans, taken into Rochelle and there confined in the same prison with the common malefactors. After a captivity of six weeks however, he had the good fortune to effect his escape, along with another Cornish youth, Mr Henry Gilbert, and in the course of a few more days was safe again aboard the *Indefatigable*.[70]

Marshall has Kempthorne's age correct but the *Indefatigable*'s 1798 muster records that he, Groube and at least some of the seamen returned to their ship on the second of March, suggesting that their captivity was closer to four months. There is no sign in the *Indefatigable*'s musters of Henry Gilbert, and thus far he has not been identified from other naval sources.[71]

---

[67] LDS P00963-1, Parish registers of St Gluvias and Mylor, Cornwall, baptisms of Emma Pellew, Belinda Kempthorne, Fleetwood Pellew, Mary Anna Kempthorne, Julia Pellew, Renatus Kempthorne, George Pellew and Harriet Kempthorne.

[68] Parkinson, *Edward Pellew: Viscount Exmouth, Admiral of the Red*, p. 135.

[69] ADM 36/13144, Muster Table of His Majesty's Ship the Indefatigable, November 1796–October 1797. The *Indefatigable*'s muster book for 1797 records that Kempthorne and the other members of the prize crew were discharged after being 'captured by the enemy in a prize' on 1 November. They were placed on the supernumeraries list for wages only until their return in March 1798.

[70] Marshall, *Royal Naval Biography Supplement*, part IV, pp. 114–16.

[71] ADM 36/13145, Muster Table of His Majesty's Ship the Indefatigable, November 1797–August 1798.

By the time he left the *Indefatigable* and transferred to the *Impetueux* with his captain, Kempthorne was one of the more senior midshipmen and in 1799 Pellew wrote to the Admiralty recommending him for a lieutenant's commission. At this stage it appears that Kempthorne had had a good, if somewhat adventurous, start to his naval career: he had benefited from a lengthy period of training under a gifted commander and survived the experience of command and captivity. However 1799 marked the start of two increasingly difficult years for Kempthorne, which were to end disastrously. Admiralty correspondence from early 1800 onwards chronicles a series of missed opportunities that highlight how vulnerable young officers were to the vagaries of chance, which frequently bedevilled their hopes of promotion.[72]

Kempthorne received his lieutenant's commission in early 1800 and was appointed to the frigate *Ceres*; however, having been at sea when his commission was issued, Kempthorne arrived in Portsmouth on 4 March to find that the *Ceres* had sailed without her new lieutenant. He wrote to the Admiralty enquiring what to do and was told he must return the commission and wait. Kempthorne wrote twice more to the Admiralty to explain that he had waited over a month but heard nothing. This correspondence was followed up by further letters sent to the Admiralty by his mother, Elizabeth Kempthorne, that reveal an almost farcical turn of events: a commission had been sent to Kempthorne's home in Falmouth rather than to Portsmouth where he was awaiting instructions. The Admiralty responded by ordering Kempthorne to join his ship immediately, but once again he found that the designated vessel had sailed. Finally, on 17 June 1800 an Admiralty Board minute appointed Kempthorne to the *Renard*[73] sloop, Captain Peter Spicer, and five days later he took up his commission.[74]

The contrast between the Admiralty's unequivocal orders and the reality of having to dash from port to port to reach one's ship can appear comical but the consequences for young officers like Kempthorne were serious and frustrating. In addition to having to pay for lodgings and travel from his half pay, Kempthorne had to watch months slip by when he was unable to use his new promotion to help his family. Young officers between commissions were effectively in limbo, and unless they had other means to support themselves, they could suffer real hardship. The reality of life for officers without commissions is clearly illustrated by C. S. Forester in *Lieutenant Hornblower*: William Bush struggles to support his sisters on his half pay

---

[72] ADM 1/2973, Lieutenants' Letters, Surname K, Number 12.

[73] ADM 3/124, ADM 3/125. In fact the minutes chronicle yet another appointment, to the *Renomme* in March, which is not discussed in the correspondence, making a total of five failed placements in the space of four months.

[74] ADM 35/1452, Pay Book of His Majesty's Sloop *Renard* 1800.

during the Peace of Amiens, and Hornblower himself is forced to eke out a living playing cards, after his commission fails to be confirmed and he is required to pay back what little wages he has received.[75]

The commander of Kempthorne's new ship *Renard*, Peter Spicer, was a protégé of Nelson who had served as a lieutenant under his command on the *Agamemnon*. His career had begun auspiciously, with Nelson applauding his 'spirited and officerlike conduct'.[76] Spicer was made master and commander around 1798, in which rank he was appointed to the *Renard* sloop. Such commands could be particularly demanding and had the potential to be the undoing of promising young officers who struggled to maintain their authority in the cramped and confined quarters of these small vessels.[77] During Kempthorne's first six months aboard the *Renard* there was considerable disagreement and dissention among the officers, which culminated in the new lieutenant being confined for contempt and disorderly conduct. Kempthorne was court martialled in September 1801 and the transcripts of the trial reveal that Spicer had considerable difficulty commanding an unhappy crew and fractious officers.[78]

At the opening of the court martial, Kempthorne was charged with having:

> frequently behaved in an unbecoming and disorderly manner and on the 5th June last neglected his duty by not coming on deck when all hands were called to weigh anchor and on the said Captain Spicer reprimanding him for so doing treated him with the utmost insolence and contempt.[79]

Rather than addressing these charges, much of the trial unexpectedly focused on an earlier incident during which Kempthorne was alleged to have struck the purser, John Miller. Evidence was presented by Miller himself, and by two other commanders, Josiah Whithorn and Robert Keen, who had both been called on board the *Renard* in July. Whithorn testified that:

> Captain Spicer had ... requested me and Captain Keen to come aboard the *Renard* and endeavour from principles of humanity the differences existing among the officers ... the gun room mess was divided and the officers at variance with one another.[80]

Whithorn went on to state that by the time they left the sloop there had been a general reconciliation and that Kempthorne had pledged that

---

[75] Forester, *Lieutenant Hornblower*, pp. 212–13.

[76] Marshall, *Royal Naval Biography*, vol. 2, part II, p. 578.

[77] Henderson, p. 221.

[78] ADM 1/5358, Records of Courts Martial, August/September 1801.

[79] *Ibid.*

[80] *Ibid.*

he would not afterwards ill-treat the purser. The revelation that Spicer required the assistance of two other captains to restore peace in the sloop's wardroom rather suggests that he failed to command his officers' duty and respect.

Apparently unprepared for the unexpected turn the trial had taken, Kempthorne does not appear to have mounted much of a defence. Consequently, despite the dubious evidence presented by the prosecution, the court found the charges against Kempthorne proven and he was dismissed the service. This disgrace would certainly have ended Kempthorne's career and aspirations but for one major factor and that was the unwavering support of Edward Pellew. He believed that not only had the trial been flawed in its process, but also that Spicer's ship had been badly run. In a letter written to Henry Dundas, 1st Viscount Melville, several years later in 1805, Pellew maintained that Kempthorne had been broken at a court martial as a result of 'falling into an irregular ship'.[81]

Pellew wasted no time in coming to Kempthorne's assistance; within weeks of the court martial the young man was back aboard the *Impetueux* and had written a lengthy memorial to the Admiralty requesting that his case be reviewed. In the memorial, Kempthorne respectfully appealed against the verdict of the court, citing abuse of process: he had not been informed of the charges against him until the day before the trial, leaving him no time to prepare an adequate defence. Kempthorne also appealed on personal grounds, stating that he had been unwell 'from long confinement and harsh treatment', adding for good measure that his family relied on him for support.[82] Pellew's hand is clearly evident in the tenor of the memorial, and his advocacy paid off: the Admiralty responded that their Lordships had examined the circumstances and were minded to recommend to the King that Kempthorne be restored to his former rank.

Pellew's most recent biographer has suggested that Kempthorne's career never fully recovered from the stigma of the trial,[83] and while this is partially true, Spicer's career arguably suffered more. Spicer left the *Renard* in 1801 and was not employed again before the Peace of Amiens left him on the beach, although by this time he had been promoted to post captain. When war broke out again in 1802, Spicer briefly commanded two ships of the line for a few months, but was then without a commission for a number of years. Eventually he was placed in charge of the Impress Service in Swansea and Cardiff before being pensioned off in 1816, having had a less than stellar career.

---

[81] ADM 1/176, Pellew to Melville, January 1805. Pellew had appointed Kempthorne as his flag lieutenant and wrote to Lord Melville seeking confirmation of the appointment.

[82] ADM 1/4799, ADM 1/2322. Memorial from Mr W Kempthorne, late lieutenant HM Navy, sent with a covering commendation from Sir Edward Pellew.

[83] Taylor, p. 267.

Prior to the breakdown of the Peace of Amiens, Kempthorne appears to have served as a midshipman on a frigate;[84] however, as soon as war broke out, he re-joined his mentor and became sixth lieutenant of Pellew's flagship *Culloden*. Finally, on 4 July 1804[85] a formal Order in Council was issued reinstating Kempthorne to the rank of lieutenant. The 1804–1805 muster books of HMS *Culloden* bear Lieutenant William Kempthorne's name alongside his former *Indefatigable* shipmates, George Bell and William Warden, the flagship's first and second lieutenants.[86]

Although Kempthorne had been restored to his former rank, it is likely that some still regarded him as tainted, as the review of his case had been conducted in private and there had been no public statement regarding the flawed trial. Despite having received a significant setback in terms of reputation and seniority, Kempthorne's career improved considerably from this point onwards. After serving for some time as the *Culloden's* most junior lieutenant, Kempthorne was appointed as first lieutenant of the frigate *Cornwallis*, Captain William Jones Lye. Writing to Admiralty Secretary William Marsden,[87] in 1805, Pellew discussed Kempthorne's commission as his flag lieutenant and later as first lieutenant of the *Cornwallis*. While the former appointment had many advantages it also meant that the young man was still very much under Pellew's wing and he may have felt he needed an opportunity to prove himself. Appointment to the *Cornwallis* as first lieutenant provided Kempthorne with a chance to prove his abilities and to lay the ghosts of the *Renard* debacle to rest.

After two years aboard the *Cornwallis*, Kempthorne, while still a lieutenant, was finally promoted to command of his own vessel, the brig *Diana*, with ten guns and forty-five men and boys. In his letter to the 1st Lord Melville in 1805, Pellew had written of Kempthorne, 'a more gallant, sober and exemplary young man I never knew',[88] and it appears that Pellew's faith in him was fully justified. From this point onwards Kempthorne's career, like that of many of his former *Indefatigable* shipmates, was characterised by the skill, courage and shrewd planning that were the hallmark of many of Pellew's young gentlemen.

In the two years between 1809 and 1810, Kempthorne enjoyed considerable success with the *Diana*. He eluded two French frigates that had chased the brig while returning from Manila to India, and he captured several impressive prizes, including the Dutch 14-gun brig *Zephyr*. The action, which demonstrated Kempthorne's inventiveness, shrewd seamanship and determination, was reported in the British

---

[84] ADM 1/176, Pellew to Melville, January 1805.

[85] ADM 12/31 Digest.

[86] ADM 36/17385, Muster Table of His Majesty's Ship the Culloden, November 1804.

[87] ADM 1/176, Pellew to Marsden, January 1805.

[88] ADM 1/176, Pellew to Melville, January 1805.

press and he was widely praised for his courage and judgement. During this period Kempthorne also found time to undertake hydrographical research charting coral reefs in the South China Sea. The *Diana* was finally condemned in 1810 and Kempthorne was promoted to commander in April 1811. Two years later, in 1813, he was appointed to command the sloop *Harlequin*, and sent to the North American station. Kempthorne had not been forgotten by his friend and patron, however, and in 1815 a minute from 'Adml Lord Exmouth for Lord Melvilles favor' includes the following request: 'Capt. Thomson (Chanticleer, N. America) and Capt. Kempthorn (Harlequin at Newfoundland) – Lord Exmouth requests may be sent out to him having no other Friends, both good officers.'[89] Pellew's request appears to have been granted, and the following April, Kempthorne was appointed to join the expedition to Algiers as commander of the *Beelzebub* bomb vessel. Kempthorne was one of the very few of Pellew's protégés that the admiral allowed to join the expedition and he was placed in a position of considerable trust. He was allocated command of a squadron of four bomb vessels that were stationed up to a mile off shore and ordered to direct their mortars and incendiary shells at the Lighthouse Battery and the citadel, without hitting any of the fleet's own ships, which lay between the bomb vessels and their target.

In the aftermath of the battle, Pellew rewarded Kempthorne's diligence and courage by appointing him acting captain of his flagship, *Queen Charlotte*, a position that was confirmed shortly after, along with the long-awaited promotion to post captain. Kempthorne's career, which had once appeared ruined, ended in modest honours, a good command and the status that accompanied it. He remained unswervingly loyal to Pellew, and in a letter sent to his former *Indefatigable* shipmate, Nicholas Pateshall, after Algiers, he wrote: 'Thank God he is now well and will long live I hope to fight his country's battles. All those who were with him will fight his for him whenever called upon I am sure.'[90] Kempthorne remained captain of the *Queen Charlotte* until 1818 when he retired from active service.

Like many retired naval officers, Kempthorne supported a number of charitable maritime causes. He attended Marine Society events which raised funds to provide poor, often orphaned, boys with the basic necessities required to send them to sea, and in March 1823 was a steward at a Society dinner held in the London Tavern.[91] Some of Kempthorne's charitable activities brought him into no doubt welcome contact with his mentor, such as the 1824 fundraising launch of the National Society for the

[89] Pellew of Canonteign Collection, Devon Records Office, Exmouth to Melville, 24 August 1814. The Captain Thomson referred to is former *Indefatigable* midshipman John Thomson.

[90] Pateshall Archive, Hereford Record Office, A95/V/N/223, Kempthorne to Pateshall, 23 October 1816.

[91] *The Morning Chronicle*, 20 March 1823.

Preservation of Life from Shipwreck which Lord Exmouth attended as vice president.[92]

Kempthorne also appears to have had business interests relating to shipping valuation and he had some involvement in the patronage of a parish living in 1828.[93] One of the last press reports to refer to Kempthorne describes a day of triumph. On 29 July 1830, Captain William Kempthorne and his friend Captain Jeremiah Coghlan attended a royal levee and both *Indefatigable* veterans were presented to the King by Robert Dundas, 2nd Viscount Melville, son of the 1st Lord Melville, to whom Pellew had written years before, asking for justice for Kempthorne.[94]

Kempthorne remained single throughout his life, and resided for some time with his sister who had married a naval purser and lived at Alphington Lodge in Exeter. It was here that Kempthorne died[95] in 1835, two years after his patron and protector Admiral Lord Exmouth. In his will Kempthorne provided modest bequests for his mother, unmarried sisters and two aunts; however his most notable bequests were to Admiral and Lady Exmouth and their son Pownoll Pellew, with whom he had served aboard the *Impetueux* in 1799. Kempthorne left instructions that a diamond brooch should be made for Lady Exmouth and rings for the two men, each bearing the inscription 'While I had life my heart was deeply impressed by your multiple kindnesses'.[96] As Exmouth and Pownoll Pellew had died two years before Kempthorne, the bequest was not fulfilled; however his will is one of the most eloquent of all the post-mortem tributes to his captain and friend. William Kempthorne was well aware of just how much he owed to the Pellews for their persistence, advocacy and enduring support and affection.

Cadogan, Coghlan and Kempthorne's social backgrounds could hardly have been more different but they are all typical of the type of young officers whose careers Pellew supported, and it is not difficult to understand his rationale for promoting such diverse protégés. Taking on the sons of influential and wealthy families brought its own rewards in a service driven by interest; recognising promising and capable seamen from the merchant service and the lower decks and promoting them to the quarterdeck provided Pellew's squadron with experienced sea officers and benefited the service more widely; and acting as protector and surrogate father to Cornish youngsters, and Falmouth boys in particular, surely appealed to Pellew's sense of duty as a Cornishman, a captain and a patriarch.

[92] *The Times*, 29 July 1830.

[93] Kempthorne to Roberts, 4 July 1829, private collection.

[94] *The Morning Post*, 29 July 1830.

[95] Find My Past, 1481A/PR/1/26, burial register, St Michael and All Angels, Alphington, 13 April 1835. Although Kempthorne died at Alphington Lodge, the burial register notes that he was 'of Brislington' at the time.

[96] PROB 11/1850, Admon of the Estate of Captain William Kempthorne.

All three of these young men benefited from their time aboard the *Indefatigable* and *Impetueux*, which provided them with sound experience of seamanship, boat actions, single ship engagements, and prize command, to say nothing of the more mundane realities of blockade duty. With the experience they had gained under Pellew's command, all were in a strong position to launch into their lieutenancies; however, once they emerged from under Pellew's wing, Cadogan and Kempthorne experienced times of real difficulty and hardship. In addition, all three suffered from trials and tribulations, both financial and emotional, in their personal lives.

Although Coghlan was the most obviously successful of the three, Cadogan and Kempthorne also contributed significantly to the success of the Royal Navy's campaigns at this time: Cadogan in the Mediterranean and Kempthorne at Algiers. Ultimately, all three fulfilled the promise of their early training, whatever human flaws they revealed. Despite their different backgrounds and career paths, Cadogan, Coghlan and Kempthorne all shared an enduring respect for Pellew and they repaid his support, patronage and friendship with lasting loyalty, love and gratitude.

6

'Boys Grown to Manhood'

EDWARD Pellew was an eloquent letter writer, and never more so than when he was angry or dismayed. Of all the many letters he wrote to Lord Spencer in the early years of his career perhaps the most dramatic is one sent in February 1799 at the end of a remarkable exchange of correspondence concerning his 'promotion' from the *Indefatigable* to the *Impetueux*. Written in the third person, with an eye to dramatic effect perhaps, this letter is nonetheless genuine in its emotional power. Pellew was well aware that he was leaving behind the best years of his life at sea and was reminded of all the young men whom he had trained as a frigate commander, the 'boys grown to manhood under me'.[1] These words apply particularly well to Henry Hart, Thomas Groube and Nicholas Pateshall, all of whom grew into experienced seamen and capable young officers during their time aboard the *Indefatigable*.

Henry Hart entered the Royal Navy in 1796 at the age of fifteen when he joined the *Indefatigable* as a Boy, First Class. Although Hart does not appear to have had any particular connection to Sir Edward Pellew prior to joining the *Indefatigable*, he went on to become a close, lifelong friend of his captain. He was also a particular favourite of Pellew's wife, Susan, and continued a close friendship with Fleetwood Pellew after his father's death. Hart served with Pellew aboard both the *Indefatigable* and the *Impetueux* and later rejoined him in India where he served as flag lieutenant of the *Culloden*. However Pellew was not Hart's only naval patron; he also served for a considerable portion of his career under Admiral Sir John Gore and accompanied him on a number of diplomatic missions. Hart had a long and successful naval and diplomatic career during which he saw service in the Channel, the Mediterranean and the East and West Indies. After his retirement from active service in 1835, Hart was knighted for his diplomatic services. He was later appointed as a commissioner of Greenwich Hospital and supported a large number of naval and social charities, which often brought him into contact with his friend and mentor Sir Edward Pellew.

Thomas Groube was one of the four[2] young gentlemen serving aboard HMS *Indefatigable* in 1797 who was born and raised in Pellew's adopted home town of Falmouth. His parents were members of prominent shipping

---

[1] Exmouth Papers, Caird Library, The Royal Museums Greenwich.

[2] James Bray, Thomas Groube, William Kempthorne and Robert Carthew Reynolds were all born in or around Falmouth.

5 Captain Nicholas Lechmere Pateshall, RN, School of Domenico Pellegrini, *c.* 1817.
Pateshall is shown wearing the uniform of a captain of three years' seniority,
which was not quite the case at that time.

and mercantile families in the town and Pellew is unlikely to have needed much persuasion to accept Groube aboard the *Arethusa* in 1794 at the age of nineteen. Groube's naval service had actually begun aboard the *Leviathan* the previous year, but he went on to serve much of his career under Pellew's command, first in home waters, and later in the East Indies where Groube was involved in a number of actions against the Dutch in Java and later served as governor of the naval hospital at Madras. After leaving the navy in 1816, Groube and his family settled in Honiton, Devon where he became deeply involved in local politics and the Independent church. Dubbed both a 'radical alderman' and 'poor man's friend' by opposing local newspapers, Groube was frequently in the midst of public controversy. Following his death in 1850, many obituaries paid tribute to Groube's naval career, his friendship with Pellew and his civic service.

Of all three, Pellew's reminiscence perhaps applies to Nicholas Pateshall more than most. Pateshall, who has already been introduced in Chapter 2, joined the *Indefatigable* in 1795 at the age of thirteen and he is unique in that he left an extensive archive of private correspondence which provides a first-hand account of his time aboard the frigate, his subsequent naval career, and his ongoing friendship with his former shipmates and captain.[3]

NICHOLAS LECHMERE PATESHALL, 1781–1856

BORN in 1781, Nicholas Pateshall was just nine when his father died, leaving his mother, Mrs Ann Pateshall, with nine children to care for. The family had an estate at Allensmore in Hereford and were reasonably well-off members of the county gentry, but such wealth was not equal to supporting six young sons without them having a profession as a source of income. Consequently, the profession chosen for young Nicholas was the sea service.

The earliest papers in the Pateshall family archive relating to Nicholas's career are an exchange of letters between his mother and one Captain Henry Lane,[4] who appears to have been a friend of the family. Lane

---

[3] Pateshall Papers, Hereford Record Office.

[4] Pateshall Papers, BD30/9/25, Ann Pateshall to Henry Lane, 27 October 1794. Although Captain Lane's relationship to the Pateshalls is uncertain, his letters make it clear that he felt a sense of obligation to the family. Lane was related by marriage to the Parminter family, who were wine merchants based in Devon and the British Factory in Lisbon, where they would have been contemporaries of both the Warden and Majendie families. Jane Majendie had been the wife of Pellew's revered former commander, Captain Philemon Pownoll, and William Warden was later to become Nicholas's shipmate aboard the *Indefatigable*. It is possible that it was these extended connections, which were underpinned by the Falmouth to Lisbon packet service, which resulted in Nicholas being placed aboard the *Indefatigable*.

provided Nicholas with accommodation and helped to equip him with the necessities for going to sea; however, as related in Chapter 2, the business did not go well, as Nicholas was a headstrong boy with a tendency to spend money too freely. No sooner had he been appointed to his ship, than Nicholas decided it was not for him. His mixed feelings and stubborn nature are all evident in the correspondence. Mrs Pateshall wrote to Captain Lane, describing Nicholas's state of mind:

> He seems, I think, very unhappy at his conduct as he repeatedly calls himself my ungrateful son.
>
> I have also hinted at the discredit that will follow if you find upon conversing with him that he really has so great an aversion as his letters seem to indicate (which are melancholy indeed).[5]

It was not the sea service *per se* that Nicholas objected to: in a letter to his brother Edmund, he argued that he had not taken against the navy; on the contrary, he longed for action and something worthwhile to do.[6] Finally Nicholas returned home in disgrace and was sent back to school where he gave vent to his high spirits by indulging in typical schoolboy pranks. A letter to his brother written in early 1795 relates tales of purchasing fighting cocks and harassing the masters.[7]

Undeterred by an unsuccessful attempt to gain Nicholas a place on a merchant ship, Ann Pateshall's luck changed when she secured a berth for her son aboard the *Indefatigable*, though it is unclear how this occurred. This was the starting point for Pateshall's transformation from a disillusioned boy to an eager young man who revelled in the challenges of life aboard ship and delighted in encouragement from his captain. When Pellew made the young man his *aide du langue* and signal officer, Pateshall wrote that this was a 'famous berth'.[8]

A number of letters survive from these early years aboard the *Indefatigable*, which reveal that Pateshall was eager to recount his adventures.

> There are 4 frigates, a cutter and a sloop of war cruising off Lisbon therefore the Admiralty has ordered we brave fellows there where we hope to give a good account of them by next Sunday.[9]

[5] Pateshall Papers, BD30/9/25, Ann Pateshall to Henry Lane, 27 October 1794.

[6] See Chapter 1.

[7] Pateshall Papers, A95/EB/40/1, Nicholas Pateshall to Edmund Pateshall, 20 March 1795.

[8] Pateshall Papers, BD30/9/45, Nicholas Pateshall to Ann Pateshall, 12 October 1795. The post of language assistant was evidently taken seriously as the account prepared by Pellew when Pateshall was finally given control of his own expenses includes tuition from a French master.

[9] Pateshall Papers, BD30/9/46, Nicholas Pateshall to Ann Pateshall, 5 December 1795.

Pateshall appears to have been awed by his heroic captain: he wrote to his mother towards the end of his first year aboard the frigate, 'we fear not while we have this brave commander Sir Edward',[10] and his stirring eyewitness account of the *Droits de L'Homme* engagement is peppered with phrases beginning 'Sir Edward says ...', 'Sir Edward thinks ...'[11]

However Pateshall's relationship with his mentor was not all smooth sailing, particularly where financial matters were concerned. In the aftermath of the *Droits de L'Homme* engagement Pateshall wrote to his brother, 'I wish our captain had had the command of the English fleet instead of the person who had it when the French fleet were out', but in the same letter he complains about Pellew controlling his allowance and making him account for everything, 'I would much rather draw my allowance from Mr Marsh than to receive it from Sir Edward'.[12]

When Pellew was finally forced to accept he must leave the *Indefatigable* and take up command of the *Impetueux*, Pateshall was one of the younger midshipmen who transferred to the ship of the line with him. In a letter to her son, Ann Pateshall expressed her desire that Nicholas should stay with Pellew.

> I read in the papers of a gentleman being appointed to succeed Sir Edward in the command of the *Indefatigable.* Of course Sir Edward's appointment will be more advantageous to him, I shall be anxious to know if he takes his officers with him, and the particulars respecting the change.[13]

Mrs Pateshall had other concerns, which had evidently been the subject of correspondence with Pellew. It appears there had been a 'misunderstanding' between Pateshall and his captain, which his mother attributed to the effect of liquor, 'the practice of drinking being too prevalent with lads in your situation'. In a letter written to her son, which suggests that Ann Pateshall and Pellew shared authority for the boy's welfare, she makes it clear that they had discussed the incident.

> I have the authority of Sir Edward to state to you the absolute necessity, even for your health's sake, to be more circumspect in your conduct, this late act of his has convinced me of his willingness to serve and encourage you.[14]

[10] *Ibid.*

[11] Pateshall Papers, A95/AP/7(1), Nicholas Pateshall to Ann Pateshall, 17 January 1797.

[12] Pateshall Papers, A95/EB/40/1, Nicholas Pateshall to Edmund Pateshall, 20 January 1797.

[13] Pateshall Papers, BD30/9/48, Ann Pateshall to Nicholas Pateshall, 2 March 1799.

[14] *Ibid.*

History has tended to remember Pellew as something of a martinet; however Ann Pateshall's letter suggests this was far from true, as she warns Nicholas that his captain has treated him too leniently: 'I fear you have hitherto presumed to trespass on his too great lenity, and he has treated you rather as man than boy.'[15] It appears that the incident in question involved Pateshall striking a seaman, dishonourable conduct for a young officer that no doubt roused Pellew's ire. Both the muster of the *Indefatigable* and documents relating to Pateshall's examination for lieutenant reveal that he was demoted to able seaman for ten months from May 1798 onwards, possibly as a result of this incident.[16]

Another letter sent at this time from financial agent J. Calvert Clark to Mrs Pateshall shows that Nicholas still had a tendency to squander his money.

> I am truly sorry to hear that your son Nicholas has been so extravagant as I had flattered myself he had kept his prize money in reserve to pay me. I think you are perfectly right to limit him in his allowance and I shall not in future pay any draught of his ...[17]

Like his *Indefatigable* shipmates who transferred to the *Impetueux*, Pateshall was initially rated able, but in early March 1799 all were restored to their previous ranks. Pateshall was reinstated to the rank of midshipman[18] and soon promoted to master's mate. Fewer letters have survived from this period; however it was another time of extraordinary action under Pellew's command. Pateshall was aboard the *Impetueux* at the time of the mutiny and also took part in a number of daring actions during the Belleisle expedition, including the destruction of the frigate *L'Insolent* and the cutting out of the *Cerbère*, led by his former *Indefatigable* shipmate Jeremiah Coghlan.

In June 1801 Pateshall was transferred 'on promotion' to the *Robust*, and then to the *Ville de Paris*, Admiral Cornwallis's flagship, where he finally attained his lieutenancy in August 1801.[19] Pateshall was almost the last among his contemporaries to gain promotion and a letter to his brother reveals he was chafing at the delay.

> I have ever since delayed in hope of having it in my power to inform you of my having received my commission as lieutenant, having finished my six years servitude, and passed my lieutenants

---

[15] *Ibid.*

[16] ADM 107/26, N. L. Pateshall, Lieutenants' Passing Certificates documents.

[17] Pateshall Papers, A95/AP/17, John Calvert Clark to Ann Pateshall, 16 April 1799.

[18] ADM 107/26, N. L. Pateshall, Lieutenants' Passing Certificates documents.

[19] ADM 107/24, N. L. Pateshall, Lieutenants' Passing Certificates.

examination ... I hope soon to have the pleasure of giving you and my mother an account of it.[20]

Pateshall's impatience was not entirely justified; by the time he transferred to the *Ville de Paris* to take up his lieutenant's commission, he had served only two days over the minimum six-year requirement, so in reality his advancement was far from slow.

Pateshall continued to serve aboard the *Ville de Paris* until she was paid off at the commencement of the Peace of Amiens. Over the course of the war, he reckoned by his own account that he had taken part in the capture and destruction of 20 enemy vessels, 468 guns and 3,937 men.[21] On being paid off, Pateshall returned to his home city of Hereford, which honoured him with the freedom of the city in May 1802, 'in consideration of his meritorious conduct in the late war'.[22] He was not quite twenty-one at the time.

Unlike many of his contemporaries, Pateshall did not spend the whole of the Peace of Amiens on half pay, as he was among those chosen to serve aboard HMS *Calcutta* during her voyage to establish a new colony in Port Phillip, Australia. This was no easy berth; the journey was long and uncertain, and the officers were responsible for the convicts who were to form the labour force for the newly settled territory. Pateshall wrote to his brother William that they were to transport 320 convicts 'beside 43 women'.[23]

In another letter written while the *Calcutta* was waiting to sail, Pateshall spoke of the reality of naval service and ambition. He knew, as every naval officer did, that war was imminent and that it would present good chances for promotion. Although Pateshall was committed to the new voyage, he was also concerned about what to do if war was declared: whether to offer his services to St Vincent aboard the *Ville de Paris*, or to Pellew, of whom he wrote a little wistfully:

> Sir Edward Pellew is appointed to the *Tonnant*, one of the finest ships of the navy, I shall offer my services to him but not with a wish to go with him as I know he has too many to provide for already.[24]

[20] Pateshall Papers, Nicholas Pateshall to Edmund Pateshall, 14 September 1801.

[21] This tally comes from the extensive notes Pateshall made for the naval biographer William O'Byrne near the end of his life, which are now preserved with O'Byrne's working notes in the British Library. Add mss., 38049, Volume XI, N-PEEL, Ff 339–43.

[22] Pateshall Papers, A95/V/N/287, Freedom of the City of Hereford, signed L. Lambe, Town Clerk.

[23] Pateshall Papers, 95/V/W/a/2, Nicholas Pateshall to William Pateshall, 26 February 1803.

[24] Pateshall Papers, A95/EB/41/S, Nicholas Pateshall to Edmund Pateshall, 13 March 1803.

Pateshall kept a journal of his voyage to Port Phillip, which has been published in Australia with an extensive introduction by the late historian Marjorie Tipping. The diary reveals that, regardless of doubts about his future career prospects, Pateshall immersed himself in the new experiences of the voyage to the Antipodes. He was a keen observer of the customs and peoples they encountered along the way, and Tipping notes that 'he commented with perception and humanity on the Aboriginals of the two settlements'.[25] He also sympathised with the plight of the convicts: 'To make these wretches happy was the wish and concern of us all, as soon as the ship was in order for so long a voyage we released upwards of one hundred from irons'.[26]

On returning from Australia, Pateshall was very fortunate to be reappointed to the *Ville de Paris*; had he remained aboard the *Calcutta* he might have been taken prisoner with his former shipmates after she was sunk in 1805.

Despite his long absence, Pateshall continued to receive news of former shipmates. In a letter to his brother Edmund, sent from the *Ville de Paris* at Torbay in January 1805, Pateshall explained that his old shipmate, Henry Hart, was sailing to India and was willing to carry any letters they wished to send to their brother who was serving there with the army.[27]

Pateshall was still anxious about his finances and the lack of opportunity for prize money that resulted from his long absence on the far side of the world, and his position on a ship of the line rather than a frigate. He wrote to his mother in August 1805: 'I am the only officer on board who has not either from prize money, or private property, much more than his pay.'[28] Consequently he was not wholly impressed with his next promotion in January 1806 to a more senior lieutenant's post, but once again aboard a ship of the line. Pateshall, who shared something of Pellew's bravado in asking favours of their Lords Commissioners, wrote to the Admiralty asking for a post in a frigate instead. Unsurprisingly, their Lordships did not grant his request.[29]

Pateshall was duly posted aboard the *Kent*, 74, Captain Garrett, where he saw service in the Mediterranean Fleet, under the command of Admiral Lord Collingwood. It was a challenging commission: Pateshall described one voyage from Minorca where 180 men fell sick with yellow fever in the space of a few hours and the ship was forced to put to sea undermanned when foul weather struck. Pateshall wrote that he was 'having to stand

---

[25] Tipping, p. 9.

[26] *Ibid.*, p. 37.

[27] Pateshall Papers, A95/V/EB/5, Nicholas Pateshall to Edmund Pateshall, 18 January 1805.

[28] Pateshall Papers, A95/V/DB/6, Nicholas Pateshall to Ann Pateshall, August 1805.

[29] ADM 1/3070, Lieutenants' Letters, Surname P.

parson, there not being one on board and it is no pleasant office I assure you'.[30] Pateshall finally had a chance to earn some prize money in 1806 when the *Kent* sailed to Lisbon where they helped to capture more than thirty prizes including a Turkish corvette.

In 1809 a new chapter of Pateshall's career began, when he was appointed as first lieutenant of the 32-gun *Hyperion*, stationed in the West Indies. Pellew wrote to Pateshall at the time, congratulating him on the opportunity that lay ahead: 'I heartily congratulate you on the prospect you have of obtaining your rank in conveying Lord Mulgrave's recommendation to Admiral Rowley.'[31] After two short commissions, Rowley acted on this recommendation and Pateshall became flag lieutenant aboard his flagship *Polyphemus*. From there he went on to his first command, the 16-gun sloop *Shark*, before being briefly appointed as acting captain of the *Polyphemus*. Unfortunately Pateshall fell victim to the West Indian climate and in November 1811 the doctors in Jamaica reported that a return to England was necessary to recover his health.[32]

Pateshall returned to sea in 1813 and commanded the sloops *Adder*, 12, and *Jaseur*, 16, on the North American station and the southwest coast of Spain. During this period he carried a series of important despatches including orders for the blockade of American ports and despatches from Wellington from the Battle of Toulouse.[33] In February 1815 Pateshall was appointed to the 20-gun *Carron*, as post captain, and stationed in Bermuda where he continued to serve until August 1816.

Years before, Pateshall had written of his ill luck in being abroad when Pellew was going to India to take up his post as Commander in Chief. Once again he found himself on the wrong side of the Atlantic in 1816 when Pellew was assembling his squadron for the bombardment of Algiers. Had he been on the right side of the ocean, it seems likely that Pateshall would have volunteered, given his continued admiration for Pellew and his relish for active engagement. Certainly Pateshall was keen to learn every detail of the engagement from his friend William Kempthorne, one of the few Indefatigables to serve at Algiers. On his return, Kempthorne wrote to his former shipmate:

> You wish me to give you more particulars of our expedition with the account of the escapes the Admiral had. I do not know that I can add

[30] Pateshall Papers, A95/EB/42/1(1), Nicholas Pateshall to Edmund Pateshall, August 1809.

[31] Pateshall Papers, A95/V/N/178, Edward Pellew to Nicholas Pateshall, November 1809. Pateshall sent a copy of this letter, together with several others from Pellew and Cornwallis, to William O'Byrne, while he was compiling his naval biography.

[32] ADM 1/2341, Nicholas Pateshall and others to Admiralty, November and December 1811.

[33] Tipping, p. 28.

all that much to the dispatches, However I will endeavour to give you some idea of it.[34]

Kempthorne went on to paint a vivid picture of the action and of Pellew's narrow escapes, including the escape of his false teeth which were knocked out and bounced across the deck, an incident which did not make it into the more grandiloquent newspaper reports, nor into those books that were later published as eyewitness accounts.[35]

Pateshall retired from active service in August 1816, returned to his family, and settled in Hereford. First, however, he spent some time travelling in Europe. Like many of his generation, he had never had the opportunity to tour the continent, as Great Britain had been at war for most of his lifetime. While in Italy he had his portrait painted, by the school of Domenico Pelligrini, an artist who had formerly lived and worked in London. Although Pateshall had only made post captain the previous year, he is pictured in the uniform of a more senior officer.

Over the course of the next decade Pateshall sought employment from the Admiralty on several occasions, but without success; however he was far from idle in retirement. Like his *Indefatigable* shipmate Thomas Groube, he immersed himself in local politics, though his political leanings were somewhat less radical. Pateshall's politics led him to become embroiled in a noted local scandal in 1833, which also made the national press. A dispute arose as a result of a parliamentary election involving one Richard Sill, a Tory lawyer from Hereford. Encountering him in the street one day, Sill attempted to provoke Pateshall by striking him and telling him to 'consider yourself horse whipped'.[36] Pateshall refused the obvious path of 'seeking satisfaction' and, following legal advice, took Sill to court. However the matter was settled amicably out of court with Sill making a public apology. Letters of support received by Pateshall at the time were united in praising his restraint, calmness and sensible approach to the incident; the hotheaded midshipman of former years was long gone.[37] Later, in 1839 Pateshall was elected mayor of Hereford, an office he filled successfully a number of times.

---

[34] Pateshall Papers, A95/V/N/223, William Kempthorne to Nicholas Pateshall, October 1816.

[35] See Chapter 9.

[36] *The Hereford Journal*, 29 January 1834.

[37] Pateshall Papers, A95/N/23, Robert Price to Nicholas Pateshall, 31 December 1833. Robert Price wrote: 'I cannot too strongly express to you the satisfaction I feel that you have not allowed your resentment, however strong or however justifiable to outweigh the calm and dispassionate judgement of your friends; if you had followed what perhaps in the first instance must be the most natural impulse of anyone under such provocation you would have done precisely that which Mr Sill most desired.'

Nicholas Pateshall never married, though at one stage he had expressed his desire to wed a cousin, Mary Lechmere; his proposal was blocked by members of the family. In the last decade of his life he lived comfortably though modestly in Hereford, his quiet existence belying the full and adventurous life he had led. He remained in touch with old shipmates and filled his time with civic duties and charitable giving.[38] When he compiled his career history for William O'Byrne's *Naval Biographical Dictionary* later in the 1840s, he included letters from both Pellew and Cornwallis, which appear to have been among his most prized documents. The action to which he devotes the most attention in his career summary is, of course, the *Droits de L'Homme*, the engagement which he left a unique eyewitness account of in the letter to his brother written almost fifty years previously.

Pateshall did receive some recognition for his naval service later in life: he reached the rank of Rear Admiral in retirement and in 1849 applied for and was awarded the Naval General Service Medal with three clasps for the engagements with the *Virginie* and *Les Droits de L'Homme*, and the *Viper* boat action. Nicholas Pateshall died on 18 October 1856 aged seventy-three; he was buried in a family grave in Allensmore and left a short will remembering family, friends and loyal servants.[39]

Pateshall's naval career may not have been stratospheric, but it was one of courage, commitment, discovery and humanity; all characteristics which he carried over into his civilian life. He retained great affection for his *Indefatigable* days and for Edward Pellew, the captain who first helped to mould a truculent schoolboy into an officer of whom the navy could be proud.

HENRY HART, 1781–1857

HENRY Hart was born in Wilmington, Kent and baptised on 1 May 1781, the eighth child of Richard Hart esquire, and his wife Susannah. The family originally hailed from Uckfield, Sussex and were said to be distantly related to the Hart Dyke baronets of Lullingstone Castle, Kent.[40] Little is known of Hart's early life before he entered the Royal Navy in 1796; the log of the *Indefatigable* records that he joined as a volunteer from the East India Company, but no evidence has survived to suggest how long he served with the Company or how he came to join Pellew's ship. Hart was initially rated Boy, First Class on joining the *Indefatigable* and he served aboard the frigate during her notable engagements with the *Virginie* and *Les Droits de L'Homme*.

---

[38] Pateshall donated to and was a supporter of the Bluecoat charity schools and also supported the creation of a Mechanics Institute during his time as mayor.

[39] PROB 11/2201, Will of Nicholas Lechmere Pateshall.

[40] O'Byrne, p. 471.

In 1799, when Pellew was forced to leave the *Indefatigable*, Hart was one of the small group of men who were permitted to transfer with their captain to his new command, HMS *Impetueux*. Hart was initially rated able seaman on joining the ship, but was restored to the rank of midshipman a few weeks later on 15 March.[41] It was only two months later that mutiny broke out aboard the *Impetueux* on 31 May, while she was anchored off Berehaven in Bantry Bay. Hart was a key witness to the short-lived mutiny, and was called to give evidence at the subsequent court martial, held aboard HMS *Prince* in the Mediterranean in June. Hart, who was midshipman of the watch on the day of the mutiny, gave a detailed account of events and identified several of the nine accused. In evidence for the prosecution, Hart testified that he observed the people coming aft to the quarterdeck and demanding a boat. The captain, still wearing his dressing gown, was called from his cabin and asked to hear their grievances. The mutineers called for a boat in order to take a letter concerning ill usage to the admiral. Pellew offered to give them a boat, accompanied by an officer, or to take the letter to the admiral himself. Both offers were refused, with the mutineers crying 'One and all!' and demanding a boat of their own. According to Hart, Pellew retorted 'That you shan't have!' and, returning to his cabin to fetch his sword, he and Captain Boys of the marines drove the men from the quarterdeck. During his evidence, Hart positively identified three of the mutineers and singled out one Stephen Walford as the leader. In addition, he testified that when the captain ordered the officers to clear the quarterdeck, he had no recollection of seeing First Lieutenant Ross ordering the men to leave. Hart's testimony, which was corroborated by ten other witnesses including the captain, was damning and despite Pellew's plea for leniency towards two of the men who had previously been of good character, three of the accused were sentenced to death, six were flogged round the fleet and only one was acquitted. Lieutenant Ross, who had done little to quell the mutiny and who was described in the mutineers' letter as having 'ever been a father to the ship', was removed to another command. Following the court martial and the execution of the ringleaders of the mutiny, discipline slowly improved aboard the *Impetueux*, though she never became such a contented and close-knit ship as the *Indefatigable*.

Hart remained aboard the *Impetueux* and participated in expeditions to Belleisle in 1799 and Ferrol in 1800. It was during the expedition to land troops at Ferrol and destroy the naval dockyard there, that Hart received his first experience of command, when he was placed in charge of one of the flat-bottomed boats used to disembark troops on a beach five miles from Ferrol.[42] Later in the same campaign, Hart also assisted in cutting out the 'desperately defended' 22-gun vessel *La Guepe* from Vigo Bay,[43] and he was

---

[41] ADM 36/128127, Muster Book of His Majesty's Ship the Impetueux.

[42] Taylor, p. 161.

[43] O'Byrne, p. 471.

also present when Jeremiah Coghlan led a detachment of boats to cut out the *Cerbère*, from Port Louis.

Like many of his contemporaries, Hart disappears from view during the Peace of Amiens; however, in June 1802 he received his lieutenant's commission and was appointed to the 32-gun frigate *Medusa*, Captain John Gore. Hart served aboard the *Medusa* for three years, eventually becoming first lieutenant. Gore had already made a name for himself as a successful frigate captain after participating in an action off Vigo Bay in 1799, when five British frigates captured the Spanish frigates *Thetis* and *Santa Brigada* carrying cargo and specie valued at over £600,000. The *Medusa* was another successful and profitable command for Gore and his crew. In addition to taking a number of notable prizes, the *Medusa* was one of four frigates under the command of Captain Graham Moore, in Hart's old ship *Indefatigable*, that were sent to intercept a flotilla of Spanish treasure ships bound for Cadiz from South America. Moore's squadron engaged the four Spanish frigates off Cape Santa Maria on 5 October 1804; one ship, the *Mercedes*, exploded after the powder magazine caught fire, but the remaining three were captured. The prizes were valued at almost £900,000; however, as Britain and Spain were not officially at war at the time, the prizes were deemed to be Droits of the Admiralty and the money went to the government. However, twelve months later the London *Gazette* announced that the sum of £160,000 would be split between the officers and companies of the four frigates that had captured the Spanish prizes.[44]

C. S. Forester dramatised this highly charged engagement in *Hornblower and the Hotspur*, where Hornblower is ordered to join Moore's squadron and intercept the Spanish flotilla. Seeing the *Indefatigable* again, Hornblower reflects on 'the ship in which he had served during those exciting years as midshipman'.[45] Typically, Hornblower sacrifices his chances of prize money by breaking away from the squadron to engage the French frigate *Félicite*, thus missing the action with the Spanish ships altogether. Henry Hart's captain, John Gore, makes a brief appearance when Hornblower meets Moore and the other captains of the squadron aboard Cornwallis's flagship, and the *Hotspur* is stationed alongside the *Medusa* as they wait to intercept the Spanish ships.

Hart had another opportunity for prize money and command just a month later in November 1804 when the *Medusa* captured the Spanish ship *Matilda* carrying a cargo of quicksilver valued at £200,000.[46] Command of the captured vessel was awarded to Hart, who brought her into Portsmouth in company with the *Medusa*.

The following year, in 1805, the *Medusa* was ordered to convey Marquess Cornwallis to India to take up his re-appointment as Governor

---

[44] *The Gazette*, 9 November 1806, p. 1402.

[45] Forester, *Hornblower and the Hotspur*, p. 256.

[46] O'Byrne, p. 471.

General. On arriving in India in July 1805, Hart immediately transferred from the *Medusa* to the *Culloden*, flagship of his former captain, and now Commander in Chief of the East India station, Admiral Sir Edward Pellew. Hart served aboard the *Culloden* until August 1806 when Pellew appointed him as acting captain of a succession of frigates: *Terpsichore*, *Duncan*, *Caroline* and *Fox*. It was while serving as commander of the *Caroline* that Hart accompanied Pellew's squadron on an expedition to destroy Dutch naval shipping in Java in December 1807. Hart was given responsibility for landing a detachment of troops under Lieutenant Colonel Lockhart and commanding the seamen on shore. While approaching the Dutch harbour at Griessie, Pellew's flagship *Culloden* grounded on a shoal. Two coastal trading vessels were seized and their cargoes jettisoned with the intention of loading the *Culloden*'s guns aboard them in order to lighten the flagship sufficiently to re-float her. Unfortunately, one of the vessels was carrying an 'extensive and variegated assortment of spirituous licquors'[47] and the *Culloden*'s seamen became so drunk that they could no longer carry out their duties. In his fury, Pellew 'swore that he would never again hoist his flag in a ship manned with such a set of drunken scoundrels'.[48] He ordered his flag to be struck and transferred his command to Hart's frigate *Caroline* until the men of the *Culloden* had sobered up sufficiently to re-float the ship.

Throughout their time in India, Hart and Pellew appear to have maintained a friendly relationship. A private letter written by Pellew in 1808 to Sir Francis Beaufort makes a veiled reference to an incident that occurred en route to the Cape.

> ... no part of my family have mentioned it, I suppose from the fear of annoying me. I must confess I was prepared for this by Henry Hart who is too honest to conceal from me what passed on your way to the Cape.

The incident appears to have involved a secretary of 'Lord George', and although it is not clear what occurred, or even which Lord George is referred to, it is apparent that Hart was a trusted confidant of the admiral.[49]

It was around this time that Hart met and married Maria Williams. Their wedding, at which Pellew was a witness, took place at St Mary's Church, Fort St George, Madras on 4 October 1808, only three days after the marriage of Pellew's eldest son Pownoll to Eliza Barlow, daughter of Sir George Barlow, Governor of Madras.

After serving four years in India as acting captain, Hart's health had begun to suffer, and he returned to England where he was appointed

---

[47] Hay, p. 155.

[48] *Ibid.*, p. 156.

[49] Huntington Library, Granville Papers, FB 1498, Pellew to Beaufort, 25 February 1808.

commander of the sloop *Thracian* and ordered to cruise off Cherbourg. Hart had been bitterly disappointed to discover on his return that he had only been appointed to the rank of commander, and he had to wait until 1811 before he was made post captain. Despite finally making post, Hart appears to have been without a command between 1811 and 1814, possibly as a result of ill health; however, from December 1814 onwards he spent almost ten months in the Mediterranean, first as captain of the 20-gun *Cyrus*, and then as flag captain to his former commander, Admiral Sir John Gore, aboard the *Revenge*, 74.

Like many young officers, Hart found himself without a command at the end of the war; however his active naval service did not end there. In August 1818 Hart was appointed as captain of the *Sapphire* and despatched to Latin America to watch over British interests in Porto Bello, Panama, which were threatened by the independence movements sweeping the continent. During his time in Panama, Hart is reported to have crossed the isthmus in two days,[50] and later he undertook a diplomatic mission to Cartagena. While stationed in the Americas, Hart also acted as a judge in a landmark case in Jamaica, which successfully prosecuted two slave traders under the Slave Felony Act for attempted violation of the Abolition Law.[51] This was the first of a number of social causes that Hart supported in later life. After spending two years in Latin America, ill health took its toll once again and Hart returned to England as an invalid in 1820.

In 1831, after ten years ashore, Hart re-joined his old friend, Admiral Sir John Gore, and returned to India, where Gore had been appointed as Commander in Chief of the East Indies and China station. Hart remained in India for the duration of Gore's command as flag captain of the *Melville*, 74. In 1833 the admiral despatched Hart in the 26-gun frigate *Imogene* on a diplomatic mission to the Imam of Muscat in Zanzibar to discuss a commercial treaty agreed with the United States the previous year. At this time America was guarding its trade with Zanzibar jealously. Hart reported that the Imam had written a public letter inviting American citizens to trade with Zanzibar and sent it to an American captain with the request that it should be published. The captain refused on the grounds that 'if we allow this to be published, everyone will hear of this place and we shall lose all our trade'.[52] Hart's mission appears to have been successful and, when he departed, the Imam gave him a fine teak-built 74-gun ship, to be presented to King William IV. When the ship, named the *Imam*, arrived in Liverpool the following year, she was reported to be carrying Arabian horses, 'buffaloes &c.' and five hundred tons of timber.[53] On his return from Zanzibar, Hart submitted a comprehensive report to Admiral Gore

[50] Lower, p. 330.
[51] *The Morning Chronicle*, 23 November 1819.
[52] Haight, p. 99.
[53] Pollock, p. 544.

and also published detailed navigation notes on the southern passage to the islands.[54]

At the end of Gore's command of the East Indies station in 1835 Hart returned to England and finally retired from active naval service. The following year, in recognition of his naval and diplomatic services, Hart was awarded a knighthood and invested as a Knight Commander of the Royal Guelphic Order of Hannover.

In the early years of the 1840s Hart visited the United States and Canada in company with Algernon Percy, then styled Lord Prudhoe, a fellow naval officer and former shipmate. It seems likely that Hart knew Percy as a volunteer and junior midshipman while they served together in India. Percy, the second son of the Duke of Northumberland, was born in 1792 and joined the navy under Pellew's command in 1805.[55] He advanced through the ranks rapidly and made post captain before his active naval service ended with the peace in 1815. Two years later Percy was raised to the Baronetage and he subsequently undertook a number of exploratory and commercial voyages to different countries around the globe, including an expedition to Egypt in 1826–1829[56] and a diplomatic and trade mission to North America and Canada in the early 1840s, when he was accompanied by Hart. The American press reported their arrival in New York en route for Halifax in July 1841,[57] and recorded some of the official functions they attended, such as a dinner given in Washington DC for the Prince de Joinville.

> At six o'clock he dined with the President in a large party, composed of the Corps Diplomatique, the members of the Cabinet, now in this city, Lord Prudhoe, brother of the Duke of Northumberland, and Sir Henry Hart, both of the Royal Navy, and many distinguished officers of our own Army and Navy.[58]

Hart returned from North America at the end of October in time to attend the wedding of Fleetwood Pellew's only daughter, Harriet, at St George's, Hanover Square. By this stage in his life Hart appears to have been very comfortably off indeed, as the 1841 census[59] shows him living in an elegant house on York Terrace overlooking Regent's Park where he and his wife Maria kept a staff of eight servants.

---

[54] *The Nautical Magazine*, vol. 4, pp. 709–11.

[55] Both Parkinson and Taylor correctly characterise Pellew's relationship with the Duke as being mutually beneficial. In return for Pellew accepting Northumberland's younger son as a trainee officer, the Duke arranged for Pownoll to be elected to parliament.

[56] Starkey and Starkey, pp. 75–84.

[57] *New York Tribune*, 19 July 1841.

[58] The president referred to is Henry Tyler. Hazard, p. 223.

[59] HO 107/677/17 Folio 8, 1841 England, Wales and Scotland Census.

During his retirement, Hart does not appear to have played such an active role in politics as some of his contemporaries; however he did support a number of conservative and Protestant causes. In 1838, he supported the Subscriptions in Aid of Irish Election Petitions, a fundraising campaign by conservatives to support Protestant candidates in the Irish elections. And in 1851 he attended a meeting of the Protestant Alliance, which resolved to petition parliament for the repeal of the Maynooth endowment act, which granted government funds to the Catholic Seminary of Maynooth.

Like many of his fellow naval officers, Hart supported a wide range of naval and maritime charities and benevolent funds, including the Seaman's Hospital and the Marine Society, of which he was appointed committee member in 1854. Several of these societies, including the Marine Society, were also supported by Pellew, and it is highly likely that Hart and Pellew met and socialised at society events.

In addition to marine societies, Hart and his wife, Lady Maria, were also involved in a number of charities to support destitute and fallen women. These included the Fund for Promoting Female Emigration: a controversial scheme established in 1849 by Sir Sidney Herbert which attempted to link philanthropy with political economy.[60] The Fund, which was patronised by Queen Victoria and Prince Albert, raised money to encourage deserving women in reduced circumstances to emigrate and paid their passage to the colonies. This was intended to have the dual benefit of aiding the women themselves, and redressing the gender imbalance of the colonies. However the society, to which Hart was a subscriber, attracted criticism from some quarters and quickly ran into financial difficulties.[61]

The London Female Mission, a charity that provided asylum and refuge to destitute women of all ages, was one of a number of associations established by David Nasmith, the Scottish founder of the City Mission Movement. The Mission was partially funded by Quakers and Congregationalists and had its headquarters in Red Lion Square where many Evangelical societies met. The cause was neither popular nor fashionable and the Mission struggled to raise funds and secure staff. Despite the charity's radical connections, both Hart and his wife were supportive members of several of the Mission's committees.

Hart continued to maintain a close personal friendship with Pellew in the later years of his life, which appears to have been based not only on their early attachment and naval experience, but also on a shared Christian faith. In an article on Hart in *The Worthies of Sussex*, published in 1865, the author adds the following footnote:

> With that brave and Christian nobleman (Pellew) he formed a friendship that endured throughout his life. In almost his last letter

[60] Alexander, pp. 110–119.
[61] Blackburn, pp. 29–31.

to Sir Henry he uses the expression – "Together we will take the cup of salvation."[62]

Although no letters from Pellew to Hart have been traced, several letters referring to Hart have survived. In a letter to his son George written in 1828, Pellew tells him that 'Harry Hart & Maria' are currently at Knaresborough, and asks him to call on them to offer his affectionate regards and to thank Hart for his letter which he will answer soon.[63]

It was not just Pellew who held Hart in affectionate regard; Susan Pellew also appears to have been particularly fond of him. Writing to Sir Francis Furling in 1831, just two years before his death, Pellew notes his wife's affection for Hart:

> Our good and worthy friend Harry Hart you will know, had the command of the Melville going to India with his old friend Sir John Gore. He is an excellent creature. From Melville he never could obtain employment; he carries with him all the good wishes of this family particularly of Lady Exmouth who liked him from a youth.[64]

Hart continued to benefit from Pellew's patronage even after the admiral's death. In 1845, Hart wrote to Prime Minister Sir Robert Peel soliciting an appointment as a commissioner of Greenwich Hospital and including a commendation from Lord Exmouth among others.

> For my past naval service it would not be proper for me to speak. I must refer you to the admiralty but I may say I served ten years with Lord Exmouth and ten years with Sir John Gore and that I commenced my naval career as a mid under the former in the year 1796 – and served through the whole war and the enclosed documents from these and other officers will say more than I dare say for myself.

> "I shall be most happy to give you any sort of testimony of that which I have long known of you, that you are deserving my highest commendation"
>
> Lord Exmouth[65]

Hart was duly appointed as a commissioner of Greenwich Hospital in 1845. Attempts were being made at the time by the hospital's governor, Sir John Stopford, to reform the terrible conditions revealed in a report by Sir John Liddell MD, Inspector-General of the Royal Hospital. In order to

---

[62] Lower, p. 329.

[63] Pellew of Canonteign Collection, 7818M/F/3/1/9, Exmouth to George Pellew, September 1828.

[64] Exmouth Papers, Caird Library, Manuscripts Catalogue, AGC/26/22, Exmouth to Furling, 25 September 1831.

[65] British Library, MS 40 573, Peel Papers, vol. 393, ff. 372–4, Hart to Peel, 12 September 1845.

facilitate these reforms Peel appointed deserving naval officers to act as commissioners. These posts had previously been held as sinecures by MPs who received £600 and a residence with the appointment.[66] Although the new commissioners supported some of Liddell's reforms, others were rejected on the grounds of cost and the hospital finally closed in 1869.

Hart was also something of an inventor and technological improver and in 1849 he patented a device to prevent chimneys smoking,[67] an innovation that was reported somewhat wryly in *The Times*:

> Our admirals in these peaceable times really do valuable civil service. From the list of patents granted in the last week we find the following, Sir Henry Hart, Commissioner of Greenwich Hospital, Rear Admiral in our navy, for improvements in apparatus for preventing what are called smoky chimneys.

The invention won the Society of Arts Medal and, shortly after, *The Times* carried an advert for the patented chimney 'as used at Greenwich hospital'.

Hart continued to socialise with naval colleagues well into his later years and he was frequently present at events such as Navy Club dinners and the Lord Mayor's banquets, which were also attended by his former shipmates, George, 3rd Earl Cadogan and Sir Fleetwood Pellew.[68]

In 1857, after a long and active retirement, Hart died at his residence at the Queen's House, Greenwich Hospital, at the age of seventy-six. He had reached the rank of Rear Admiral in retirement and was survived by his wife Lady Maria. As the couple appear to have had no children, he bequeathed his estate to Lady Maria and to his nephew, Henry Hart of Beddingham, Sussex. Henry Hart was one of only seven of the *Indefatigable* midshipmen who had lived long enough to receive the Naval General Service Medal, with two clasps for the *Droits de L'Homme* engagement and *Cerbère* boat action.

THOMAS GROUBE, 1774–1850

THOMAS Groube was born in December 1774 in Falmouth to Samuel and Catherine Groube, née Boulderson, and was baptised the following month in January 1775.[69] He was the youngest of four children, and was still only ten years old when his father died in 1785. Groube's family, on both paternal and maternal sides, was well established in Falmouth's

---

[66] Ferguson, pp. 21–2.

[67] *The Repertory of Patent Inventions Enlarged Series*, vol. 13, pp. 87–8.

[68] *The Morning Post*, 22 June 1849.

[69] LDS P00172-1, record of baptism, King Charles the Martyr, Falmouth, 11 January 1775, Thomas, son of Samuel Groube and Catherine, née Boulderson.

maritime and commercial communities: the Groubes[70] were merchants who originally hailed from London, and several of the Bouldersons[71] were captains in the Falmouth packet service. With such a background Groube would have been an ideal protégé for Pellew.

Groube's naval service began in 1793 when he joined the 74-gun *Leviathan*, Captain Lord Hugh Seymour, serving for nine months in the Mediterranean during the republican siege of Toulon. The fact that Groube was rated able, rather than volunteer, for the duration of his service aboard the *Leviathan*, suggests that he may well have had some sea-going experience prior to joining the Royal Navy. In 1794 Groube joined Pellew for the first time aboard the *Arethusa*, before following him into the *Indefatigable* in 1795. This was a formative period of Groube's career and he shared in the many successes of both frigates. Apart from a brief two-month spell as able seaman in 1795, Groube was rated as master's mate for the majority of his time aboard the *Indefatigable*, although he was promoted to acting lieutenant in the final days of Pellew's command.

In late 1797 Groube was placed in command of one of the *Indefatigable*'s prizes; however the vessel was recaptured by the French and he and his prize crew were taken to La Rochelle as prisoners. Six months later Groube and his fellow midshipman, William Kempthorne, managed to escape in unknown circumstances, and by May 1798 they were back aboard the *Indefatigable*.[72]

On joining the *Impetueux* with Pellew in 1799, Groube reverted to the rank of master's mate for several months before taking his lieutenant's examination in what must have been somewhat fraught circumstances. Groube's certificate shows that he passed his examination in Port Mahon Bay, Minorca on 22 June 1799,[73] just two days after the court martial that condemned to death three leaders of the mutiny which had taken place aboard the *Impetueux* earlier in March. The captains who examined Groube aboard the *Neptune*, Charles Stirling and William Wolsely, had also formed the court for the trial, which took place aboard the *Prince*, under the presidency of Rear Admiral Collingwood and Admiral Charles Cotton.[74] Groube was just ten days over the six years' minimum service required to take his lieutenant's examination and he must have prepared for his exam

---

[70] PROB 11/1136, Will of Samuel Groube, Merchant of Falmouth, November 1784.

[71] Boulderson Family of Falmouth, Cornwall, England, http://freepages. genealogy.rootsweb.ancestry.com/~jray/boulderson/index.htm.

[72] ADM 35/13144, ADM 35/13145, Muster Tables of His Majesty's Ship the Indefatigable, November 1796 to October 1797 and November 1797 to August 1798.

[73] ADM 6/97, Lieutenants' Passing Certificates, 1797.

[74] ADM 1/5349, Impetueux Court Martial, June 1799.

in the turmoil of the aftermath of the mutiny and the tense atmosphere of the trial.

After passing for lieutenant, Groube continued to serve aboard the *Impetueux* until the ship was paid off at the commencement of the Peace of Amiens and, so far, no evidence has come to light of his activities during the short-lived peace. As soon as war recommenced in March 1803, Pellew was appointed to command the *Tonnant*, a fine 80-gun ship of the line, and before long Groube was commissioned as one of her lieutenants alongside his former *Indefatigable* shipmates, William Warden and George Bell. Groube continued to serve under the *Tonnant*'s subsequent commander, Captain William Henry Jervis, but was invalided out by a bout of ill health, which forced him to return home to recuperate for much of 1805. A letter to the Admiralty in May of that year gives an insight into his condition:

> I have to request with extreme regret that you will be pleased to acquaint their lordships of the Admiralty that the scrofulous affection on my neck still continues, without the least disposition to heal and I am sorry to say the faculty is of the opinion that it will take a considerable time if ever ... consequently I become a very unfit subject for sea service ... where I should be liable to frequent wet jackets and salt provisions, which would considerably increase the malady.[75]

At this point it seems that Groube was confronting the possibility that his naval career might be coming to a premature end, and his letter goes on to request that he might be given a posting with the Sea Fencibles at Falmouth so that he might continue to have some opportunity to serve. Fortunately Groube recovered sufficiently to receive a commission in the autumn of 1805 and he became lieutenant of the 44-gun *Woolwich*,[76] which sailed for the East Indies, where Pellew was Commander in Chief, and a number of Groube's former *Indefatigable* shipmates were stationed.

Pellew clearly valued Groube's service as he appointed him as first lieutenant of his flagship *Culloden* in August 1806. In this capacity Groube saw action commanding a division of boats in a successful mission to capture and destroy Dutch forces in Batavia Roads. The following year, in early 1807, while still a lieutenant, Groube was appointed to his first acting command: the 36-gun French frigate *Psyche*, which had been captured from Pellew's friend Jacques Bergeret off the Malabar coast in February 1805. Later that year, Groube was appointed to command the *Duncan*, 38, and the sloop of war *Victor*, 18, both of which had previously been commanded by former Indefatigable Henry Hart. While commanding the *Victor*, Groube was involved in a second successful action at Griessie in Java against what remained of the Dutch forces.

---

[75] ADM 1/2898, Lieutenants' Letters, Surname G, 5 May 1805.

[76] *Ibid.*, November 1805.

During his time as Commander in Chief, Pellew had developed a naval hospital in Madras, and Groube was appointed governor there in October 1808. He may have received this commission for health reasons, though the appointment could also indicate his commander's faith in his abilities ashore as well as afloat.

Like many young officers stationed in India, Groube was thrust into the expatriate communities of the great cities of Madras and Calcutta, with their culture of parties, receptions and balls, which were something of a marriage market for young women who had travelled to India with their families. Although Pellew was not above match-making on behalf of his eldest son Pownoll, he distrusted the young ladies of Madras, writing to his friend Alex Broughton:

> All boys are in great danger in India ... I never permit Pownoll or Fleetwood to sit twice at Table with the same young Lady, for they really push them upon the boys in so bare faced a manner they can hardly get off without saying soft things.[77]

Three of the former Indefatigables did indeed succumb to the charms of the young ladies of Madras: Pownoll Pellew and Henry Hart both married at St Mary's Church, Fort St George, Madras, during the same week in December 1808, and six months later, Groube married Anna Maria Watson, a young widow, on 13 June 1809.[78] The first two of the Groubes' children were later born and baptised in Madras.

A month after Groube's marriage, his promotion to the rank of commander was confirmed, though he continued to serve ashore at the hospital for a further eighteen months. Pellew wrote of Groube's promotion in a letter to Francis Beaufort, who had also served on the East Indies station for a time. This is one of a number of letters the admiral wrote to Beaufort updating him with news of his former shipmates and colleagues. It also provides evidence of the central role Pellew often played in maintaining the network of friendship that bound his young officers together.[79]

An anecdote of Mr and Mrs Groube at this time appears in a book called *The Cabin Boy* by one Billy Pitt, who came from the same neighbourhood as Groube, but received a somewhat frosty reception on visiting the couple.

> I made myself known to a young lady, with whose family both my father and myself had been on the most intimate terms for many years; I was in master's uniform and the young lady did not recollect

---

[77] Pellew to Broughton, 10 January 1807, in Parkinson, *Edward Pellew: Viscount Exmouth, Admiral of the Red*, pp. 370–1.

[78] India Office Registers of Births, Marriages and Deaths, St Mary's Church, Fort St George, Madras.

[79] The Huntington Library, Beaufort Papers, FB 1499, Pellew to Beaufort, 16 November 1809.

me. I called the next day to see her brother-in-law, Captain Groube, governor of the hospital, and an old Falmouth acquaintance, who married a sister of the young lady above mentioned. Being in a master's uniform I was received with icy coldness by her and with not quite so warm as I expected from him. I took Tiffin with him, and afterwards he showed me round the hospital and stammered out some sort of apology for his wife's behaviour, but 'no naval officer under the rank of Commander was taken the slightest notice of by the ladies in India and it would be unreasonable to expect her to break through the general rule.'[80]

By the time this book was published in London in 1840, Groube was in his mid-sixties and deeply involved with the political and charitable work to which he devoted much of his life ashore. It is impossible to know whether Groube knew of the book, or what he might have thought of it, but the picture Billy Pitt paints of a young couple caught up in the self-serving snobbery that characterised the British enclave in India might well have been one he came to regret; it certainly does not accord with the couple's later life in Britain.

In 1811, the family left India and returned to Britain, and in August 1812 Groube took up his last naval commission when he was appointed commander of the 16-gun brig-sloop *Calypso*. The *Calypso* was stationed in the Baltic where she played an important role during the siege of Danzig. Groube was also responsible for conveying Lord Walpole to St Petersburg and, as a result of his service in the *Calypso*, he finally made post captain in June 1814. Like many of his contemporaries, Groube's active naval service came to an end as the fleet was scaled down at the end of the Napoleonic Wars and he found himself surplus to the peacetime requirements of the Royal Navy.

After the war, Groube and his family settled in Honiton in Devon where he and Anna Maria had several more children and he became involved in local and church politics. The couple were both involved in the Independent church and Groube's politics and faith were very much entwined during this period of his life. It is not clear whether the couple were already involved with the Independent or Congregational church when they returned to Britain around 1812. Although their wedding took place in St George's Church, Madras, this does not necessarily imply that the couple were Anglican as there was no legal provision for marriage outside of the Anglican system at that time, other than for Jews and Quakers. Similarly, the baptisms of their children are not necessarily indicative of their denomination: their eldest son George was baptised in Madras, no record of their next two children's baptisms has been found, their fourth child was baptised at Above-Bar Independent Church in Southampton, and their youngest four were baptised in the Anglican parish

---

[80] Pitt, pp. 165–6.

6 Gravestone of Rear Admiral Thomas Groube and his wife Anna Maria,
by George Nicolle. This simple headstone in the churchyard at Honiton
Congregational Church provides a striking contrast with Warden's memorial.

church in Honiton between 1817 and 1824. There is other evidence that suggests that the couple became deeply involved with the Independent church while they lived in Honiton from about 1816 onwards. Both their wills, which were written in 1842 and 1851, were witnessed by William Wright, minister of the Independent chapel at Honiton from 1818[81] to 1851.[82] Another clue to the Groubes' Congregational membership is their gravestone, which survives to this day in the churchyard of Honiton Congregational Church. The memorial is moving in its simplicity: a small stone with an arched top, it has three oval stone bosses carved with just their names, date of death and, in Groube's case, his naval rank. The headstone is plain and unpretentious and seems a far cry from the social aspirations of the affected young couple Billy Pitt met in Madras. Indeed involvement with the Congregational church would in itself have limited their social ambitions as it denied certain privileges open to members of the established church. Horatio, one of Thomas and Anna Maria's sons, entered the Christian ministry but, as he was barred from studying at Oxford or Cambridge, he completed his studies in Edinburgh instead.

This social disjunction is again revealed in press accounts of a notorious church affair that Groube intervened in during the 1840s. Around this time Honiton received a royal charter instituting the new offices of mayor and aldermen. Thomas was duly elected as an alderman; however he also held the ancient and largely symbolic position of Honiton portreeve. Reverend James Shore, an Anglican curate, had been dismissed from his post by the Bishop of Exeter, and smeared in the press for holding views that were too independent and evangelical. Shore's supporters agreed to petition parliament on his behalf but their attempt to get the mayor to call a meeting failed. *Woolmer's Exeter and Plymouth Gazette*, a conservative local paper, gives an account of what happened next:

> The dissenter sympathisers with Mr Shore were then obliged to resort to a most extraordinary proceeding in order to gain their object ... the recent royal charter ... has not abolished the old office of portreeve. The present holder of the obsolete portreevalty is Captain Thomas Groube RN, one of the radical aldermen of the town council ... Alderman Groube decided to fly in the face of his municipal chief and has fixed *a meeting* to take place this day.[83]

Despite the outrage of the conservative press, the meeting went ahead with Groube in the chair. By invoking the traditional privileges of the portreeve,

---

[81] The Surman Index, digitised by Dr Williams' Centre for Dissenting Studies, first indicates Wright as the minister in Honiton in 1818.

[82] 1851 Census, Household of William Wright, HO107/1868 folio 196 schedule no. 144 for 15 Eaton Place, St Sidwell, Exeter.

[83] *Woolmer's Exeter and Plymouth Gazette*, 23 September 1848.

Groube was able to overrule the mayor, and provide Shore with a platform from which to clear his name.

As a serving naval officer, Groube was a post captain of several years' standing; in retirement he attained the rank of Rear Admiral, and in civic society he was respected as a bold and brave veteran of the wars with France. With his naval rank and social standing as a 'radical alderman', Groube had a strong platform from which to campaign on radical community issues including the income tax and opposition to the Corn Laws.

Although no known letters survive between Groube and Pellew from this period, it appears likely that they remained on good terms despite their widely differing political outlooks, as contemporary biographies and press articles often refer to Pellew as Groube's friend. An undated letter written from Pellew to Lord Sidmouth is addressed from 'Honiton' where the Pellews appear to have been staying at the time.[84] As the town is a very short journey from Pellew's own home in Teignmouth it is possible that the purpose of their stay was to visit the Groubes. Hospitality, both offered and received, continued to characterise Pellew's relationships with his former officers throughout his life.

Groube lived long enough to apply for the Naval General Service Medal, with clasps for the *Virginie* and the *Droits de L'Homme* engagements, and in 1849 he qualified for the rank of Rear Admiral in retirement. Thomas Groube died on 25 January 1850 at home in Honiton aged seventy-five, 'beloved and regretted by all'.[85] His obituaries paid tribute to his naval career, inevitably mentioning Pellew and the *Indefatigable*, and to his civic service in Honiton, describing him as 'that true friend of the poor man'.[86] There is a touching similarity in accounts of Pellew's and Groube's funerals, though they took place seventeen years apart. Both were simple affairs, lacking in pomp and ceremony; however, as a mark of respect, the shops closed in their home towns of Teignmouth and Honiton. Quiet endings for two adventurous lives lived in public service.

---

[84] Exmouth Papers, Box 23, Pellew to Sidmouth.

[85] *Exeter Flying Post*, 31 January 1850.

[86] *The Western Times*, 15 February 1850.

7

Diversity and Responsibility

DURING his own lifetime Pellew was regarded not only as one of the outstanding frigate captains of the era but also as a consummate and versatile sea officer. These were qualities that he looked for in his own officers and men, and they were often to be found in young men who came to the Royal Navy from the merchant service. The navy attracted skilled merchant recruits as it offered them the possibility of honour, gentility, wealth and a chance of bettering themselves.[1] The advantage was not all one way; the navy also benefited significantly from the recruitment of officer candidates from the merchant service. In the case of the *Indefatigable*, merchant recruits leavened the frigate's cohort of midshipmen with adaptable and experienced sea officers who had valuable practical and navigational experience. Such recruits were ideally suited to service with detached frigate squadrons where their flexibility, resourcefulness, and knowledge of coastal waters and harbours could be exploited to the full during shore operations, cutting out expeditions and taking and crewing prizes. Regardless of their background, Pellew nurtured many merchant recruits throughout his lifetime and supported their careers as they progressed through the commissioned and warrant ranks of the service. Of those that served aboard the *Indefatigable*, several were to become his lifelong friends, and one a member of his extended family.

Alexander McVicar is unusual among the *Indefatigable*'s merchant recruits as he transferred between the Royal Navy and the merchant service several times throughout his career. By the time he joined the *Indefatigable*, McVicar was already an experienced and versatile seaman whose skills were recognised and valued by Pellew. During the Peace of Amiens, McVicar returned to the merchant service before rejoining the navy when hostilities resumed. He went on to serve at Trafalgar, in the North Sea and the Baltic. After retiring from active service McVicar continued to engage in maritime commerce and served as Admiralty Commissioner for the Harbour and Docks of Leith.

Another versatile merchant recruit was John McKerlie; in addition to holding the rank of midshipman, at various periods McKerlie served as the *Indefatigable*'s quarter gunner, boatswain and schoolmaster. Despite losing his arm during the *Droits de L'Homme* engagement, McKerlie had a

---

[1] Rodger, *The Command of the Ocean: A Naval History of Britain 1649–1815*, pp. 264–5.

distinguished naval career, serving at Trafalgar, off Heligoland, and on the Scheldt. He was seconded from the navy at the request of Thomas Telford to work on a survey of communication routes between England and Ireland. At the end of the war, McKerlie returned to his native Wigtownshire where he built a successful career in merchant shipping before returning to the navy at the age of sixty to captain the controversial experimental frigate *Vernon* during sea trials in the Mediterranean.

John Thomson, the son of the *Indefatigable*'s first lieutenant, had a lengthy and wide-ranging naval career during which he saw active service in almost every corner of the globe. He was present during the attack on Ferrol, helped to land Abercromby's troops at Aboukir, assisted in the recapture of the Cape, accompanied Popham on his ill-fated expedition to Buenos Aires, carried the declaration of war at the outbreak of the War of 1812, and harassed American shipping from Halifax to Charleston. Thomson was also feted by Nelson for his determined bravery during a bloody engagement off Toulon. After retiring from active service, Thomson developed business interests in the fishing industry in Leith and finally moved to Ireland to serve as an Inspecting Commander of the Coast Guard. Thomson remained close to the Pellew family and married Pellew's niece shortly after the end of the war.

John Gaze began his naval career when Pellew pressed the crew from the merchant vessel he was serving on and then encouraged him to enlist as a volunteer. Gaze forged a successful career as a distinguished sailing master and he and Pellew became 'inseparable',[2] serving together for almost their entire careers from 1793 onwards. Gaze was master of Pellew's flagships in India, the North Sea and the Mediterranean, and rose to the warrant rank of First Master to the Commander in Chief. When Pellew launched the expedition to Algiers it was Gaze who accompanied him as Master of the Fleet. After retiring from active service, Gaze served as Master Attendant at Sheerness Dockyard. His long and meritorious service was recognised when he was appointed to the rank of Master and Commander, a notable distinction for a warrant officer.

Although details of George Chase's early life and career are obscure, he appears to have joined the Royal Navy from the merchant service around 1793. Like many merchant recruits, Chase was a versatile individual who served as midshipman, sailmaker's mate and quarter gunner. As with Gaze, Chase followed the warrant career path and went on to have a long career serving as master gunner. Although his career followed a different route from many of his shipmates, he was clearly trusted and valued by Pellew, who appointed him as his personal coxswain over three commands.

[2] ADM 6/126, Pellew to Admiralty, 21 July 1809.

ALEX MCVICAR, 1768–1840

ALEXANDER McVicar was born in Leith on 29 October 1768,[3] the sixth of eight children born to William McVicar and his wife May Berry. William is described in his son's baptismal record as a sailor, though it is unclear whether he served with the merchant or royal marine.

McVicar's lieutenant's passing certificate[4] records that he entered the Royal Navy at the age of just nine when he joined the 20-gun hired armed ship *Leith* as a gunner's servant in March 1778. The fact that he entered the service at such an early age suggests that he may have gone to sea with a family member or acquaintance; however it is equally possible that his name was carried on the ship's books. According to his certificate, McVicar spent two years aboard the *Leith* before transferring to a second hired armed ship *Alfred*. From there, he moved first to the 16-gun brig-sloop *Pylades*, in October 1782, where he was rated able seaman, and then to the *Myrmidon* where, in January 1785, he was promoted to the rank of midshipman at the age of fifteen.

At this point, McVicar's first phase of naval service came to an end and ten years were to pass before he re-joined the Royal Navy. McVicar's whereabouts from 1785 to 1796 are unknown but it seems highly likely that he joined the merchant service. In marginal notes written in the family copy of Edward Osler's biography of his father, Admiral Lord Exmouth, Fleetwood Pellew recorded that: 'Capt Bell and Capt Thomas Groube were both taken from a West Indiaman. Capts Gaze and McVicar the same (merchant vessels).'[5]

McVicar re-entered the navy in 1796 when he joined the *Indefatigable* as a volunteer at Falmouth on 18 February.[6] By this stage he was twenty-seven years old and already an experienced seaman. Pellew clearly acknowledged this experience and McVicar was immediately rated midshipman. Over the course of the next four years Pellew made good use of his skilled recruit and McVicar's entry in the *Indefatigable*'s 1797 muster reveals multiple instances of re-rating and promotion: 'Midshipman till 7th June, then master's mate to 4th September then Mid to 27th September then MM to 30th Oct then Mid to 11th December then MM.'[7] It is only by examining the records of the squadron as a whole that the full picture is revealed

---

[3] Scotland's People, OPR Birth 692/02 0060/0271, records of baptism, South Leith Parish Church, 1 November 1768, Alexander, son of William McVicar and Marjory 'May', née Berry.

[4] ADM 107/21, A. McVicar, Lieutenant's Passing Certificate.

[5] Pinhey, p. 23.

[6] ADM 36/13143, Muster Table of His Majesty's Ship the Indefatigable, January–October 1796.

[7] ADM 36/13144, Muster Table of His Majesty's Ship the Indefatigable, November 1796 to October 1797.

of McVicar's initially confusing muster entry, and his part in a series of personnel movements that illustrates how Pellew managed his squadron.

McVicar's first two re-ratings took place in the summer and autumn of 1796 during a phase of promotions which saw the *Indefatigable*'s acting sailing master, John Thomson (2), as the muster describes him, move to *La Revolutionnaire* as acting master. This was a short temporary promotion as Thomson returned to the *Indefatigable* three months later. During Thomson's absence, his place as acting master was taken by former merchant seaman George Bell, a position that he had occupied on previous occasions. Later, Bell himself was seconded to the *Jason* as acting master for a short period of two months. On 10 December 1796, the *Indefatigable*'s first lieutenant, Richard Pellow, was discharged 'on promotion', setting off a complex chain of subsequent re-ratings. The following day, John Thomson, the ship's second lieutenant and father of John Thomson (2), was promoted to first lieutenant. John Norway, third lieutenant, was then promoted to second, and George Bell, sailing master, was advanced to acting third. Meanwhile, John Thomson (2), son of the Lieutenant Thomson, was promoted from master's mate to acting sailing master, and finally, McVicar himself was promoted to master's mate.

These temporary promotions and re-ratings are part of a pattern, visible throughout the muster and pay books of the squadron, that highlights Pellew's strategic use of key personnel on short-term assignments. By filling in for one another, skilled officers, who had often gained their experience in the merchant service, could be shared with other ships that may have lacked officers as a result of sickness, injury or secondment to prize crews. Lower down the scale, this strategy also provided men like McVicar and Thomson with opportunities for advancement.

Pellew made good use of his junior officers, while at the same time providing them with opportunities to hone their skills, by placing them in command of prize crews. Generally the log and muster of the *Indefatigable* does not record the names of crew despatched in prize vessels, unless they had the misfortune to be re-captured. Such was the fate that befell Alexander McVicar and five of his shipmates in January 1797 when a prize he was commanding was re-taken by the French. McVicar's younger shipmate Nicholas Pateshall refers to the loss of this prize in a letter to his brother dated 20 January 1797. Pateshall explained that: 'The most valuable of our prizes which I mentioned in my last was retaken by a French privateer within 5 miles of Falmouth in which I lost a worthy messmate[8] and two other midshipmen.'[9]

Not only did McVicar lose his prize, but he and his crew were also absent

---

[8] The three men Pateshall refers to are George Tippett, Alex McVicar and James Bray.

[9] Pateshall Papers, A95/EB/40/1, Nicholas Pateshall to Edmund Pateshall, 20 January 1797.

from the *Indefatigable* during the *Droits de L'Homme* engagement. Pellew did not take the loss of his valuable prize, and equally valuable officers, lightly and he wrote to the Admiralty requesting temporary command of an additional vessel to find and retake the prize, a request the Admiralty refused.[10] Luckily, the prize crew's captivity was short-lived, as they were soon transferred to a cartel and handed over to the *Phoebe* and thence to their 'proper ship', as the *Phoebe*'s captain referred to the *Indefatigable* in his supernumeraries list.[11]

Despite the apparent failure of the mission, Pellew appears to have regarded McVicar's conduct as exemplary, as, soon after his return in early July 1797, he was put forward for his lieutenant's examination. During his examination McVicar was unable to present his journals and captains' certificates from the *Pylades* and the *Myrmidon* as these had been lost 'owing to his being taken in a prize belonging to the *Indefatigable*'.[12] The fact that McVicar took his journals and certificates aboard the prize may suggest that he initially intended to sit his examination for lieutenant at an earlier date. Indeed it is quite possible that Pellew despatched him in the prize in order to enable him to return to England to present himself for examination.

Within weeks of McVicar passing his lieutenant's examination, Pellew wrote to Lord Spencer recommending him for promotion. Spencer's reply was encouraging, but typically non-committal: 'I will set Mr McVicar's name down on my list of Candidates for Promotion, and shall be glad to take as early an opportunity of giving him a Commission as prior Engagements will permit.'[13] In the meantime, Pellew himself promoted McVicar to acting lieutenant of the *Indefatigable*. McVicar finally had his commission confirmed in September 1798, and he left the *Indefatigable* to take up the position of lieutenant of the armed ship *Sally*. Pellew was evidently keen to keep his adaptable officer and, even before McVicar had left the frigate, he had written to Spencer on the subject, eliciting a somewhat weary reply: 'I shall have no objection to Mr McVicar being restored to you by and by.'[14] A minute of the Admiralty Board records that McVicar was indeed reappointed to the *Indefatigable*, as third lieutenant, in January 1799, only three weeks before Pellew received notification of his unexpected promotion to the *Impetueux*. As the Admiralty did not permit Pellew to transfer any of his lieutenants to his new command, McVicar remained aboard the *Indefatigable*.

---

[10] ADM 1/2315, Captains' Letters, Surname P, 1797.

[11] ADM 36/13221, Muster Table of His Majesty's Ship the Phoebe; ADM 51/1197, Captain's Log of His Majesty's Ship the Phoebe.

[12] ADM 107/21, A. McVicar, Lieutenant's Passing Certificate.

[13] Exmouth Papers, Box 2, MSS/92/027, Spencer to Pellew, 25 September 1797.

[14] Exmouth Papers, Box 2, MSS/92/027, Spencer to Pellew, 1 October 1798.

In McVicar's case, promotion to the commissioned ranks of the Royal Navy did not preclude further merchant service. In 1802, with the advent of the Peace of Amiens, McVicar wrote to the Admiralty requesting leave of absence to captain the merchant schooner *Hazard* on the Leith to Danzig route and later to take her to Malaga.

Merchant commands of this nature were mutually beneficial for both parties; not only did the lieutenant acquire valuable experience of command and familiarity with coastal waters, ports and merchant shipping routes, he also gained knowledge of the types and capabilities of merchant vessels that detached frigates often sought to take as prizes. Contacts established in merchant ports during trading voyages may also have been useful to the Admiralty for gathering intelligence when hostilities resumed.

At a time when many Royal Navy lieutenants found themselves beached on half pay, McVicar's ability to re-enter the merchant service provided him with additional financial benefits and security, and in April 1803, following his voyages to Danzig and Malaga, he was able to marry Margaret Reid, the daughter of a Leith merchant.

After the breakdown of the Peace of Amiens, McVicar returned to the Royal Navy and served as lieutenant of the *Minotaur* at the Battle of Trafalgar. The *Minotaur* and the *Spartiate*, where McVicar's shipmate John McKerlie was also serving, were the rear two ships of Nelson's division and came late to the battle, having been hampered by light airs. However, when they did engage, they were able to rake Admiral Dumanoir's 80-gun *Formidable*, manœuvring into position to protect the vulnerable *Victory* and isolating the Spanish *Neptuno*, forcing her to strike.[15]

Following Trafalgar, McVicar was stationed in Yarmouth for a number of years, where his eldest daughter, the first of ten children, was born in 1807 and where his former *Indefatigable* shipmate, James Bray, was based at the time. Later, in 1809, McVicar's experience of northern waters was put to good use when he was appointed to command the 18-gun ship-sloop *Rover*. In October of that year, *The Lancaster Gazette* reported:

> That active and zealous officer Captain McVicar, while acting commander of His Majesty's ship *Rover*, on a seven weeks cruise, on the coast of Norway and Jutland, took and destroyed eighteen sail of the enemy's vessels, and only lost one marine killed, the bosun and one seaman wounded. In making one of the above captures, the *Rover* chased so close to the shore, within two feet of her own draft, under the fire of the enemy, the crew having abandoned the vessel, and the *Rover*'s boats being all detached on other service, several seamen of the *Rover* volunteered swimming to take possession of the prize, which they effected, unhurt, under a heavy fire from the enemy on land.[16]

---

[15] Robson, p. 139.

[16] *The Lancaster Gazette*, October 1809.

Between 1813 and 1815, McVicar commanded the *Apelles*, a 14-gun brig-sloop based in his home port of Leith on the North Sea station. During this period McVicar was successful in taking a number of prizes, and he demonstrated his adaptability once again when he was commissioned by the Admiralty to undertake sea trials of new ship's compasses patented by Leith watchmaker, George Alexander.[17] McVicar was finally appointed to the rank of post captain in 1817 but he appears to have left the service around this time. McVicar remained settled in his home town of Leith, where he continued to engage in maritime commerce. In 1825 he was one of a number of gentlemen who formed a committee to establish a company to supply fish to the markets of Edinburgh.[18] Though retired from active service, McVicar continued his association with the Royal Navy and served as Admiralty Commissioner for the Harbour and Docks of Leith when the new Leith Dock Commission was established in 1826.

Alexander McVicar's long, varied and successful career finally came to an end in May 1840 when he died at North Leith at the age of seventy, leaving a modest estate valued at £1,838.[19]

JOHN MCKERLIE, 1775–1848

JOHN McKerlie[20] was born in 1775 at Glenluce, Wigtownshire, and baptised on 12 August. His father, also John McKerlie, was employed as a stonemason; however the younger McKerlie chose a quite different career path. Marshall's *Naval Biography* relates that McKerlie first went to sea 'when very young'[21] with a friend of his father's who was employed in the Baltic trade. Although there is no indication of how long McKerlie remained in the merchant service, Marshall records that he made several voyages across the Atlantic.[22]

McKerlie entered the navy in April 1794, as a volunteer rated able, when he joined Pellew's *Arethusa*[23] from the receiving ship *Royal William*. The following year, when Pellew left the *Arethusa*, McKerlie transferred with him to the *Indefatigable*. Like many of Pellew's recruits from the merchant service, McKerlie appears to have been a versatile and experienced individual who made a valuable addition to the crew. For his first two years aboard the *Indefatigable*, McKerlie was rated quarter gunner; however during this period he also served as the frigate's schoolmaster, though at

---

[17] *The Repertory of Arts, Manufactures, and Agriculture*, vol. 23, pp. 330–4.

[18] *Caledonian Mercury*, 15 October 1825.

[19] Edinburgh Sheriff Court Inventories, SC 70/1/59.

[20] McKerlie's name is variously spelled McKerlie, M'Kerlie and MacKerlie in contemporary documents and reports.

[21] Marshall, *Royal Naval Biography Supplement*, part III, p. 186.

[22] *Ibid*.

[23] ADM 107/24, J. McKerlie, Lieutenant's Passing Certificate, 1 August 1800.

the age of twenty-two he cannot have been much older than the boys he tutored. It appears that McKerlie was both literate and numerate, and this, together with his previous sea-going experience, would have made him a good choice for the position of the frigate's schoolmaster.

McKerlie was still rated quarter gunner at the time of the *Droits de L'Homme* engagement and he was the only one of the young gentlemen to be injured in the action, receiving a wound in his thigh and losing his right arm. Following the *Droits de L'Homme* engagement McKerlie was promoted to midshipman, a rank he held for over a year before being appointed acting boatswain in August 1798. McKerlie was one of a series of acting boatswains who served aboard the *Indefatigable* following the dismissal by court martial of boatswain John Skene for neglect of duty in May 1796.[24] McKerlie served in this capacity for six months until January 1799 when he reverted to his former rank of midshipman and master's mate. By this stage, Pellew knew that he would have to leave the *Indefatigable* and it is possible that this eleventh-hour re-rating was intended to ensure that McKerlie would be able to accompany him to the *Impetueux*.

Aboard the *Impetueux*, McKerlie had numerous opportunities to prove his abilities. In addition to participating in multiple boat actions during the Belleisle expedition of 1800, McKerlie was also given command of a prize ship intended to land troops during the aborted operation. When the attack was abandoned, Pellew appointed McKerlie to the frigate *Thames* as acting lieutenant, and wrote to Lord Spencer asking the Admiralty to confirm this position. Spencer declined; as McKerlie had not passed his examination for lieutenant, he could not fill the vacancy in the *Thames*. McKerlie did finally pass the examination and receive his lieutenant's commission in October 1800.

Marshall includes an anecdote from this period of McKerlie's career, relating that when he had not been informed of his role in the Belleisle attack, he asked Captain Pellew and General Maitland how he was to be deployed during the debarkation. Pellew is reported to have replied:

> McKerlie you have lost one hand already, and if you loose the other you will not have anything to wipe your b******* with; you will remain on board with the first lieutenant and fight the ship as she is to engage an 8-gun battery.[25]

Unlike many of his shipmates, McKerlie remained afloat during the Peace of Amiens, serving first with the Channel Fleet and later on the Newfoundland station. He then went on to join the 74-gun *Spartiate*, Captain Laforey, as lieutenant, and served in this capacity at the battle of Trafalgar.

Following Trafalgar, McKerlie was promoted to the rank of commander; however, at this point he returned to Scotland to settle 'private affairs'.

---

[24] ADM 1/5336, Skene Court Martial.

[25] Marshall, *Royal Naval Biography Supplement*, part III, p. 187.

In 1806 McKerlie wrote a series of letters to the Admiralty from the port of Garlieston in Wigtownshire, regarding a pension for the loss of his arm. In the correspondence, McKerlie explained that Pellew had advised him to apply to Chatham for a pension to compensate for the injury sustained during the *Droits de L'Homme* engagement. He duly received an annual pension of £7 13s 4d; however this had been stopped when he was promoted to lieutenant in 1800. As a result, he asked their Lordships' 'liberal protection and support' to petition for further compensation.[26] The Admiralty, misunderstanding his request, replied that he should have a commission at the next available opportunity. McKerlie politely clarified his request, adding a somewhat indignant postscript: 'Sir, in your last you had addressed to Lieut Jno McKerlie but you had been mistaken I Am a Captain.'[27] The Admiralty's response was terse, and informed McKerlie that 'their lordships do not interfere with the regulations established by the chest of Greenwich'.[28]

By December 1806 McKerlie had concluded his personal business and wrote again to the Admiralty, this time eloquently requesting a commission.

> ... as I am but a young man and very anxious to follow my profession until I am rendered incapable from old age or infirmity from following up any advantage I may be to my King and country.
>
> I have therefore to beg your lordships will think me worthy of the command of one of his Majesty's sloops of war either upon the home or the foreign station but rather would prefer a warm station on account that I have lost my right arm with that brave officer Sir Edward Pellew in the *Indefatigable* engaging the *Droits de L'Homme* and with whom I served the whole of my times as midshipman, and my arm being but badly amputated it does not so well agree with a cold climate.
>
> But I am perfectly ready and willing to serve upon any station their lordships may think fit to employ me on ... I hope your lordships will employ me again where I can be a benefit to my country and an honour to myself is the most ardent wish of your most obedient and humble servant.[29]

It is unclear how the Admiralty responded to this request; however around this period McKerlie was seconded from the navy to work with Thomas Telford surveying harbours, roads and bridges for an 1809 parliamentary report on communications between England and Ireland, via the west of Scotland.[30] Telford personally requested McKerlie as 'a

---

[26] ADM 1/2151, McKerlie to Marsden, 6 March 1806.

[27] ADM 1/2151, McKerlie to Marsden, 11 March 1806.

[28] *Ibid.*, corner note.

[29] ADM 1/2151, McKerlie to Admiralty, 10 December 1806.

[30] Telford and McKerlie, 1809.

proper person to be thus employed' owing to his being 'well acquainted with the country, as well as with the harbours and packets'.[31]

McKerlie returned to active naval service as commander of the brig *Calliope* from 1808 to 1813, during which time he served on the North Sea station, participating in the capture of Flushing and the Walcheren expedition. For a time this service brought him back under Pellew's command as he was appointed Commander of the North Sea fleet blockading the Scheldt between 1810 and 1811. McKerlie's conduct on the Scheldt was considered so gallant that Admiral Sir Richard Strachan awarded him the north coast of Holland and Heligoland as a cruising ground, during which time he captured a large number of merchant vessels and privateers. By 1813 McKerlie had been put in command of the squadron of ships stationed off Heligoland, where he was instrumental in overseeing the defence and retreat from Cuxhaven and responsible for destroying enemy shipping on the Braak. McKerlie returned to Britain at the end of 1813 but, despite finally being awarded the rank of post captain, he was unable to obtain another command and returned home to Garlieston. In 1816 he finally received a pension for the loss of his arm and in the same year he applied to accompany Pellew on the expedition to Algiers. In a personal letter to McKerlie, Pellew declined his request, adding: 'Had you been there I know your ship and your fin would not have been out of hail of your old commander and friend EXMOUTH.'[32] McKerlie was one of many friends and former colleagues whose service Pellew refused, as he considered the expedition to Algiers to be so hazardous.

Following the end of his naval career, McKerlie turned his attention to merchant shipping in his home port of Garlieston. Between 1823 and 1826 he built, owned and operated a number of merchant vessels operating between Garlieston, Liverpool, London and Ireland. McKerlie was clearly a successful member of the thriving Wigtownshire community; he served as a local magistrate, enjoyed country pursuits and was regarded as being an excellent shot despite the loss of his right arm.[33] Around this time McKerlie married Herriot Stewart and the couple went on to have one child, a daughter, Lilias.

One final late opportunity for naval service came McKerlie's way in 1834 when he was appointed as captain of the experimental frigate, *Vernon*, designed and built in 1832 by the controversial Surveyor of the Navy, Sir William Symonds. It seems likely that McKerlie's appointment came about through his association with the Earls of Galloway. Sir James Graham, First Lord of the Admiralty, was the grandson of the 7th Lord Galloway who had built the port of Garlieston in the 1760s, and the 8th Lord Galloway was an Admiral who had served as one of the Lords Commissioners of the

---

[31] Marshall, *Royal Naval Biography Supplement*, part III, p. 188.

[32] *Ibid.*, p. 194.

[33] Boyd, p. 121.

Admiralty in 1805. A memoir published by a Mr Mark Boyd in 1871 relates that McKerlie was awarded the *Vernon* commission after joining the First Lord on a shooting party on his uncle's estate.[34]

All Symonds's ships divided opinion and none more so than the *Vernon*. At the age of sixty McKerlie seems an unusual choice for such a contentious command; however it is possible that with his connection to Lord Galloway, in addition to being a veteran of both Trafalgar and the *Droits de L'Homme* engagement, he may have been regarded as a safe pair of hands, metaphorically if not literally.

McKerlie took command of the *Vernon* in July 1834 and spent the next three years putting the ship through her paces in sea trials in the Mediterranean. McKerlie was enthusiastic about his new command and the *Vernon* initially performed well in trials against a test squadron, which took place off Malta in 1835. However she faced a stiffer challenge with the arrival of the 74-gun *Barham*, Captain Corry, at the end of the year. Corry was a popular captain and had something of a reputation as a crack yachtsman.[35] At the end of the first round of trials, Graham wrote to Symonds: 'The *Barham* had a great advantage in being so lately out of dock, and I hear Corry is a better jockey than old M'Kerlie.'[36]

Despite Corry's jockeyship and the determination of the *Vernon*'s officers, the trials proved to be inconclusive. The controversy surrounding the *Vernon* rumbled on and the perception grew that *Barham* had proved to be the superior vessel. This prompted the officers of the *Vernon* to issue a public declaration in 1837 stating that they considered the 'magnificent ship' to be 'a *perfect* man of war in every respect'.[37] First among the signatories was John McKerlie, Captain. The declaration was one of McKerlie's last acts as captain of the vessel he had once described as 'the finest ship in the world'. McKerlie's devotion to the *Vernon* is illustrated by the fact that he bequeathed the watch book he had kept during the Mediterranean trials to his daughter, who later presented it to the Admiralty.

Following his retirement from the service, McKerlie returned to Garlieston, before eventually moving to the handsome Corvisel House, in nearby Newton Stewart. In 1847 he was one of the *Indefatigable*'s eight surviving veterans who received the Naval General Service Medal with the *Droits de L'Homme* clasp. The following year, in 1848, Rear Admiral John McKerlie died at Corvisel House at the age of seventy-three.

---

[34] *Ibid.*

[35] Sharp, p. 176.

[36] *Ibid.*

[37] *The Nautical Magazine and Naval Chronicle* for 1837, pp. 328–9.

7 Captain John Thomson, RN, artist and date unknown, probably after 1815.
Thomson is wearing captain's uniform and the Sultan's Medal
for Egypt, awarded to him for an action in 1801.

JOHN THOMSON, 1774–1835

ALTHOUGH John Thomson spent a relatively short but eventful period serving under Sir Edward Pellew's command, his naval career and later civilian life are closely bound up with those of his commander and he represents a good example of the support that Pellew provided to recruits from the merchant service and the sons of friends and fellow naval officers.

Thomson, the son of a naval warrant officer, also John Thomson, and his wife Jean, was born in Leith on 21 August 1774.[38] As with many of his contemporaries, Thomson's lieutenant's passing certificates falsified his date of birth to make him appear four years older. According to his certificates, Thomson entered the Royal Navy in March 1792 as master's servant aboard the *Viper* cutter. As he would have been only seven at the time, it appears more than likely that his name was entered on the *Viper*'s books, and subsequently on those of the cutter *Monkey*, to give him almost four years' additional sea time. There is a gap in Thomson's service record between February 1786 and December 1793, at which point he joined the *Arethusa* as an able seaman, serving alongside his father, a lieutenant aboard Pellew's frigate.[39] The fact that Thomson was immediately rated able suggests that he had some sea-going experience before joining the *Arethusa* and it seems probable that, like his father, he spent some time in the merchant service prior to December 1793.

When Pellew was given command of his own squadron in 1795, both father and son transferred with him from the *Arethusa* to the *Indefatigable*, where Thomson was rated able, midshipman and master's mate in quick succession. Thomson had an opportunity to demonstrate his courage and seamanship the following year when he attempted to take one of the *Indefatigable*'s boats alongside the stricken *Dutton* when she was wrecked off Plymouth in January 1796. Pellew clearly valued the younger Thomson's skills and experience as he appointed him acting lieutenant of the frigate *Revolutionnaire* between June and October 1796. On returning to the *Indefatigable*, Thomson was promoted to acting sailing master in December 1796 as part of the same chain of promotions that saw his father promoted to first lieutenant and Alex McVicar to master's mate.

---

[38] Scotland's People, 692/01 0030 0276, North Leith Parish Registers. 'John Thomson, carpenter, and Jean Ridpath of this parish, spouses, had a son born 21 August and baptised 6 September 1774 named John.' Although John Thomson senior's occupation is listed as 'carpenter', cross-referencing the parish register with his will provides corroborating evidence that this is the correct John Thomson.

[39] The ship's musters identify Thomson as John Thomson (2), in order to distinguish him from his father, who is referred to as John Thomson (1). The names of both men are frequently spelled 'Thompson' in Admiralty records.

Thomson proved his worth again only a month later when he and his shipmate John Gaze played a crucial role in saving the *Indefatigable* during the engagement with *Les Droits de L'Homme*. One of the French 74's final broadsides caused devastating damage to the frigate's masts and rigging, with one shot cutting the main topmast shrouds right through. Had the mast gone by the board, the ship would surely have been lost; however both were saved by the prompt actions of Thomson, who clinched the end of a hawser around the mast head, while Gaze went aloft to cut away the damaged topgallant yard. In his despatch following the engagement, Pellew acknowledged 'Thomson the master' as one of the officers who had 'abundant claims' on his gratitude and to whom he owed 'infinite obligations'.[40]

Thomson passed his examination for lieutenant in April 1797 and left the *Indefatigable* to take up his first lieutenant's commission aboard the ship of the line *Vengeance*, Captain Thomas Macnamara Russell, in the West Indies. After serving two years in the West Indies, Thomson returned to the familiar waters of the Channel to join the 74-gun ship of the line *Renown* in late 1799. During this period, Thomson, together with Lieutenant Burke, also of *Renown*, led a number of boat actions and cutting out expeditions along the coast of France. They succeeded in cutting out several *chasse marées* laden with brandy, wine and stores for the fleet at Brest, and destroyed a fort at the mouth of the Quimper river. Thomson and Burke led a third attack at Noirmoutier which destroyed a number of armed vessels; however, as the tide ebbed, their own boats were left aground, exposing them to the fire of the onshore batteries. They escaped by dragging a large fishing boat and the ship's barge through the mud and back out to sea; however several men were killed and wounded and seventy-six were left stranded and taken prisoner by the French.[41]

In August 1800, *Renown* joined a squadron of ships, including Pellew's *Impetueux* and their former ship *Indefatigable*, now under the command of Henry Curzon, to launch an attack on the Spanish port of Ferrol. Following this action, *Renown* sailed for the Mediterranean where Thomson saw active service at Aboukir in March 1801. Thomson was one of a number of officers who were responsible for landing the first detachment of General Abercromby's troops under heavy fire at Aboukir Bay. He was subsequently awarded the Sultan's Gold Medal for Egypt (2nd class), in recognition of his service.[42]

During the Peace of Amiens, Thomson continued to serve aboard *Renown* before transferring to the 32-gun frigate *Narcissus*, Captain Donnelly, towards the end of 1803. The *Narcissus* was stationed in the

---

[40] *The Gentleman's Magazine*, vol. 67, part 1, pp. 240–1, Pellew to Nepean, 17 January 1797.

[41] Stanhope Lovell, pp. 8–9.

[42] Quinan, www.pellew.com/Family%20Tree/Thomson.htm.

Mediterranean with Nelson's fleet blockading Toulon. In July 1804 Thomson led a party of boats from the *Narcissus*, *Seahorse* and *Maidstone* in an attack on twelve laden settees moored below the shore batteries at La Vandour in the Bay of Hyères. The French were fully prepared for the attack: the vessels were hauled in and secured to the shore and the boarding party came under heavy fire from the ships, shore batteries and even the houses of the town.[43] Thomson and his men succeeded in towing out one of the settees and destroying the others, but the action cost 'several valuable lives'; four officers and men were killed and twenty-three others wounded, some severely.[44] Despite acknowledging that the 'importance of this service may be little', Nelson commended the 'determined bravery' of the officers and men.[45] Nelson's despatch appeared in the *Gazette*[46] and Thomson was awarded a Lloyd's Patriotic Fund sword worth £50.[47]

In late 1805, the *Renown* joined a squadron commanded by Sir Home Riggs Popham and proceeded to the Cape of Good Hope, with two infantry brigades led by Sir David Baird, in order to retake the colony from the Batavian Republic. Baird met minimal resistance and the commandant of Cape Town surrendered only days after the British troops landed in January 1806. Following the success of the mission, Popham turned his attention to South America. Believing that the inhabitants of Buenos Aires and Montevideo could be encouraged to throw off the Spanish colonial yoke with assistance from the British, Popham proceeded on an unauthorised mission to the River Plata in April 1806. Popham's plan initially met with success: Buenos Aires was captured with little opposition and over a million dollars of specie, gold and silver, part of the capitulation settlement, was shipped back to Britain aboard the *Renown*. Thomson, however, remained behind; Popham had appointed him as Port Captain of Buenos Aires and placed him in command of a captured Spanish ship, *Neptuno*.[48] The success of the mission was short-lived. Barely seven weeks after they had surrendered, the citizens of Buenos Aires retook the city and imprisoned the British troops, Thomson included.[49] Despite reinforcements arriving in February 1807, the British failed to recapture Buenos Aires and were forced to withdraw from the entire region in order to secure the prisoners' release. Eventually, in October 1807, Thomson and the captured British troops were freed and returned to England.

---

[43] *The Naval Chronicle*, vol. 12, p. 316, Donnelly to Nelson, 11 July 1804.

[44] *Ibid.*

[45] *The Naval Chronicle*, vol. 12, pp. 315–16, Nelson & Bronte to Marsden, 12 August 1804.

[46] *The Gazette*, 15742, p. 1238, Nelson & Bronte to Marsden, 12 August 1804.

[47] McGrath and Barton, p. 121.

[48] Cobbett, pp. 541–2.

[49] Rodger, *The Command of the Ocean: A Naval History of Britain 1649–1815*, p. 548.

Following his return, Thomson did not have to wait long for another commission: in June 1808 he was appointed as lieutenant of the 74-gun *Swiftsure*, Captain John Conn, and sailed for Halifax where he rejoined his former commander, Sir John Borlase Warren. In May the following year, Thomson was promoted to commander, but he had to wait almost six months until he received his first command, the 16-gun brig-sloop *Colibri*. In the interim, Thomson served briefly as Port Commander of Halifax.[50] Excepting a short period as acting flag captain for Warren aboard the *Santo Domingo*, Thomson remained in command of the *Colibri* until 1813. Warren's first commission as Commander in Chief of the North American station ended in 1810; however Thomson continued to benefit from his interest, or rather that of his wife. In June 1812, Lady Borlase Warren wrote an extraordinary personal letter to Pellew, berating him for failing to act on Thomson's behalf.

> Dear Sir Edward
>
> I have this day a letter from Captain John Thomson of HMS *Colibri*, from North America, which disappointed me much, as from all I had entreated you expecting him, and your own apparent wish to serve him, I concluded you would have long ere this have added this sloop to your fleet. I quite depended on your exertions in his favour and I am persuaded that the Commander in Chief of the Mediterranean Fleet would not have been refused that request of the Admiralty Board. You ought to have insisted upon it, that he might have the chance of your being able to Post him. Indeed I am quite angry with you. It is so unlike an old friend, so unlike what I expected of you! And we must quarrel forever unless you immediately demand of the Admiralty Board that the *Colibri* to join your fleet. I shall only quarrel with you, for you know I am much too sincerely attached to your dear Lady Pellew and your children, to give up the comfort of their friendship, but you are a very naughty admiral indeed and poor John Thomson, who has for years been devoted to you, is suffering from it. Altho' you have been so forgetful of your promise to me about J Thomson, I yet believe you will be sincerely sorry to hear our beloved daughter is still a great invalid if it pleases the Almighty to preserve her to us over this summer we must try a warm climate ... Sir John has run up to town for the Installation or would assist in this scolding letter, for it is no joke, that we are all <u>quite angry</u> with you therefore you must hasten to reform.
>
> Adieu, Adieu!!
> C. Warren[51]

---

[50] ADM 9/3/819, Memorandum of the Services of Captain John Thomson.

[51] Pellew of Canonteign Collection, un-catalogued, Warren to Exmouth, 2 June 1812.

It is not clear whether Pellew was chastened by Lady Warren's rebuke, and interceded on Thomson's behalf. Although Thomson did not make post at this time, the *Colibri* was a successful command by any measure. At the outbreak of the War of 1812 Thomson carried the declaration of war from New York to Halifax, and between July 1812 and September 1813 the *Colibri* took a large number of prizes.[52]

Thomson's successful run in the *Colibri* finally came to an end in August 1813. While reconnoitring Port Royal Sound south of Charleston, the sloop grounded on a sandbar and had to be abandoned. The subsequent court martial found that the loss of the *Colibri* was attributed to sand having suddenly accumulated over the bar, and Captain Thomson, his officers and company were acquitted of all blame.[53]

After being exonerated by the court martial, Thomson was immediately appointed commander of the 16-gun sloop *Rattler* for a short period between September 1813 and May 1814. He then returned briefly to England before being appointed to his penultimate command, the 10-gun brig-sloop *Chanticleer* in the West Indies in August 1814.

Perhaps mindful that the war was drawing to a close, or fearing another dressing down from Lady Warren, Pellew exerted his influence on Thomson's behalf in 1815. A minute for Lord Melville's favour requesting promotions and transfers for various deserving officers and men, includes: 'Capt. Thomson (*Chanticleer*, N. America) and Capt. Kempthorn (*Harlequin* at Newfoundland) – Lord Exmouth requests may be sent out to him having no other Friends, both good officers.'[54]

Whether as a result of Pellew's intervention, or in recognition of his exemplary service, Thomson finally made post captain in July 1815. His final act of naval service, as captain of the 74-gun *Venerable*, was to transport Admiral Sir Philip Durham, the outgoing Commander in Chief of the Leeward Islands station, home to Britain as the war ended. In May 1816, John Thomson's long and active naval career came to an end, his retirement pension secured by his eleventh-hour promotion to post captain.

Following his retirement from the Royal Navy, Thomson strengthened his ties with the Pellew family when he married Pellew's niece, Constantia Henrietta Spriddle, in Falmouth on 19 December 1816. Following their marriage it appears likely that the couple lived for a time in Thomson's home town of Leith as he had inherited property, and possibly also business interests, from his parents who had died there in the early 1800s.

---

[52] In the space of three weeks between 23 July and 13 August 1813 the *Colibri* took six American vessels: *Gleaner*, 6 guns and 40 men; *Catharine*, 14 guns and 88 men; *Polly*, 4 guns and 35 men; *Buckskin*, 1 gun, 3 swivels and 32 men; *Dolphin*, 1 gun, 1 swivel and 28 men; *Regulator*, 1 gun and 40 men; and *Dolphin*, 2 guns and 48 men. *The Naval Chronicle*, vol. 28, pp. 256–8.

[53] ADM 1/5438, *Colibri* Court Martial.

[54] Pellew of Canonteign Collection, 7818M/SS/1, Minute of Admiral Lord Exmouth for Lord Melville's favour, 'about 24/8/1815'.

Although Thomson's business activities have not been fully traced, in 1825 he subscribed to the committee established by Alex McVicar to supply fish to the markets of Edinburgh. Thomson may have been involved with the fishing industry for a number of years, as Pellew's household accounts from 1818 record an item 'Paid Capt. Thomson for fish'.[55]

In April 1827 Thomson and his family moved to Ireland where he was appointed as Inspecting Commander of the Coast Guard at Westport, County Mayo.[56] Thomson may have had existing connections to Ireland, not only through the navy, but also through his membership of the Edinburgh auxiliary branch of the Irish Evangelical Society.[57] Thomson remained in Ireland until his death in 1835 at the age of sixty.

JOHN GAZE, *c.* 1779–1851

JOHN Gaze appears to have been born in north Norfolk in the late 1770s, but his exact date and place of birth remain obscure. The *Indefatigable*'s 1797 muster[58] records Gaze's age as twenty-one and his place of birth as Hickling, a small village north of the port of Yarmouth on the Norfolk Broads; however there is no baptism of a boy with this name in the Hickling registers in 1776, though two boys named John Gaze[59] were baptised there in 1779 and 1780.[60] Though it cannot be proved with certainty, it seems unlikely that either is the young man who served aboard the *Indefatigable*. Gaze's naval career began in February 1793 when he joined Pellew's earlier command, the *Nymphe*. He was initially rated able seaman, before being re-rated quarter gunner and quartermaster within a matter of weeks of joining the frigate. Had Gaze been born in 1779/80 he would have been around the age of fourteen at the time, not an improbable age for a boy to be serving aboard a frigate; however his rapid re-rating suggests that he was somewhat older. Gaze was around eighteen when he joined the *Nymphe* and the muster lists his place of birth as North Yarmouth, though all subsequent musters give his place of birth as Hickling. It is possible that

---

[55] Pellew of Canonteign Collection, 7818M/E/2/1/3/1, Right Honorable Lord Viscount Exmouth in Account with Toulmin & Copeland.

[56] *Woolmer's Exeter and Plymouth Gazette*, 30 June 1827.

[57] *Caledonian Mercury*, 12 March 1825.

[58] ADM 36/13144, Muster Table of His Majesty's Ship the Indefatigable, September 1796 to October 1797.

[59] The surname Gaze is relatively common in the area and there appears to be an extended family with various children being born around the same time with similar sets of family forenames.

[60] LDS Registers, FHL 1526819, item 18, Hickling Parish Registers, John, son of John and Margaret [Fisher], baptised 14 December, and John, son of John and Mary [Chase], baptised 10 September 1780.

Gaze himself was unsure where he was born, or that he had been brought up in Hickling and came to think of it as his place of birth.

Many years later, Gaze gave his own account to George Pellew of how he came to meet his father and join the Royal Navy. While correcting errors and omissions in Edward Osler's life of Lord Exmouth, George Pellew relied on Gaze's knowledge of his father's career at sea and recorded the following:

> From this time (1793) Captain Gaze[61] must be regarded as an eye witness of almost all my father's services, he having first joined at Portsmouth from having been the mate of Mr Lacon's – the brewer of Yarmouth – merchant vessel *Venus*: and when Cap Pellew had pressed all the men on board her, he sent for Gaze next day and said 'I cannot press you, but if you will enter the service, I will place you on the Quarter Deck and take care of you.' This offer Gaze accepted and never left him afterwards.[62]

In a letter written to the Admiralty Board in July 1816, Pellew himself described how he first took Gaze under his patronage following his good conduct on the *Nymphe*.[63] Although this does not quite tally with Gaze's own account of their meeting, it seems possible that Pellew may have encouraged Gaze to volunteer in order to earn the £5 bounty and later, realising that he was a competent seaman and valuable asset, made the promise that Gaze recounted many years later.

A comprehensive record of Gaze's career from 1797 to 1816 has survived in his master's service record[64] which contains a chronological career summary, the Trinity House certificates he received on passing his master's examinations, Admiralty correspondence and letters, and testimonials from captains with whom he served. Among these letters are several from Pellew, which demonstrate the support he provided to deserving officers, whether commissioned or warrant, and the loyalty and friendship he received in return.

Gaze passed his first master's examination, qualifying him to serve as master on sixth rate ships, in February 1797[65] and soon after was appointed as master of the 16-gun brig-sloop *Kangaroo*, Captain the Hon. Courtney Boyle.[66] As was often the case, Gaze's transfer to his new ship was neither swift nor smooth. Still aboard the *Indefatigable* in April 1797, Gaze wrote to

---

[61] On retirement as Master Attendant of Sheerness in 1846, Gaze's services were recognised by his promotion to Master and Commander, hence George Pellew referring to him as 'Captain' in 1848.

[62] Pinhey, p. 19.

[63] ADM 6/146, John Gaze, Records and Certificates of Masters, Ga-Go.

[64] *Ibid.*

[65] *Ibid.*, Trinity House Certificate, 2 February 1797.

[66] *Ibid.*, Admiralty order, Sir Richard King, 21 February 1797.

the Admiralty asking if his seniority on the master's list could be dated from the order appointing him to the *Kangaroo* rather than from the date he was able to join the ship.[67] Gaze also enclosed a letter from Pellew enquiring if he would be entitled to half pay at master's rate while waiting for his confirmation, and announcing that he intended to employ Gaze as master of the *Indefatigable* as soon as he was sufficiently qualified.[68] As Gaze was then qualified only to serve as master aboard sixth rates, he needed to gain sufficient experience at this level before progressing to becoming master of fifth rates such as the *Indefatigable*.

Gaze finally joined the *Kangaroo* in May 1797, but it was not long before he rejoined the *Indefatigable* as acting master in the autumn of 1798, and had his warrant confirmed shortly thereafter. When Pellew was forced to leave the *Indefatigable* to take command of the *Impetueux*, Gaze continued to serve as the frigate's master under her subsequent two captains, Henry Curzon and Matthew Scott.[69] Both were successful commanders and the *Indefatigable* continued to take a large number of prizes. Although sailing masters may not be the stuff of legends as frigate captains are, John Gaze clearly played a vital role in establishing the *Indefatigable*'s reputation as a famously successful frigate.

When the *Indefatigable* was paid off in October 1801 in advance of the Peace of Amiens, Gaze remained on her books while she was laid up in ordinary through the spring of 1802. As Pellew was himself on the beach at this time, he was not in a position to help secure a more promising commission for Gaze; however, Captain Edward Brace,[70] formerly Gaze's commander on the *Kangaroo*, requested that he join him as master of the sixth rate *Camilla*. The reply on the reverse of Brace's letter indicates that his request should be turned down as no competent master was available to replace Gaze on the *Indefatigable*;[71] however, despite the Admiralty's initial objections, Gaze was able to serve as master of the *Camilla* for several months during 1802.[72]

With the breakdown of the Peace of Amiens and Pellew's return to sea as captain of the 80-gun *Tonnant*, Gaze was reunited with his patron and also his old shipmate Jeremiah Coghlan when he became master of Coghlan's 10-gun cutter *Nimble*, attached to Pellew's Channel Fleet squadron. Gaze served aboard the *Nimble* for fifteen months until he was appointed as Pellew's sailing master, joining former Indefatigables Thomas Groube and William Kempthorne aboard the *Tonnant*, stationed off the coast of Spain.

---

[67] *Ibid.*, Gaze to Admiralty, 17 April 1797.

[68] *Ibid.*, Pellew to Admiralty, 16 April 1797.

[69] *Ibid.*, Statement of the Services of John Gaze.

[70] Brace replaced Boyle as commander of the *Kangaroo* in July 1797.

[71] ADM 6/146, Brace to Admiralty, 14 January 1802.

[72] *Ibid.*, Trinity House Certificate for Masters of Fourth Rates, 2 February 1799.

In 1804 when Pellew was appointed as Commander in Chief of the East Indies station and raised his admiral's flag aboard the *Culloden*, he requested Gaze as his sailing master. The request was confirmed and Gaze served as master of Pellew's flagship for the next five years. Pellew showed his gratitude for his friend's faithful service in a reference he wrote in August 1809 around the time Gaze qualified as master of second rate vessels.[73]

> He has entitled himself to my entire approbation upon every occasion of active employment by the zeal and attention which has uniformly shown to his duty and as possessing the most complete knowledge in his profession. I recommend him as a most meritorious officer.[74]

When Pellew's commission in the East Indies came to an end in 1809, Gaze returned with him to Europe and continued to serve as master of his flagships: *Christian VII* on the North Sea station and later the *Caledonia* in the Mediterranean from 1811 onwards. In 1810, Gaze had passed his final master's examination enabling him to serve as master of first rates, and from this point onwards his title was First Master to the Commander in Chief. For a short period during Pellew's Mediterranean command in 1814, Gaze was appointed to the dockyard at Port Mahon, before returning to sea for the remainder of the war as master of Pellew's final flagship in the Mediterranean, the 98-gun *Boyne*.

In 1816 when Pellew was charged with the Algiers mission, many of his former officers requested to join the fleet; however most were refused as Pellew knew that the mission was likely to result in great loss of life. Of the former Indefatigables Pellew only permitted his trusted companions John Gaze and William Kempthorne to accompany him.

Prior to the departure of the fleet, questions appear to have been raised regarding Gaze's suitability for the appointment of Master of the Fleet. Although the original query has not survived in the Admiralty archives, Pellew's response is an eloquent testimonial of his high regard for Gaze.

> I have received your letter of the 19th instant requesting me to give my opinion as minutely as possible with respect to the Nautical Skill and acquirements of Mr John Gaze (33) Master of the Fleet under my Command.
>
> I have only to observe that I took him under my patronage in 1793 for his good conduct in the Action with the *Nymph*, since which we have been almost inseparable; this I think is the highest encomium I can bestow on him. Yet I have no hesitation in stating that his professional skill as well as his Integrity as a man is seldom surpassed, and if I had thought the Board were unacquainted of the high esteem

---

[73] *Ibid.*, Trinity House Certificate for Master of Second Rates, 7 August 1809.

[74] ADM 6/126, reference written by Pellew for John Gaze, August 1809.

in which I hold the merits of Mr Gaze I should have made it known to them long before.[75]

Pellew appears to have assuaged whatever concerns had been raised and Gaze accompanied him to Algiers. This final victory marked the end of Gaze's long and distinguished sea-going career.

Even after retiring from active service at sea, Gaze and Pellew continued their close association; in 1816 Gaze was appointed as Assistant to the Master Attendant at Plymouth Dockyard, while his patron became Commander in Chief, Plymouth. Subsequently, in 1832, the same year that Pellew was appointed Vice Admiral of the United Kingdom, Gaze became Master Attendant at Sheerness, a post he held until his retirement in 1846. In 1824, he married Ann Susannah Gibbons, the daughter of a banker from Staffordshire, and the couple went on to have one son, John Pellew Gaze.

While Gaze was serving as Master Attendant at Sheerness he and his family had a lucky escape when one of the portable magazines aboard HMS *Camperdown* exploded, causing extensive damage and resulting in the death of one seaman and a young woman who was among a group of visitors. Several other seamen and visitors were injured, among them 'Mrs Gaze, the lady of Mr John Gaze, Master Attendant of HM Dock there, and Master Gaze'.[76] Fortunately their injuries were only superficial.

Pellew and Gaze had indeed become inseparable over the many years they served together, forging a deep and abiding friendship and enduring personal and professional respect. This friendship continued even after Pellew's death; Gaze remained close to the family and, as a result of their long shared service, he was regarded as the authoritative repository of Pellew's naval service and life at sea. George Pellew, Sir Edward's third son, acknowledged Gaze's 'Long acquaintance and confidential intimacy with my father and the deep interest he took in all that related to his public services'.[77]

At the end of his long naval service Gaze was rewarded with the Naval General Service Medal with four clasps, including one for the *Droits de L'Homme* engagement and another for Algiers,[78] and promotion to the commissioned rank of Master and Commander. He retired to Fareham in Hampshire and died there in February 1851.[79] An obituary that appeared shortly after his death described Gaze as 'the gallant deceased ... one of the most distinguished masters in the navy',[80] citing his exemplary management of Pellew's flagship at Algiers, along with the inevitable reference to *Les Droits de L'Homme*. Writing about Algiers, Pellew

---

[75] ADM 6/126, Pellew to Admiralty, 21 July 1809.

[76] *The Times*, 15 July 1843.

[77] Pinhey, p. 6.

[78] ADM 171/8, Medal Rolls, Royal Navy General Service Medal.

[79] Civil Registration of Deaths, ancestry.co.uk, 1851, vol. 7, p. 51.

[80] *The Kentish Gazette*, 25 February 1851.

himself had commented, 'Our old friend John Gaze was as steady as a rock',[81] a statement that might have been equally true of their professional relationship in general and their long and abiding friendship.

GEORGE CHACE, *c.* 1773–1840

ALONGSIDE John Gaze, George Chace is the only other of the *Indefatigable*'s young gentlemen who followed the warrant career path, rather than going on to become a commissioned officer. Indeed he is included in this study only by virtue of the fact that he served as a midshipman aboard HMS *Indefatigable* for a short period in February and March 1796.[82]

Evidence of Chace's early life is scant and has been pieced together from a few official Admiralty documents and civil records. There is currently more documentary evidence for the later stages of Chace's life than for the earlier, as he lived just far enough into the era of civil registration for both his marriage in 1839[83] and death in 1840[84] to be recorded, and his burial record appears in the digitised archives of Stoke Damerel churchyard.[85] An annotated copy of Chace's will has also survived, attached to a claim his widow submitted to the Pension Office for outstanding pension money.[86] This will is written on the Admiralty's standard form for recording seamen's wills, which was generally used for simple bequests, or in the case of serious illness or imminent death at sea. In addition to these civil documents, a detailed record of Chace's later career survives in the archives among the certificates of service for warrant officers.[87]

George Chace appears to have been born in London some time between 1771 and 1775; however his exact date and place of birth are unknown and the date of his entry into the Royal Navy is similarly obscure. Chace joined the *Indefatigable* in 1794 having previously served with Pellew aboard both the *Nymphe* and the *Arethusa*. His entry in the *Indefatigable*'s muster book records his place of birth as London, and his date of birth as 1771, making him twenty-six on joining the ship. However his death certificate and the burial register give his age in 1840 as sixty-five, which would suggest a later birth date of around 1775. Chace's entries in the muster books of the *Nymph*, *Arethusa* and *Indefatigable* are all internally consistent regarding

---

[81] Osler, p. 322.

[82] ADM 36/13144, Muster Table of His Majesty's Ship the Indefatigable.

[83] George Chace and Elizabeth Roach, Marriage Register entry no. 253, 14 February 1839, Parish Church of Charles the Martyr, Plymouth.

[84] Death of George Chace, gunner in HM Navy aged 65, 10 December 1840, Register of Deaths entry, no. 393, Parish of Stoke Damerel.

[85] Burial Register, 16 December 1840, Stoke Damerel Parish Church.

[86] ADM 45/12/9, Will of George Chance and pension claim.

[87] ADM 29/3, Entry books of certificates of service: Gunners 1817–1839.

age and place of birth, but there is no indication where in London he might have been born and, thus far, no baptism or other birth record has been found.

On first joining the *Nymphe* in 1793, aged around twenty-three, Chace was initially rated able, before rapidly being re-rated as sailmaker's mate, then quarter gunner. This strongly suggests that he had some prior sea-going experience before joining the *Nymphe*, but the frigate's muster does not cite any previous ship or supernumeraries list and merely records his place of appearance on the ship as Portsmouth. A handwritten note added to Chace's will lists the ships *Nymphe*, *Arethusa* and *Indefatigable* along with the annotation 'Captain Edward Pellew, later Lord Exmouth'. A fourth vessel, *Cormorant*, is also listed, but it is not clear what part this ship played in Chace's service history. The likelihood that Chace's career in the Royal Navy began before he joined the *Nymphe* is corroborated by the seven years of service recorded in his gunner's passing certificate issued in 1797, which would suggest he first entered the navy in 1790.[88] There is also a strong possibility that Chace may have been another capable recruit from the merchant service.

Like many of the other young gentlemen who had prior experience at sea, Chace was re-rated several times and served in a number of roles including able seaman, sailmaker's mate, quarter gunner and midshipman; however, for the majority of the time he served aboard Pellew's three frigates he held the position of captain's coxswain. Although there are no surviving letters from Pellew that mention Chace by name, other than official correspondence referring to his service record and conduct which was required documentation for candidates for the office of master gunner, the fact that he served as captain's coxswain across three commands would suggest that Pellew regarded him as a reliable and trustworthy individual.

Chace's career as master gunner began soon after the *Droits de L'Homme* engagement when he took his master gunner's examination on 22 February 1797. Although he passed successfully, he did not receive his warrant until later that year when he left the *Indefatigable* in July, discharged 'on promotion'[89] to the *Bristol*. At the time, the *Bristol* was moored on the Thames, just 'down from the Tower',[90] serving first as a hospital and later as a prison ship. This was the beginning of almost thirty years' service as a master gunner, during which time Chace served almost continuously, as is indicated by his pension record.[91]

Chace's career reflects a very different progression from those of his shipmates who went on to become commissioned officers; his career path

[88] ADM 6/127, George Chace, Gunner's Passing Certificate.

[89] ADM 36/13144, Muster Table of His Majesty's Ship the Indefatigable.

[90] ADM 102/99, Muster Table of His Majesty's Ship the Bristol.

[91] ADM 359/47A/208, George Chace, Certificate of Service and Pension Record.

is characteristic of warrant officers, and particularly of standing officers, such as carpenters, gunners, pursers and boatswains, who often remained with a single ship throughout its lifetime in service. In all the twenty-nine years of Chace's naval service he spent most of them, roughly twenty years, on ships that were laid up in ordinary. During this twenty-year period, he served on four ships, and in one case, that of the *Jupiter*, he seems to have been appointed to her almost before her hull was laid down.[92]

In 1826, Chace finally retired from the service as a superannuated gunner and settled in Devonport where there was a large community of warrant officers and their families. It was common for superannuated gunners to be involved in examining new applicants for the rank of master gunner[93] and it is quite possible that he undertook such responsibilities.

In 1839 Chace married Elizabeth Roach, who was herself the widow of a gunner, John Roach[94] of the *San Josef* gunnery training ship at Plymouth. Chace's marriage certificate describes him as a widower but, thus far, documentary evidence of his first marriage, or of any children that may have resulted, has not been found. Chace died only one year after his marriage, in 1840, and was buried in Stoke Damerel, the parish that served Devonport Dockyard. Following his death, his widow Elizabeth filed a claim[95] for pension money outstanding at the time he died, and it is from this claim that the annotated copy of Chace's will has survived.

George Chace's career path differed markedly from the majority of his former *Indefatigable* shipmates, and fewer traces have been left from which to reconstruct his naval service. However there is one important regard in which Chace's life was similar to many of his fellow Indefatigables: in his chosen field of service, his career was dedicated, long and successful. Though Chace spent much of his service on ships in ordinary, for three memorable years he was part of that capable and close-knit cadre of officers and men that crewed the *Indefatigable* when Pellew was at the peak of his career as a fighting frigate captain. Chace's name may be absent from the network of correspondence that bound these men together, but the fact that he served as Pellew's personal coxswain throughout this period testifies eloquently to the high regard in which he was held by his captain.

---

[92] ADM 6/192, Succession books of standing officers.

[93] Chace himself was examined by one active and two superannuated gunners.

[94] John Roach and Elizabeth Colepack, Marriage Register entry no. 43, 5 October 1837, Parish Church of Charles the Martyr, Plymouth.

[95] ADM 45/12/9, Will of George Chace.

8

Friends, Family and
the Falmouth Connection

LIKE many sea captains of the age, Pellew drew heavily on his home community and a wide circle of family and friends in order to man his ships. Although Pellew was born in Dover, his roots were planted firmly in Cornwall where his family originated and where he himself grew up. In the earlier part of his career, Pellew had particularly strong connections to Falmouth where the Western Squadron was based and where his own young family were born and raised. Although Pellew famously resorted to recruiting a band of Cornish tin miners to crew his first frigate, the *Nymphe*, he was able to draw many more promising recruits from the thriving port town of Falmouth.

The final cohort of the *Indefatigable*'s young gentlemen fall roughly into two groups: those who were related to friends and family of Pellew, and those who belonged to the close-knit Falmouth maritime community. Like William Kempthorne, James Bray's father earned his living in the Falmouth packet service, though their family backgrounds could not have been more different. Bray's father, a surgeon in the packet service, belonged to a family of prominent Catholic clergy and scholars who held influential positions in both Ireland and France. William Warden's connection to Falmouth is rather more tangential; however, as he was the son of a Lisbon merchant, it is possible that his connection to Pellew came about via the Falmouth–Lisbon packet and the trade links it supported.

Throughout his life, Pellew had a reputation for promoting the sons of family, friends and influential patrons, often beyond their abilities, and in this regard the young gentlemen of the *Indefatigable* were no exception. In addition to carrying the names of his own two sons on the ship's books, he also accepted on board the son of his friend and fellow Cornish frigate commander, Robert Carthew Reynolds, along with a young relative of his wife, Susan Frowd, and another youngster with family connections to his closest friend and confidant, Alex Broughton. There is no question that Robert Reynolds junior and Philip Frowd were deserving of the confidence Pellew placed in them; both were gallant and enterprising young officers. Richard Delves Broughton, however, was a rather different kettle of fish; described by Pellew himself as an 'odd fellow', young Broughton had a short and turbulent naval career which ended with him being court martialled and dismissed the service.

While this group all benefited from Pellew's patronage, they did not benefit from his famous luck: all five died before they reached their prime.

Frowd succumbed to disease in the West Indies, Warden died of exposure at sea in the Indian Ocean, Bray was killed when his ship was wrecked off the coast of Halifax, and Broughton's troubled life ended in unknown circumstances in India. Reynolds had the distinction of being the only one of the *Indefatigable*'s 1797 young gentlemen to have died of wounds sustained in action. He was buried with all due ceremony on HMS *Diamond Rock* off Martinique, the only man ever to be interred there.

JAMES BRAY, 1778–1812

JAMES Bray was baptised in Falmouth in June 1778, the eldest of four children born to James Bray and Margaret Fullerton. Bray senior was a surgeon on His Majesty's packet boats stationed at Falmouth, and served aboard the Lisbon packet *Hanover*[1] in the mid-1780s. With his connections to the Falmouth packet service, Bray appears to have been a typical recruit to Pellew's squadron; however in some regards his background was very different from that of his fellow Cornish shipmates. Bray's father had been born in Fethard, County Tipperary, into a family of prominent Catholic scholars and clergy; his uncle, Thomas Bray, was a Catholic prelate who served as Archbishop of Cashel from 1792 to 1820,[2] and his sister Margaret became a nun in the Presentation Convent in Cork. The family also had connections to the clergy in France through Bray's grandmother, Margaret Power. One of Margaret's brothers owned property near Avignon, and served as canon at Cassel in Flanders and as chaplain to the French Ambassador in Rome in 1765, and her nephew was the first vice president of Maynooth College.[3] Despite such prominent Catholic lineage, James Bray senior and his wife Margaret Fullerton married in the Anglican tradition and all their children were baptised in Falmouth parish church.

Bray initially entered the Royal Navy when he joined the *Arethusa* as an able seaman at the age of sixteen, one week before the end of Pellew's command. He immediately transferred to the *Indefatigable* where he was initially rated as able before being promoted to midshipman only a fortnight later. Bray's rapid promotion suggests that he had some prior sea-going experience, which would not be unexpected for a young man from Falmouth with connections to the packet service. Bray's service aboard the *Indefatigable* was not uneventful; however he was missing from the frigate on the night of the *Droits de L'Homme* engagement, as he was one of the crew of the prize captained by Alex McVicar that was re-taken by the French within five miles of Falmouth. Bray's captivity was mercifully

---

[1] *The Medical Register for the Year 1783*, p. 57. James Bray senior's entry in the Medical Register appears opposite the entry for physician J. Harry M.D. (Leyden 1778), father of *Indefatigable* midshipman John Harry.

[2] Stephen, p. 241.

[3] O'Donnell.

brief; together with McVicar, he was transferred to a cartel and soon restored to his 'proper ship' via HMS *Phoebe*.[4]

Like the *Indefatigable*'s other older midshipmen, Bray did not follow Pellew to the *Impetueux* in 1799; instead he transferred to the ship of the line *Canopus*, captained by another Falmouth-born officer, Bartholomew James.[5] Bray served aboard the *Canopus* as master's mate for five months, until the end of James's command, and then transferred to the 32-gun frigate *Alcmene*, Captain Sir Henry Digby. Like Pellew, Digby was a popular and accomplished frigate captain, and the *Alcmene* was a particularly lucrative command. Bray was lucky enough to be serving as midshipman aboard the *Alcmene* in October 1799 when she was one of three frigates that pursued and captured the Spanish treasure ship *Santa Brigada* off the coast of Galicia. The ship was carrying an immensely valuable cargo, which included 1,400,000 dollars,[6] and the prize money subsequently paid out was staggering. Each captain was awarded over £40,000, while Bray, as a midshipman, stood to receive £791.[7]

Bray passed his examination for lieutenant in March 1801; however details of his naval career between 1801 and 1806 are scarce. In May 1806 he was appointed to join the sloop *Dauntless* at the Nore, but it appears that he suffered a period of ill health around this time as he wrote to the Admiralty from his home in North Yarmouth on 18 May apologising for being unable to join the *Dauntless* due to 'severe indisposition', adding that he would be sufficiently recovered to travel in a day or two.[8] It seems unlikely that Bray did indeed join the *Dauntless*, as on 28 May he was appointed to the 28-gun frigate *Nemesis*, and joined the ship in Spithead two days later. Unfortunately for Bray, he was superseded by another lieutenant a week later, prompting him to write to the Admiralty pointing out the considerable expense he had incurred travelling by land to join his ship in time, and trusting that their Lordships would take into account the hardship of his case and allow him to remain.[9]

Bray's prospects appear to have improved by 1807 when he was appointed as lieutenant of the 38-gun frigate *Shannon*, Captain Philip Broke. In April of that year the *Shannon*, together with the *Meleager*, Captain John Broughton,[10] was sent north to Greenland to protect the

---

[4] ADM 36/13221, Muster Table of His Majesty's Ship *Phoebe*. ADM 51/1197, Captain's Log of His Majesty's Ship *Phoebe*.

[5] Laughton, pp. 203–204.

[6] Marshall, *Royal Naval Biography*, vol. 1, part II, p. 763.

[7] W. James, *The Naval History of Great Britain from Declaration of War by France in 1793 to the Accession of George IV*, vol. 2, p. 523.

[8] ADM 1/2766, Lieutenants' Letters, Surname B 238.

[9] ADM 1/2766, Lieutenants' Letters, Surname B 239.

[10] There does not appear to be any clear relationship between Captain John Broughton and Bray's *Indefatigable* shipmate Richard Delves Broughton.

whale fishery.[11] The ships reached the ice in early May but pressed on. *Shannon* cruised around the coast of Spitzbergen and in late June reached Magdalena Bay[12] where Broke and his officers conducted a thorough survey of the bay.[13] After sailing west to Greenland in late July, the two ships returned south to Shetland before arriving back in Yarmouth at the end of September.

In October 1807, shortly after Bray's return from the Arctic, he married Mary Lane Tyler, the daughter of a gentleman[14] from Gorleston, Suffolk, and the couple made their home in South Town, Yarmouth.[15]

Bray continued serving aboard the *Shannon* following his marriage, though it is not clear for how long, and his whereabouts between 1808 and 1812 remain obscure. In the early part of 1812 he was appointed as commander of the 14-gun brig *Plumper*[16] and sent to Halifax to counter the threat of US privateers. Initially this proved to be a profitable cruise, and the *Plumper* was successful in taking a considerable number of prizes around the Bay of Fundy, including three privateers in as many days between 16 and 18 July.[17] Earlier that month, Bray had also captured the merchant vessel *Margaret*, which was then recaptured by the US privateer *Teazer*. The *Margaret* was carrying two letters from Bray which the US press lost no time in publishing, no doubt to highlight the speciousness of British naval commanders and the poor conditions suffered by British seamen.

> I took out of the latter vessel two bags, said to contain 2000 dollars, for the better security thereof; and, as dollars are things which speak for themselves, I shall share them out as soon as I can. So I will thank you to send me a scheme of sharing as soon as you can ... and I will thank you to ask the Admiral if I shall send him his share in cash or bills from St. Johns. Lieutenant James Bray, 6 July 1812.

---

[11] Broke kept a detailed Remarks Book chronicling this voyage, which is published in Brighton's 1866 biography, *Admiral Sir P. B. V. Broke: A Memoir.*

[12] Now Magdalenefjorden.

[13] Voelcker, p. 84.

[14] Mary's father William died in 1818; his will describes him as a 'gentleman' and reveals that he left considerable property.

[15] Ancestry.org, film no. 1585963, item 3, p. 156, parish registers of Gorleston Parish Church, 14 October 1807.

[16] Both Marshall and *The Naval Chronicle* identify the *Plumper*'s commander as Lieutenant Josias Bray who served as lieutenant of the *Achille* at Trafalgar and went on to command revenue cutters after the war; Marshall, *Royal Naval Biography*, vol. 4, part II, p. 150. However it is clear from Admiralty documentation that the commander of the *Plumper* was in fact Lieutenant James Bray.

[17] *Fair Trader*, 1-gun schooner, twenty men; *Argus*, 1-gun schooner, twenty-three men; *Friendship*, 1-gun schooner, eight men.

... there is no difficulty in sharing them (the dollars), and our people are very poor, some of them having had no money for these nine years past. Lieutenant James Bray, 7 July 1812.[18]

Bray's profitable cruise came to an end in December 1812 when, after accompanying a convoy of six merchant vessels to Halifax, the *Plumper* set out for St John's carrying a number of passengers and a considerable quantity of specie. In the early hours of the fifth of December the *Plumper* ran ashore below steep cliffs south of Dipper Harbour in the Bay of Fundy. The brig quickly broke up in heavy seas and forty-two of her passengers and crew were drowned, including Bray and most of the officers. The following day, the naval schooner *Bream* and government sloop *Brunswicker* sailed to Dipper Harbour where they picked up thirty survivors from the foot of the cliff. Initial press accounts of the disaster were confused, with some reporting erroneously that Bray and his officers had survived; in fact the only officer to survive the wreck was a midshipman, named Hall.[19]

Three months later, in March 1813, Bray's will was proved by his executor and father-in-law, William Tyler, and Mary Bray, still living at their home in South Town, applied to the Admiralty for a widow's pension.[20] Mary received her pension the following year, in 1814, at which point she returned home to her native Suffolk and remarried.

WILLIAM WARDEN, 1782–1807

WILLIAM Warden was born in Lisbon in 1782, to George Warden and Elizabeth Barclay, whose families had been long-standing members of the British Factory community for several generations; he was baptised on 2 March 1782.[21] William's great-great-grandfather, also William Warden, was the King's Master Shipbuilder in Portugal[22] in the late 1720s; his mother's family were established merchants, and both families maintained business interests in Portugal and Britain.

Like his shipmate, Robert Reynolds, it is difficult to ascertain with certainty when exactly Warden joined the Royal Navy, as the date of baptism accompanying his lieutenant's passing certificate was falsified to make him appear three years older.[23] The certificate records that Warden joined the *Nymphe* as captain's servant in 1783 at the age of fourteen, though in reality he was only eleven at the time. He then transferred to

[18] *Newport Mercury*, 25 July 1812.

[19] *The Examiner*, p. 23.

[20] ADM 6/352, Widows Pensions.

[21] LDS, C88000-1, baptism of William Warden.

[22] PROB 11/765, Will of William Warden Senior, probated 1750.

[23] ADM 107/23, William Warden, Lieutenant's Passing Certificate, 31 August 1799.

the *Arethusa* in 1783, where he was re-rated as volunteer, and thence to the *Indefatigable* in 1795.

It is quite possible that Warden did indeed go to sea at the age of eleven; however it is also possible that his name was carried on the ships' books. In either case, it seems likely that there was some connection between the Warden and Pellew families. No correspondence has survived to establish this connection with certainty; however there were close ties between Falmouth and Portugal, resulting from the Falmouth–Lisbon packet route, one of the most important links between Britain and her strategically and economically significant continental ally. It is also possible that a more personal connection existed through Pellew's former captain and mentor, Philemon Pownoll, as both he and the Wardens had married into a prominent family of Lisbon wine merchants, the Majendies.

On joining the *Indefatigable* in 1795, Warden was initially rated volunteer, before being rated able five months later and then being made midshipman in October 1795 and yeoman of the sheets in June 1797, a position he held for two years.[24]

Like several of the younger midshipmen, Warden transferred with Pellew from the *Indefatigable* to the *Impetueux* in 1799, where he was rated midshipman until he passed his examination for lieutenant in August of that year at the age of sixteen.[25] Following his promotion, Warden was appointed as lieutenant of the 36-gun frigate *Decade*,[26] bound for the West Indies; however it was not long before Pellew was applying to the Admiralty to have Warden returned to the *Impetueux*, and in March 1801 he was appointed as second lieutenant,[27] a position he held until the ship was decommissioned during the Peace of Amiens.

When war recommenced in 1803, Warden rejoined his former captain and several of his shipmates aboard the *Tonnant*, serving in the Channel and the Mediterranean. Around this time, Warden made out a will leaving all his possessions to a Miss Eliza Hollingsworth of Stoke Damerel, Plymouth.[28]

Warden was one of a number of the former Indefatigables who accompanied Pellew to the East India station when he took up the position of Commander in Chief in 1804. Warden was appointed as second lieutenant of Pellew's flagship *Culloden*, alongside his former shipmates, George Bell, first lieutenant, Will Kempthorne, sixth lieutenant, and John Gaze, master. The following year, the Indefatigables were joined by another former messmate, Henry Hart.

---

[24] *Ibid.*

[25] *Ibid.*

[26] ADM 12/86, Digest for 1800, William Warden promoted and appointed to *Decade*, 18 January 1800.

[27] ADM 1/3197, Warden to Admiralty, 7 March 1801.

[28] PROB 11/1507, Will of William Warden.

Warden left the *Culloden* in September 1806 when he was promoted to acting commander of the 16-gun sloop *Rattlesnake*, which had previously been briefly commanded by Pellew's sixteen-year-old son Fleetwood.[29] Early in January the following year, the *Rattlesnake* was involved in a controversial engagement when Warden encountered the 16-gun French privateer *Les Deux Sœurs* off the island of Cheduba in the Bay of Bengal. A tense standoff ensued until the privateer ran aground and became disabled. The crew abandoned the ship leaving the captain and second lieutenant aboard, at which point the *Rattlesnake*'s boat crew boarded and destroyed the privateer. The French seamen were recovered from Cheduba and, together with their captain, De Jean Hilaire, transported to Kedgeree as prisoners of war.

Two months later, in March 1807, Sir George Barlow, Acting Governor General of India, received a letter from Captain Hilaire complaining that during the destruction of *Les Deux Sœurs* and the capture of her men, Warden had behaved in 'a manner so little consistent with propriety'.[30] In a florid twenty-six-page letter of complaint, Hilaire pressed a number of serious charges against Warden. According to Hilaire, *Les Deux Sœurs* did not strike her colours in consequence of any act of the *Rattlesnake*, as the officer commanding the *Rattlesnake*'s boat did not board until the privateer had been abandoned by all but himself and his lieutenant, and the signal raised for assistance. After removing the two officers to the *Rattlesnake*, Captain Warden and his men then seized the shipwrecked mariners from the shore of a neutral country, firing on some as they fled. In addition to violating Cheduba's neutrality, Hilaire claimed Warden had deceived him and his men by leading them to believe that they would be treated as persons claiming assistance, rather than prisoners of war. Hilaire stated that he had written a letter for Warden to carry on shore to his men assuring them that if they surrendered they would not be regarded as prisoners of war. This letter had been written in French, but Hilaire declared that he had translated it to Warden several times.

After the French were removed from Cheduba, Warden granted Hilaire permission to return to the island to retrieve a trunk containing his 'private papers, a little money and my effects'. Several days later, the *Rattlesnake* arrived in Kedgeree and Warden summoned Hilaire, stating that it had been reported that he was in possession of a large sum of money obtained from a prize. Warden ordered all the prisoners to be searched, then embarked in his boat, leaving the French crew

> to the mercy of men (I can no longer call them officers) who, without mere respect even for themselves, commenced a search such as most

---

[29] *The Asiatic Annual Register*, 1807, p. 204.

[30] British Library, IOR/F/4/264/5853, February–July 1807, Complaint of Captain De Jean Hilaire of the French privateer Les Deux Sœurs regarding the conduct of Captain William Warden of HMS Rattlesnake.

certainly has never been made before. The Surgeon and I were the only people whose persons were spared from examination, the rest without distinction underwent a personal search even to the most indecent violation of natural concealment.[31]

Some gold and silver was found on the seamen and Hilaire's trunk was found to contain 1,200 pieces of gold and 340 pieces of silver taken from the privateer's prize. Hilaire stated that, with much reluctance, Warden gave up a little of the money to the captain and men, 'the remainder was deposited without ceremony in a little trunk which Captain Warden took with him and of which I have never since heard any more'.[32]

Complaints of such impropriety against a British naval officer were treated with the utmost gravity and four weeks later, on 2 April, Barlow's secretary forwarded a lengthy summary of the complaint to Warden, requesting 'any explanation which you may think proper ... for the purpose of superseding the necessity of a representation of Captain de Jean Hilaire's complaints to his excellency Sir Edward Pellew'.[33] Warden's response was immediate and unequivocal. Hilaire had been the first to violate the supposed neutrality of Cheduba by firing on the *Rattlesnake*'s boat and later admitting that he initially took the sloop for a merchantman and would have taken her for a good prize. Warden enclosed Hilaire's disputed letter and explained that the French captain had indeed translated it for him twice, telling him that it advised the men to consider, as he did, 'that it was better for them to give themselves up as prisoners of war'. For good measure, Warden added:

> on my oath I will declare it ... whether the letter is different to what he interpreted I do not know, but the Government are very welcome to it, had I had the least idea that it was offering them not to be prisoners of war, I certainly should not have taken it.[34]

On translation, it was found that Hilaire's letter advised the crew that as it was Warden's intention to 'take or destroy' them, he thought it his duty to lessen the hardships of their situation 'which will no doubt be taken into consideration at the proper time and place in such manner as to preclude being considered as prisoners of war'. The letter concluded by telling the men to 'consider that you think best to do, at all events do not expose any effects, particularly my papers and what is in my trunk, which may become of great use to us'.[35]

Warden also denied firing on the French mariners, and explained that when he landed on Cheduba, far from having to seize them by force, they

---

[31] *Ibid.*, p. 24.

[32] *Ibid.*, pp. 25–6.

[33] *Ibid.*, p. 36.

[34] *Ibid.*, p. 49.

[35] *Ibid.*, pp. 60–1.

came willingly. Fearing that the natives would take them as slaves, they had been looking out for the *Rattlesnake*'s boats 'day after day' and some had even been prepared to try swimming off to the ship.[36]

Regarding the money, Warden stated that he learned of the hidden money from the French midshipmen who had spoken of 400 dollars they were due to receive as their share of prize money 'plundered from the Arabs'. On asking Hilaire about the money, he replied that he had only a little, whereupon Warden informed him that even if it was only a trifling sum he must give it up to prevent being searched. Warden ordered his first lieutenant to retrieve the money and then left the ship. On his return, the lieutenant told Warden that Hilaire had 'behaved very ill' when his trunk was searched and four bags of money found. Also that the French officers, when informed of the search,

> behaved very improperly, the First Lieutenant particularly by immediately pulling off his cloaths and throwing them down on the table of the gunroom even his shirt he pulled off, although he was repeatedly told he was acting contrary to what was wished.[37]

The men were also searched for money and 'the places where they contrived to stow it was really strange'. Some had hidden coins in their hair, others had concealed them in their clothing and one was later discovered to have swallowed some. After retrieving the money, it was counted in the presence of the first lieutenant, the purser, Hilaire and his surgeon. Hilaire was told to retrieve any that was private property belonging to him or his men and the remainder was placed in a trunk and forwarded to the Naval Agent in Calcutta.

Having answered Hilaire's complaints, Warden concluded by accusing Hilaire of being a 'Pirate who had the audacity to claim that which he has so shamefully plundered'.[38]

Aware that he did not have the authority to decide on the matter, Barlow referred the matter to Pellew's judgement in his capacity as Commander in Chief of His Majesty's Naval Forces in India. On 9 May, Barlow forwarded the correspondence to Pellew along with a lengthy minute of his own.[39] As an 'act of justice' towards Warden, Barlow expressed the opinion that the charges against him were without foundation and that Hilaire's letter to his men absolutely disproved the truth of his assertions against him.

It is not difficult to imagine Pellew's reaction on receiving Barlow's correspondence. Pellew would go to extraordinary lengths to protect his men and would no doubt have regarded such a slur on the reputation of one of his own trusted officers as a grave accusation. Warden was after all

---

[36] *Ibid.*, pp. 49–50.
[37] *Ibid.*, pp. 53–4.
[38] *Ibid.*, p. 57.
[39] *Ibid.*, pp. 61–6.

8 Memorial to William Warden, South Park Street Cemetery, Kolkata.
Pellew's tribute is still clearly visible on Warden's memorial today.

one of Pellew's Indefatigables, one of the boys grown to men under him. His esteem for the young man was clear and indeed while Warden was busy penning his response to Hilaire's accusations, Pellew had already promoted him to post captain of the 38-gun frigate *Sir Francis Drake*.[40]

Unfortunately Warden was never to take up his new command and Pellew never had the satisfaction of clearing his name. William Warden died of 'excessive fatigue and exposure' during a violent gale on a passage from Madras on 5 June 1807;[41] he was twenty-five years old.

Pellew may not have been able to clear the charges against Warden before his death; however, to underline his faith in his young officer, and to dispel any questions that may have lingered over his conduct and reputation, Pellew forwarded a copy of Warden's report of the engagement with *Les Deux Sœurs* to the *Naval Chronicle* on 8 September, along with a note expressing 'the highest approbation of Lieutenant Warden's persevering and judicious conduct in overcoming the local difficulties attending the destruction of the vessel'.[42]

Pellew appears to have been deeply moved by Warden's death and, as evidence of his esteem and affection, he erected a handsome memorial to him at Calcutta, which can still be seen today. The poignant inscription on the memorial reads:

> To commemorate the private worth and public merits of this promising Officer this monument is erected by his Commander in Chief as a tribute of regard to his memory.[43]

The monument is evidence of Pellew's regard for Warden and also perhaps his desire to make a visible public statement confirming his appreciation of the young man.

Warden had amassed a fortune of several thousand pounds at the time of his death,[44] but three years were to pass before probate was granted in 1810, by which time Eliza Hollingsworth had married and become Eliza Millman.[45] The will gives no indication of Warden's relationship to Eliza, but it is not too far-fetched to speculate that she may have been his fiancée or sweetheart. Whatever hopes Warden may have had for Eliza, she benefited handsomely from his untimely death.

[40] *The Asiatic Annual Register*, 1807, p. 204.

[41] *The Naval Chronicle*, vol. 18, 1807, p. 519.

[42] *Ibid.*, p. 234.

[43] Derozario, p. 83.

[44] British Library, L-AG-34-27-388, folio 7, British India Office Records of Inventories and Accounts of Deceased Estates.

[45] PROB 11/1507, Will of William Warden.

PHILIP FROWD, 1779–1802

PHILIP Frowd was born in Wiltshire on 30 May 1779,[46] the son of William and Elizabeth Frowd, and he has the unusual distinction of being baptised twice within three months of his birth,[47] first in Market Lavington and again in Brixton Deverill.

Philip was one of at least five siblings in a branch of the widespread Frowd family, prominent members of the Wiltshire squirearchy from whose ranks were drawn a large number of clergy.[48] Early in the eighteenth century the family had bought the lease on a manor at Brixton Deverill[49] and it is possible that Philip's second baptism may have resulted from a desire to have a son's name recorded in the register of their home parish. The muster book of the *Indefatigable*,[50] however, records Philip Frowd's place of birth as Market Lavington, where his first baptism was registered.

Pellew's wife Susan had been born into another branch of the Frowd family from the neighbouring village of East Knoyle, so it is no surprise that when the decision was made to send young Philip to sea, the family sought to make good use of this 'interest'. Philip's older brother, Anthony Edward, also joined the service, and went on to become a naval surgeon. Philip Frowd's first ship was not one commanded by Edward Pellew, however, but by his brother, Captain Israel Pellew. According to Frowd's lieutenant's certificate documentation, he entered the service in October 1793 at the age of fourteen when he joined the 24-gun sixth rate *Squirrel* as captain's servant. Only two months later, in December 1793, he transferred to Edward Pellew's new command, the *Arethusa*, where he served first as captain's servant and later as midshipman.[51] Frowd accompanied his captain to the *Indefatigable* in 1795, and retained the rank of midshipman until he was rated ship's corporal in June 1797. This role involved assisting

---

[46] Both baptismal entries give the same date of birth and parents' names. Register entries for Market Lavington, Wiltshire, 3 July 1779, and Brixton Deverill, Wiltshire, 29 August 1779.

[47] This is not normal practice for the Church of England but it may be that Philip was simply 'received into church' on the second occasion, having his details recorded in the parish of his parents' home. This particular branch of the Frowd family had children born and baptised in three parishes around the edge of Salisbury Plain: Market Lavington to the east, Edington to the north and Brixton Deverill to the west.

[48] Pellew's chaplain aboard the *Queen Charlotte* during the Bombardment of Algiers was a John B. Frowd, though his relation to Philip Frowd is unknown. Naval General Service Medal Roll.

[49] Brixton Deverill Manors, p. 10 n. 58, www.victoriacountyhistory.ac.uk.

[50] ADM 36/13143, Muster Table of His Majesty's Ship the Indefatigable.

[51] ADM 107/23, Philip Frowd, Lieutenant's Passing Certificate, 30 November 1799.

the master at arms to maintain discipline and security aboard ship and Frowd is the only one of this cohort of young gentlemen to hold this rank.

Frowd continued as the *Indefatigable*'s corporal until 1798 when he transferred to Israel Pellew's 32-gun frigate *Cleopatra* where he was re-rated first as midshipman and subsequently as master's mate. The frigate was stationed briefly in the Channel, where she took the French privateer *Emilie*, then on the Halifax station where she cruised over a wide stretch of the American coast. In October 1799 Frowd left the *Cleopatra* to briefly join the *Lynx*; this was effectively a passage home to England to enable him to sit his examination for lieutenant, which he passed on 30 November 1799.[52]

Frowd's connections and experience stood him in good stead. His first commission as lieutenant was aboard the 38-gun frigate *Boadicea* under the command of Captain Sir Richard Keats, a close friend of the Pellews.[53] Keats was a captain in a similar mould to Pellew: a daring, successful frigate commander, with an excellent reputation for seamanship. Shortly after Frowd joined the *Boadicea*, the ship was involved in a mission to bring supplies and ammunition to Belleisle for the French royalist opposition in the Vendée. Frowd was optimistic about their prospects and wrote to a former *Cleopatra* shipmate, Lieutenant Taylor, still on the Halifax station:

> there is now a large squadron of frigates. Those ships [are] fitting out for that Service. But Sir Edw I hear is to be kept with the grand fleet, which Lord St Vincent is expected every day to take the command ... it is the General opinion at home that a Peace must soon take place. Indeed, 'tis impossible they can hold out much longer. You may expect by every Packet to hear of Louis the 18th being on the throne of France.[54]

Although Frowd's career as an officer started well, there is evidence that he was not in the best of health. By 16 November 1801 Frowd was writing to the Admiralty from the hospital in Plymouth, informing them that he had been there since 22 October after having been transferred there from his ship, *Prince*, because of debility. He continued to explain that the physician and surgeon at the hospital thought that he 'can no more benefit from medicine but that country air may accelerate my recovery'.[55]

The frustration at delays suffered by young officers who were at the mercy of Admiralty bureaucracy surfaces in Frowd's next letter which he wrote following a 'survey' of his health which he had requested earlier.

---

[52] *Ibid.*

[53] Taylor, p. 77.

[54] Frowd to Taylor, 30 December 1799. Manuscript letter sold by Mullock's Specialist Sporting Auctioneers, www.invaluable.com/auction-lot/maritime-naval-french-revolution-rare-naval-1-c-t4nu4aarmg.

[55] ADM 1/2875, Lieutenants' Letters, Surname F, no. 126, Frowd to Admiralty, November 1801.

Having been a considerable time at this hospital ... the recovery of my health which I have not been able to accomplish and a survey having been held on me ... their opinion that it may be established if I am permitted to retire to the country.[56]

The reply notes sketched in the corner of this letter record that their Lordships do not appear to have received a report on Frowd and that he should be informed that the correct method for submitting letters is through the hospital governor. There is no further mention of this case in the Admiralty archives[57] so it is impossible to know whether Frowd was ever granted leave to go to the country and recuperate.

Frowd appears to have recovered sufficiently to serve alongside his brother Anthony aboard the 36-gun frigate *Blanche* in the West Indies. Although the *Blanche* had a successful cruise and took many prizes before she herself was captured in 1805, both Frowd and his brother succumbed to yellow fever, which ended the lives of so many seamen on the West Indies station. *The Naval Chronicle* recorded their deaths in a short and melancholy entry: 'At Jamaica, Mr A Froud, surgeon, and his younger brother Lieutenant P Frowd, of the Blanche. The same letter conveyed to the parents the death of two sons, both under thirty years of age.'[58] Philip Frowd was buried in Port Royal cemetery, Jamaica, and is commemorated by a memorial paid for by his younger sister Harriot, which can still be seen in St Peter's church today. The inscription reads:

Sacred to the memory of Lieutenant Philip Frowd of the Royal Navy who died here of the yellow fever, April 15, 1804 in his twenty fourth year. This is placed as a token of affection by his disconsolate sister, Harriot Frowd of Weymouth, Dorsetshire, England.[59]

Other than the brief news of Sir Edward in Frowd's letter to his friend Lieutenant Taylor, no other correspondence exists to record the link between Frowd and Pellew; however it is clear that both Sir Edward and his brother Israel did much to shape the young man's career. Although Frowd had an almost textbook early naval career, and his untimely demise was one suffered by many thousands of seamen, unusually, he was the only one of the young gentlemen who served aboard the *Indefatigable* in 1797 to succumb to disease.

---

[56] ADM 1/2875, Lieutenants' Letters, Surname F, no. 127, Frowd to Admiralty, December 1801.

[57] ADM 12 series, Index and Digests.

[58] *The Naval Chronicle*, vol. 12, 1804, p. 166.

[59] Memorials at St Peter's Church, Port Royal, Jamaica, www.jamaicanfamilysearch.com.

RICHARD DELVES BROUGHTON, 1784–1806

RICHARD Delves Broughton is unique among the young gentlemen of HMS *Indefatigable* as, despite the best efforts of both Pellew and his family, he has the unfortunate distinction of being the only one of this cohort whose career ended in ignominy and disgrace.

Pellew had a close personal interest in Delves Broughton, which stemmed from the boy's connection to his old friend Alex Broughton. Pellew and Broughton had forged a lifelong friendship while serving together as midshipmen during the American War of Independence. Although Broughton left the service shortly after, and Pellew spent most of his life at sea, their friendship endured and was sustained by regular correspondence.

Richard Delves Broughton's relation to Alex Broughton remains unclear, leading some of Pellew's biographers to speculate about the young man's parentage and legitimacy. Parkinson refers to a 'certain mystery'[60] surrounding him, while Taylor goes further and suggests that Dick, as he was known, may have been Alex Broughton's illegitimate son.[61]

In point of fact, there is no doubt as to Delves Broughton's parentage. He was baptised in 1784 in the parish of Eccleshall, Staffordshire,[62] the youngest of thirteen children born to the Reverend Sir Thomas Broughton and his wife Lady Mary, and there is no suggestion that he was anything other than a legitimate and recognised son of the family.

According to Delves Broughton's lieutenant's passing certificates, he began his naval career in 1795 at the age of eleven as an able seaman aboard the unrated gunboat *Augusta*.[63] This seems a rather improbable posting for a boy so young, and it is likely that it was added to his certificates to increase his time at sea. Delves Broughton's certificates also falsified his date of birth to make him appear three years older; a statement signed by Joseph Rathbone, minister of Eccleshall Parish, Staffordshire, in January 1802, certified that Delves Broughton was born on 11 January 1781.[64] Rathbone had indeed been perpetual curate of Eccleshall in the early 1780s; however he died in 1784, eighteen years before he ostensibly certified young Delves Broughton's date of birth.

Delves Broughton's next listed posting was to the *Indefatigable* where he served as a volunteer from January 1796 to March 1798, at which point he was rated midshipman. When Pellew left the *Indefatigable* in early 1799,

---

[60] Parkinson, *Edward Pellew: Viscount Exmouth, Admiral of the Red*, p. 206.

[61] Taylor, pp. 109–10.

[62] Staffordshire County Council Digitised Parish Records, findmypast.com.

[63] ADM 107/27, Lieutenant's Passing Certificates, Richard Delves Broughton, 6 January 1802.

[64] *Ibid.*

Broughton accompanied him to the *Impetueux* where he served, again as midshipman, until July 1800.

Throughout the period that Broughton served aboard the *Indefatigable* and *Impetueux*, Pellew regularly updated Alex Broughton on the boy's progress. Pellew's letters to Alex Broughton were returned to the family by his son, Bryan Sneyd Broughton, in 1833; however much of the correspondence that relates to Delves Broughton is heavily redacted. In a letter to George Pellew dated April 1833, Sneyd Broughton wrote:

> You will perceive that I have scratched out some few lines of some of your father's letters and my reason for so doing is that persons, now living, were mentioned as they might not wish anyone to see.[65]

Despite the redactions, it is clear from Pellew's letters that young Delves Broughton was 'an odd character' with an eccentric streak. In one letter, Pellew described him as 'the most extravagant dog in cloathes I ever saw, a new coat lasts him a fortnight and a new hat a week',[66] and in another instance Pellew wrote that he had been sleeping on his chest for a whole voyage as he had lost his hammock.[67] Despite other peculiarities, it appears that Delves Broughton had at least some merit as a young officer, as Pellew trusted him sufficiently to join the crew of a prize vessel captured by the *Impetueux*. Pellew may have given Delves Broughton considerable leeway, and been tolerant of a degree of eccentricity, but he was not a man to knowingly entrust a prize to unreliable crew members.

Despite his somewhat erratic behaviour, Delves Broughton's career continued to progress and in July 1800 he was appointed to the *Ville de Paris*, the flagship first of Earl St Vincent, Commander of the Channel Fleet, and subsequently of Admiral Cornwallis. Initially Delves Broughton was listed as a supernumerary, and it is possible that he may have been ashore in hospital at the time. On an earlier occasion, Pellew had written to Alex Broughton that Dick had a serious health problem from which he had recently recovered: '... poor Dick has been very near Kicking great care and nursing has bro't him about'.[68] Whatever the case, Delves Broughton remained with the flagship until November 1801 when he joined the 36-gun frigate *Doris*, Captain Charles Brisbane. Just a month after Delves Broughton left the *Ville de Paris*, his former *Indefatigable* shipmate Nicholas Pateshall joined Cornwallis's flagship.

---

[65] Exmouth Papers, Caird Library, MSS/92/027, Box 22, Bryan Sneyd Broughton to George Pellew, April 1833.

[66] Parkinson, *Edward Pellew: Viscount Exmouth, Admiral of the Red*, p. 204.

[67] Exmouth Papers, Caird Library, MSS/92/027, Box 22, Pellew to Broughton, 7 January 1799.

[68] Pellew to Broughton, 6/19 July 1800. Quoted in Parkinson, *Edward Pellew: Viscount Exmouth, Admiral of the Red*, p. 244.

In January 1802 Delves Broughton passed his examination for lieutenant, but it was not long before his career began to unravel. Early in 1804 while serving as lieutenant of the sloop *Autumn*, Captain Samuel Jackson, Delves Broughton was court martialled for neglect of duty and un-officer-like conduct.[69] The court heard that Delves Broughton had been suspended from duty in December 1803 following repeated bouts of drunkenness and neglect of duty, and that he was frequently so intoxicated that he could not take charge of the watch. The charge of un-officer-like conduct related to allegations that he spent most of his time sitting in the galley with the men, rather than with his fellow officers.

Delves Broughton's family were horrified about the effect a court martial would have on their good name, and his father wrote a desperate letter to Earl St Vincent, hoping to forestall a public trial.

> My son Richard's conduct ... has been such that I fear he will be brought to some public disgrace. Trusting to the friendly intention towards him I have experienced from your lordship ... I thought it candid to make this communication of most earnest entreaty that out of regard to me and to my family you would have the goodness to dismiss him the service without bringing him to any public trial.[70]

St Vincent may have evinced 'friendly intention' towards the young man in the past, but such behaviour could only have one outcome. His reply, though predictably brief, could be regarded as St Vincent's motto in all things naval: 'Acquaint him that this would not be for the good of discipline in the service'.[71] In the event, having made no defence, the court martial found Delves Broughton guilty and he was dismissed the service.

Despite the apparent finality of the verdict, Delves Broughton's naval career did not end there. Not long after the court martial, he joined the 36-gun frigate *Penelope*, commanded by his brother-in-law, Captain William Robert Broughton, who had already distinguished himself as an explorer of some repute.[72]

In 1805, while serving as midshipman aboard the *Penelope*, Delves Broughton wrote his will,[73] leaving one thousand guineas to his sister Jemima, and the rest of his wages, chattels, land and estate to his brother Thomas.

Delves Broughton did not remain aboard the *Penelope* for long; in July 1805 the muster records his discharge 'per order'. At this point, Delves Broughton disappears from Admiralty records; however in August 1805 he

---

[69] ADM 1/5365, Delves Broughton Courts Martial, January 1804.

[70] ADM 106/1456, Broughton to St Vincent, Promiscuous Correspondence, Surname B, 1802–1804.

[71] *Ibid.*

[72] Laughton, p. 466.

[73] PROB 11/1468, Will of Richard Delves Broughton, 1805.

reappears as a cornet in the 22nd Regiment of Light Dragoons, a regiment raised for service in India.[74] Delves Broughton's cornetcy was obtained 'by purchase' and may represent one last effort by his family to forge a career for the young man and keep him out of trouble.

Whether Delves Broughton embarked for India willingly or not, and whether he found himself better suited to a career in the military than the navy, is unclear, as he died less than two years later in 1806.[75] The cause of Delves Broughton's death is unknown; he may have succumbed to fever or to drink, or he may have suffered a recurrence of previous health problems. At the time of his death, it was believed that Delves Broughton had died intestate[76] and a sale of his possessions to set against his estate was arranged in Madras in July 1807. Although the items included no less than nine shirts, ten waistcoats and eighteen pairs of pantaloons, the sale achieved only £29 and exceeded his innkeeper's debts by only £7.[77] Amongst the items sold were a handful of books, including a handbook for cavalry officers and a copy of Lord Chesterfield's *Letters to his Son on the Fine Art of becoming a Man of the World and a Gentleman*, a popular volume of advice for young gentlemen on navigating the nuances and pitfalls of society, which might well have been a gift from the young man's family in a moment of optimism.[78]

Pellew, who was stationed in Madras at the time, would no doubt have been aware of events, and it is possible that a redacted letter written to Alex Broughton in July 1807 referred to the circumstances of the young man's death.[79] During the few short years Delves Broughton spent in India, he would have been part of the same social milieu of naval, military and civilian personnel, where so many of his former *Indefatigable* shipmates were advancing their careers, getting married and generally fulfilling all that their mentor could have hoped for them. Although it was long since

---

[74] *The Gazette*, 20 August 1805, p. 1046.

[75] British India Office Records Online, BL-BIND-005137383-00394, Burial Register, Fort St George, Madras, 8 November 1806.

[76] British India Office Records Online, BL-BIND-L-AG-34-29-207-0040, Probate Records, 1807.

[77] British India Office Records Online, BL-BIND-L-AG-34-29-211-00136, Probate Records, 1807. The excessive number of items of clothing recalls Pellew's observations on Delves Broughton's dress habits almost ten years earlier.

[78] British India Office Records Online, Wills and Probate. These two books, along with one other, were bought at the auction by one Ramaswamy Brahman, most likely Ramaswamy Brahman, a civil servant with the Treasury in Madras at the time. Brimnes, p. 149.

[79] Pellew to Alex Broughton, 22 July 1807. Parkinson, *Edward Pellew: Viscount Exmouth, Admiral of the Red*, p. 377. At the end of this letter is a sentence beginning 'your young friend Dicky as I told you ...' Parkinson notes that two further lines are redacted.

Delves Broughton had been under Pellew's command, it was in his nature to feel both responsibility and regret for the young man's untimely demise.

By any measure, Richard Delves Broughton's career was not a success; he was the only one of the *Indefatigable*'s young gentlemen not to forge a successful naval or civilian career and he has been remembered as one of Pellew's notable failures.[80] However it is typical of Pellew's perception of himself as both patron and patriarch, and his fierce loyalty to his friends, that he felt he owed it to Alex Broughton to promote the career of his young élève. Ultimately, however, neither Pellew's patronage, St Vincent's former friendly intentions, nor a purchased commission, were enough to save the flamboyant but troubled young man from an early death.

ROBERT CARTHEW REYNOLDS, 1782–1804

ROBERT Carthew Reynolds junior was born at Penair, Cornwall and baptised on 30 December 1782, the eldest son of Jane Vivian and Lieutenant Robert Carthew Reynolds, a Cornish Royal Naval officer, and close friend of Edward Pellew. As with so many of his shipmates, it is unclear exactly when young Robert first joined the Royal Navy. Documents associated with his lieutenant's passing certificates[81] record that he entered the service in 1793 when he joined Pellew's frigate *Nymphe* as captain's servant. This date must be regarded with some caution, however, as the documentation also includes a handwritten note signed by both a curate and a churchwarden certifying that Reynolds had been christened in 1777, falsifying his age by five years.[82] It is possible that Reynolds did indeed enter the *Nymphe* as captain's servant at the age of ten, as Reynolds senior was temporarily without a command around this time, and Pellew would no doubt have been happy to accept his friend's son aboard his ship; however it is equally likely that young Reynolds was present in name only. According to the documentation, Reynolds transferred with Pellew to the *Arethusa* and thence to the *Indefatigable* where he was rated first as volunteer, then as able seaman, before being promoted to the rank of midshipman on 6 March 1796 at the age of just thirteen.

It seems probable that by this stage Reynolds was indeed at sea and was aboard the frigate on the memorable night of the *Droits de L'Homme* engagement when the *Indefatigable* and his father's ship, the *Amazon*, chased down the French 74 and ran her into Hodierne Bay. One can only imagine young Reynolds's reaction when the crew of the *Indefatigable* realised the peril of their situation that night, and his feelings on returning to their home port of Falmouth only to learn that his father's ship had been

---

[80] Taylor, p. 160.

[81] ADM 107/23, Robert Carthew Reynolds, Lieutenant's Passing Certificate, 6 August 1799.

[82] *Ibid.*

wrecked alongside their gallant opponent in Hodierne Bay. Unlike the unfortunate crew of *Les Droits de L'Homme*, Captain Reynolds and his men survived the wreck of the *Amazon* and were taken prisoner by the French. Pellew did his utmost to broker an exchange to free Captain Reynolds, but eight months were to pass before he returned to England to face a court martial for the loss of the *Amazon*. Captain Reynolds and his officers were acquitted with the highest commendation and two months later he was appointed to command the 44-gun frigate *Pomone*. Five months later, in April 1798, Reynolds junior left the *Indefatigable* and joined his father aboard the *Pomone*, serving first as midshipman and then as acting lieutenant. Reynolds passed his examination for lieutenant in August 1799 at the age of just sixteen, though his falsified certificates made him out to be twenty-one.[83]

Reynolds's whereabouts between 1800 and 1804 are uncertain; however it is likely that, as with many of his contemporaries, he found himself on the beach during the Peace of Amiens. By 1804 Reynolds was serving in the West Indies as lieutenant of the 74-gun *Centaur*, flagship of Commodore Sir Samuel Hood. Hood had been ordered to blockade Fort Royal on French Martinique and his attention fell on Diamond Rock, a volcanic plug that occupies a strategic position in the straits of St Lucia. In order to command the straits, Hood determined to occupy the rock and garrison the position with 120 sailors and marines from the *Centaur*. With considerable ingenuity, a number of 18- and 24-pound guns were hauled up the sheer face of the rock and positioned in five batteries commanding the straits. Hood then commissioned the rock as a sloop and placed HMS *Diamond Rock* under the command of Lieutenant James Wilkes Maurice, first of the *Centaur*.[84]

In order to deflect attention from the difficult operation of fortifying the rock, Hood launched a diversionary expedition to cut out the French brig-sloop *Le Curieux* from Fort Royal harbour. On the morning of 4 February 1804, Lieutenant Robert Reynolds led seventy-two men in four of the *Centaur*'s boats into the entrance of Fort Royal harbour where *Le Curieux* was lying close under Fort Edward. The brig, crewed by one hundred men, put up a fierce fight but, despite being seriously injured, Reynolds and his men carried the prize. Hood's report to the Admiralty praised Reynolds, who

> boarded over her quarter in a most gallant manner ... The enemy made a warm resistance at the first onset but the spirited and superior valour of this brave officer and his supporters drove them

---

[83] *Ibid.* At the time that Robert Carthew Reynolds left the *Indefatigable*, his younger brother Barrington Reynolds joined the frigate.

[84] Stuart and Eggleston, pp. 42–59.

forward, where a second stand was made which was carried with equal gallantry.[85]

An account of the action subsequently published in *The Naval Chronicle* by Reynolds's second in command, Lieutenant George Edmund Byron Bettesworth,[86] also praised his conduct and credited him with the original plan of action.

> The lot fell to Lieutenant Reynolds, than whom there could not have been a more gallant officer; he, by fortunate chance, first volunteered it (with Lieutenant Bettesworth and Mr Tracey)[87] and was in consequence offered the preference; the event has shown how well he merited the confidence reposed in him by the Commodore; he was, with Richard Templeman, a Seaman, first on board.[88]

On returning to the Diamond Rock squadron, Reynolds was immediately promoted to commander of the prize. Unfortunately he never took up his new command; he did not recover from his wounds, and, after lingering for six months, he died on 3 September 1804, at the age of just twenty-one. Reynolds's dying wish was to be buried on Diamond Rock, a request that Hood granted, and several days later he was interred with due ceremony in one of the caves on the rock. *The Naval Chronicle* later carried an affecting account of his burial written by an officer who attended.

> With sorrow I inform you of the melancholy intelligence of the death of the brave Captain Reynolds (son of Captain Carthew Reynolds) of His Majesty's Sloop Curieux, who obtained the command of her for his gallant conduct in cutting her out from under Fort Edward, Martinique, having received seven wounds in the conflict. His remains are deposited on the Diamond Rock, Martinique and where a stone will perpetuate his memory. His funeral was conducted with as much ceremony as time would allow and with that solemnity which real worth ever inspires. The whole of the Officers of the Centaur and every Man and Boy in the Ship, who had been witness to his gallant exploits, attended; the band played the Dead March, which drew tears from every eye in the Ship.[89]

---

[85] Hood to Nepean, 6 February 1804. *The Naval Chronicle*, vol. 12, 1804, p. 65.

[86] Bettesworth later served as captain of the *Crocodile*, where he disrated the troublesome Midshipman Richard Badcock. Bettesworth died in 1808 and was unable to testify at George Cadogan's court martial.

[87] Tracey was Commodore Hood's secretary.

[88] A.B. to Mr Editor, 10 September 1804. *The Naval Chronicle*, vol. 12, 1804, pp. 380–2.

[89] Extract of a letter from Barbados. *The Naval Chronicle*, vol. 12, 1804, p. 423.

Robert Carthew Reynolds was the only man ever to be interred on Diamond Rock, and the only one of this cohort of the *Indefatigable*'s young gentlemen to die of wounds sustained in action.

Lieutenant Maurice continued to hold Diamond Rock for a further eight months until Napoleon himself ordered Admiral Villeneuve to recapture the position. In May 1805 a fleet of sixteen French and Spanish ships, commanded by Captain Cosmao-Kerjulien, blockaded the rock for fifteen days, cutting off all supplies. Maurice and his men withdrew to the summit of the rock and continued to defend their position from the bombardment of two 74s, a frigate, a corvette, a schooner, and eleven gunboats until lack of water forced them to surrender on 2 June. The garrison were briefly held as prisoners of war by the French before being exchanged and repatriated. Maurice was court martialled for the loss of his 'ship', but exonerated and commended for his gallant conduct.

Although several of the young gentlemen featured in this chapter had some connection to the port town of Falmouth, they all had very different social backgrounds, and no evidence has surfaced to suggest that they knew each other prior to serving aboard the *Indefatigable*. Indeed the only connection that links all five of these men together is Pellew himself, who took them on to his books and into his ships as a favour to colleagues, friends and family. Unlike many of their fellow *Indefatigable* shipmates who lived on into ripe old age, there is little evidence of networks of friendships evolving between these young men, primarily due to their unfortunate early deaths. It is ironic that although this group may have benefited early in their lives from Pellew's patronage, they did not share his famous luck, and all died before reaching their mid-twenties. Although they are the only ones of the *Indefatigable*'s 1797 cohort who died early in their careers, the causes of their deaths are typical of the early nineteenth-century navy: disease, shipwreck, storms and wounds sustained in action. Bray, Warden, Frowd, Delves Broughton and Reynolds may not have left a legacy of naval and public service as many of their shipmates did, but the memorials that still stand in Kolkata and Port Royal are an enduring reminder of promising lives cut sadly short, and in this regard their legacy is perhaps more typical of the many thousands of young gentlemen who lost their lives serving in the Royal Navy during the French Revolutionary and Napoleonic Wars.

9

'Faithful and Attached Companions'

IN his comprehensive work on frigate command in the Napoleonic Wars, *The Star Captains*, Wareham has explored the close affinity and camaraderie that often developed among frigate crews, particularly when they served together across multiple commands under the leadership of gifted and charismatic captains.[1] Through independent cruising, crewing and taking prizes, undertaking cutting out expeditions and shore-based operations, frigate service allowed young officers to gain considerable experience at a young age and to forge a shared identity that often persisted long after crews were paid off and dispersed to other ships of the fleet. Wareham quotes Captain Abraham Crawford's reminiscence that 'those of the frigate school' differed widely from crews of ships of the line, sloops and gun brigs: 'Of this they seemed themselves aware, avoiding as much as they could an intimacy with the others and forming as much as possible, a society apart.'[2]

There is no doubt that the officers and men who served under Pellew's command aboard the *Nymphe*, the *Arethusa*, and the *Indefatigable* developed a strong shared identity that bound them together, even after Pellew was forced to relinquish command of his beloved frigate and the crew were scattered across the fleet. Unfortunately no personal correspondence dating from this period has been found from the young gentlemen who followed Pellew from the *Indefatigable* to the insubordinate ship of the line *Impetueux*. Even Nicholas Pateshall, who wrote so enthusiastically when he joined Pellew's crew, is silent. However it is not hard to imagine that the Indefatigables would indeed have formed a society apart from the mutinous crew of the *Impetueux*. Certainly one of the Indefatigables, Henry Hart, was a witness for the prosecution at the court martial of the *Impetueux* mutineers, and Osler tells a, possibly apocryphal, tale that when the hour came to execute the condemned men, Pellew distinguished the conduct of the Indefatigables from that of their shipmates.

> Addressing a few words, first to the men who had followed him from the *Indefatigable*, and afterwards to the rest of the crew, "Indefatigables," he said, "stand aside! Not one of you shall touch the rope. But you, who have encouraged your shipmates to the crime by

---

[1] Wareham, p. 52.
[2] Crawford, p. 240.

which they have forfeited their lives, it shall be your punishment to hang them."[3]

This incident is echoed in two episodes of the Hornblower television series produced in 2001, 'Mutiny'[4] and 'Retribution',[5] which are loosely based on C. S. Forester's novel *Lieutenant Hornblower*. In both episodes, the division between the Indefatigables and the ill-disciplined crew of the ship of the line *Renown* is distinct. Former *Indefatigable* midshipmen Lieutenant Hornblower and Lieutenant Kennedy, and ratings Matthews and Styles, now promoted to boatswain and boatswain's mate, hold themselves aloof from the ineffectual officers and disorderly Renowns until tensions erupt with brutal consequences.

While there is ample evidence that the historical crew of HMS *Indefatigable* did indeed forge a close and lasting camaraderie, it is perhaps ironic that arguably the most famous alumnus of Pellew's frigate school, the fictional Horatio Hornblower, is the quintessential 'Man Alone'. As conceived by his original creator C. S. Forester, Hornblower was to be:

> the captain of a British frigate – not of a ship of the line ... Nor would Hornblower be the captain of a mere sloop
>
> ... too cynical about his own motives, too aware of his own weaknesses, ever to know content ... a man of considerable character so that, even though despairing – hopeless – he could maintain the struggle with himself and not subside into self-satisfaction or humility.
>
> ... a man of marked ability; he must also have the quality of leadership – that would develop out of his perceptiveness and sensitivity.
>
> Besides being self-conscious he would be shy and reserved ...[6]

Hornblower's ability and leadership qualities are certainly characteristics shared by many of his historical shipmates; however he lacks their close-knit camaraderie and friendship. Although Forester's Hornblower is adored by his men and feted by the Admiralty, he conspicuously lacks friends and, with the exception of the stoical William Bush, he rarely bonds with his fellow officers. In his transition from page to screen, however, Hornblower acquires some of the more sociable characteristics that distinguished graduates of Pellew's frigate school. In the television adaptation of the novels, the youthful Hornblower forms a close friendship with Midshipman Archie Kennedy, a character who makes only a fleeting appearance in Forester's novels.[7] Having first met

---

[3] Osler, p. 185.

[4] T. R. Bowen, *Mutiny* screenplay, 2001.

[5] B. Rostul, *Retribution* screenplay, 2001.

[6] Forester, *The Hornblower Companion*, pp. 87–9.

[7] Forester, *Mr. Midshipman Hornblower*, pp. 81–2, 116–17.

aboard the decaying ship of the line *Justinian*, Hornblower and Kennedy's friendship develops aboard the *Indefatigable* as they experience crewing prizes, cutting out expeditions, shore operations and captivity. Later, when Hornblower and Kennedy find themselves serving as lieutenants under the unstable Captain Sawyer of the ship of the line *Renown*, the bond of friendship forged aboard the *Indefatigable* endures and Kennedy ultimately lays down his life to save his shipmate.

In many ways, the close friendship that develops between Kennedy and Hornblower in their televisual incarnation is perhaps more representative of the type of relationships that formed among long-serving frigate crews, than is Forester's archetypal Man Alone. It is certainly typical of the close and enduring bonds that formed between Hornblower's historical counterparts. For the young gentlemen of HMS *Indefatigable*, the bonds they forged in Pellew's exemplary frigate school persisted throughout their naval service and long into their civilian lives.

Clearly the seventeen young gentlemen presented in this study were not the only junior officers to serve aboard the *Indefatigable* at this time. The *Droits de L'Homme* engagement may be an iconic point in time, but selecting a group of men from a single point in the ship's timeline isolates them from many of their shipmates. They were of course part of a much wider network of volunteers, midshipmen and master's mates with whom they no doubt formed equally close bonds. There are several young officers who left and entered the *Indefatigable* immediately before and after the *Droits de L'Homme* engagement, who have been excluded from this study by very narrow margins indeed, and there are a significant number who would have been shipmates from earlier and later commands: from senior master's mates who were promoted just prior to George Chace joining the *Nymphe*, to junior volunteers who joined the *Impetueux* in the final year of Pellew's command. While it is highly likely that these men also formed long and lasting friendships, with each other and with their captain, those that served aboard the *Indefatigable* on the night of the *Droits de L'Homme* engagement shared in an experience that intensified these bonds of camaraderie. In addition, such was the fame of the action, that 13 January 1797 provides a convenient point in time that can be used to trace this particular group of officers through Admiralty archives, civic records and contemporary press articles.

Most of these officers, as we have seen, had relatively successful naval careers, and, for those who lived on after the war, prosperous and productive civilian lives. With the arguable exceptions of the Honorable George Cadogan, who unexpectedly inherited his prominent family title, and Jeremiah Coghlan, who became famous for his naval exploits, few of these men became widely recognised 'names' like so many of the previous generation of naval officers, and consequently, little of their personal correspondence has survived for posterity. Had the war continued, it is likely that many of them would have reached senior rank, in which case more documentary evidence might have survived. As this was not the case, the lives of these officers have been pieced together from disparate and often scant sources. Relatively little personal correspondence has survived for even the two most prominent Indefatigables, Cadogan and Coghlan: a house fire in the late nineteenth century destroyed most of the 3rd Earl Cadogan's personal archive, and Coghlan burned many of his letters in a state of anxiety about them falling into the wrong hands, which haunted him during a period of ill health in 1836. Later that year, Coghlan wrote to George Pellew, who was collating information for his planned biography of his father:

> With respect to your dear Father's correspondence the most important of it, at least, was destroyed during an alarming illness last winter. The medical men holding out no hope of my recovery and fearful lest they should get into bad hands I had it committed to the flames in my bedroom, painful as it was to my heart to part with anything that bore his beloved and honoured name.[8]

There is no indication as to the identity of the 'bad hands' Coghlan was referring to, but it seems that he was something of an anxious character with a tendency to suspect the worst. Over twenty years previously, Susan Pellew had referred to this trait in a letter to her husband:

> I am always sorry you did not put Fleetwood into Alcmene instead of Coughlin – how is it dear that you always think you have Enemies projecting evil for you and yours? It is a sad Alloy to Your Comfort and nine times out of ten ill founded – Jerry has this propensity too, but in this instance it may be for his Advantage.[9]

Despite continued ill health, Coghlan was rather more sanguine later in 1836, admitting to George Pellew that some of his father's correspondence had indeed survived, but that it would require sorting out.

> My Dear Dean
> I have been so very unwell ever since the receipt of your letter of the 18th that it has been quite impossible for me to undertake the selection of that part of your dear father's letters which may be thought worth a place in your forth coming work.
> The whole are mixed with a mass of other documents from the various flag officers I have served under during the war besides many from governors of several colonies where I have been stationed and others from publick bodies in various parts of the world.[10]

---

[8] Exmouth Papers, Box 22, Coghlan to George Pellew, 29 July 1836.

[9] Exmouth Family Archive, 7818M/F/1/5-6, 9-10, Susan Pellew to Edward Pellew, 13 March 1814.

[10] Exmouth Papers, Box 22, Coghlan to George Pellew, 24 August 1836. This is the same letter in which Coghlan made his apparently unfulfilled promise about taking 'half an hour' to tell the true story of the *Dutton*.

For whatever reason – either Coghlan's ongoing infirmity or his fear of material falling into 'bad hands' – he never did deliver the promised material to George Pellew and a considerable body of evidence for his continued friendship with both Pellew and his former shipmates, disappeared. Among the papers of Nicholas Pateshall, the one Indefatigable for whom a substantial personal archive has survived, there are several letters from Coghlan; however Pateshall's side of the correspondence, which might have been among Coghlan's 'mass of other documents', has been lost.

Despite the myriad ways in which personal letters and papers are so easily subject to loss or destruction, the partial evidence that has survived gives considerable insight into the bonds that united Pellew and the boys who grew to men under his command.

It is of course Nicholas Pateshall's remarkable archive that paints the most vivid picture of Pellew as captain, mentor and father figure to the young boys who joined his frigate school in the mid-1790s. The mixture of awe, pride, affection and occasional resentment, which must have been typical of many young volunteers, is vividly evoked in Pateshall's early letters. Ann Pateshall's letters to her son also provide a unique parental view of what she considered to be Pellew's rather lenient approach to mentoring his young charges. Although Mrs Pateshall clearly disapproved of the prevalence of alcohol consumption among the 'lads in your station',[11] invitations to the captain's table to learn the mores and customs of naval dining and drinking were an essential aspect of the young officers' training and helped to build strong collective ties between young men who often came from disparate social backgrounds.[12]

Forester vividly illustrates the educational benefits of dining at Pellew's table in *Hornblower and the Hotspur*. Invited to dine with Pellew and Cornwallis aboard the *Tonnant*, Hornblower, while 'cautiously on guard about his manners', learns much about conjuring a lavish dining experience from meagre cabin stores and naval rations.

> He helped himself at random – one name meant no more to him than another – and went on to make an epoch-making discovery, that Wensleydale cheese and vintage port were a pair of heavenly twins ... Almost simultaneously he made another discovery which amused him. The chased silver fingerbowls which were put on the table were very elegant; the last time he had seen anything like them was as a midshipman at a dinner at Government House in Gibraltar. In each

---

[11] Pateshall Papers, BD30/9/48, Ann Pateshall to Nicholas Pateshall, 2 March 1799.

[12] Another instance of this sociability is John Smyth's account of returning to the *Tonnant* and receiving an invitation to join the captain and officers in drinking a toast to Pellew's wedding anniversary. Smyth Papers, D/CB/4/14/4, John Smyth to John Gee Smyth, 14 June 1803.

floated a fragment of lemon peel, but the water in which the peel floated – as Hornblower discovered by a furtive taste as he dabbed his lips – was plain sea water. There was something comforting in that fact.[13]

In addition to these on-board social occasions, it is clear that Pellew also extended such hospitality to his officers ashore. From the early years of the 1790s when Pellew and Susan opened up their growing household in Falmouth to William Kempthorne's struggling family, to the large hilltop home full of grandchildren in Teignmouth, passing references in letters and household accounts[14] attest to the continued presence of Indefatigables in the lives of the Pellews. It may well be because of the warmth and hospitality that extended beyond the confines of the ship and terms of duty at sea that so many of the condolence letters sent to Fleetwood Pellew after his father's death use the word 'kindness'. And it was a kindness that was reciprocated; in the same letter in which Pellew shared with Francis Beaufort news of his friends serving on the East India station,[15] including Thomas Groube and George Bell's promotions, he also passed on thanks from both himself and Susan: 'I feel myself greatly obliged to you for the attention you have paid to Lady P who writes me how sensible she is of your civilities.'[16]

Not only does Nicholas Pateshall's archive provides a unique source of information about the young gentlemen's initial service aboard the *Indefatigable*; it also presents invaluable evidence of the networks of friendships that continued to bind the former Indefatigables together throughout their later lives. During this later period, Pateshall's correspondence is supplemented by additional sources, such as contemporary press reports which, though brief, nonetheless present a wider picture.

During the Peace of Amiens, the *Indefatigable*'s young gentlemen were widely dispersed: a few continued to serve in the Royal Navy, some entered the merchant service, and many, like their captain, found themselves on the beach. However, when hostilities resumed and Pellew was appointed first to the *Tonnant* and later to the *Culloden* on becoming Commander in Chief of the East India station, the rapidity with which a number of the Indefatigables were appointed to serve on Pellew's flagship or in his squadron strongly suggests that a network of communication existed that kept the young gentlemen in contact with each other and with their captain. Of course Pellew's rising seniority, particularly after his arrival in India, also meant that, unlike his desperate struggle to keep his people with him

---

[13] Forester, *Hornblower and the Hotspur*, pp. 128–33.

[14] Pellew of Canonteign Collection, 7818/E/2/1/3/1 and 7818/E/2/1/3/2, Account of Lord Exmouth with Toulmin and Copland.

[15] Huntington Library, FB 1498, Pellew to Francis Beaufort, 25 February 1808.

[16] *Ibid.*

when he transferred to the *Impetueux* in 1799, he now had considerable influence in choosing his own officers and men.

By the end of the French Revolutionary War, all the *Indefatigable's* young gentlemen had passed their examinations and qualified variously as lieutenant, master or gunner. When hostilities resumed, following the collapse of the Peace of Amiens, they were all successful in securing commissions, which dispersed them across the globe. While some spent much of their naval career in home waters, other Indefatigables were posted at various stages to the East and West Indies, North and South America, the Baltic, the Cape, the North Sea, Greenland and New South Wales. Despatches took many months to travel between the Royal Navy's far-flung foreign stations and news of former shipmates was harder to come by; however the surviving documentation reveals glimpses of how the Indefatigables maintained their social networks. For example when Henry Hart was appointed as first lieutenant of the *Medusa* and posted to the East India station, Nicholas Pateshall took advantage of his friend's new commission to send letters and parcels to his brother Sandys who was serving with the army there. Writing to another brother, Edmund, in January 1805, Pateshall noted:

> The *Medusa* frigate is about to sail for the East Indies with Lord Cornwallis. The first lieutenant of her is an old messmate of mine, by name Henry Hart, who will take charge of any letters or other things for Sandys, I intend writing to him by this post upon the subject.[17]

No archival source of personal correspondence belonging to Henry Hart has yet been found, otherwise the letter Pateshall wrote to his friend might have survived, perhaps alongside correspondence from other former shipmates and his captain. A footnote in *The Worthies of Sussex*,[18] published in 1865, refers to correspondence between Hart and Pellew, which seems to have been extant at the time, but unfortunately, if Hart's personal papers have survived, they have not yet been located.

This extended network of shipmates and friends also meant that former Indefatigables who served together later in their careers had a network of colleagues they had known for many years who could be trusted and relied upon. William Warden's will is evidence of this; in 1804, while lieutenant of the *Tonnant*, Warden wrote his will and asked two of his current shipmates and former Indefatigables, Thomas Groube and John Gaze, to act as witnesses, and he appointed a third, Jeremiah Coghlan, to act as his executor.[19] It is quite likely that some of the other young gentlemen also

---

[17] Pateshall Papers, A95/V/EB/S, Nicholas Pateshall to Edmund Pateshall, 18 January 1805.

[18] Lower, pp. 329–30.

[19] PROB 11/1507, Will of William Warden, formerly Lieutenant of HM Ship *Tonnant*, late Commander of HM Sloop *Rattlesnake*. When Warden's will

made wills at this time; however, as they lived much longer than Warden and grew to have families for whom they had to make provision, they are likely to have revised their wills at a later date and destroyed earlier versions which may have mentioned shipmates they were close to at the time.

Pellew seems to have played a pivotal role in sustaining his officers' communication networks, as a result of his senior naval rank and personal interest in his protégés' careers. As a Commander in Chief he had access to the most efficient communication channels the service could offer and he was also on the receiving end of official despatches detailing promotions, appointments and other more general news of the service. He regularly forwarded news of promotions to friends and colleagues, as he did when telling Francis Beaufort about George Bell and Thomas Groube's commissions, and he also passed on congratulations or commiserations to junior officers who had been successful or frustrated in their hopes for promotion. An instance of this is evident in two letters sent on consecutive days in November 1809: one to Nicholas Pateshall congratulating him and wishing him 'all possible good fortune, I am, dear Pateshall, very sincerely your well wisher',[20] and another to Francis Beaufort, a close friend of several of the 1797 cohort, offering sympathy on his lack of advancement.

> I wish in offering my thanks I could likewise offer my congratulations on obtaining the reward you have so long deserved from the service and which I assure you no man on earth more sincerely wishes for you than I do.[21]

Pellew may not have been able to provide Beaufort with the rewards he undoubtedly deserved; however it was primarily as a result of his actions while Commander in Chief of the East India station that Pellew gained his, not undeserved, reputation for partiality and nepotism. His blatant over-promotion of his own sons, Pownoll and Fleetwood Pellew, was misguided at best and irresponsible at worst and it is not hard to imagine that such favouritism must have resulted in a degree of frustration and jealousy among other more deserving junior officers. However, if this was the case, there does not appear to have been any lasting personal animosity directed towards the Pellew brothers from their contemporaries in the service. Indeed the condolence letters written to Fleetwood after the admiral's death reveal not only love and respect for Pellew, but also genuine warmth and affection towards Fleetwood himself. George Cadogan and William Kempthorne also enquired affectionately after Pownoll Pellew who

---

was proved in January 1810, the legatee, Eliza Millman, née Hollingsworth, was granted administration, as Jeremiah did not appear. This is understandable as he was stationed in the West Indies at the time.

[20] Pateshall Papers, A95/V/N/170, Pellew to Pateshall, 25 November 1809.

[21] Beaufort Papers, FB 1499, Pellew to Beaufort, 26 November 1809.

appears to have been in poor health at the time.[22] In a short but very telling exchange of correspondence with Fleetwood Pellew after his father's death, Cadogan wrote to confirm that he would be visiting Fleetwood at home the following day and added an enquiry: 'I cannot resist the inclination I feel to address a few lines to my dear old friend your brother, unless you have any objection to my doing so from the fear of agitating his mind.'[23]

Henry Hart seems to have developed a particularly close and long-standing friendship with Fleetwood Pellew. Many years later, in 1841, Hart was one of what the press archly referred to as 'a select circle' who attended the wedding of Fleetwood's only daughter, Harriet, to Horatio William Walpole, 4th Earl of Orford.[24]

The period of Pellew's East India command provides a striking example of the complex network of personal and professional relationships that united the Indefatigables as a distinct community where long-standing friendships flourished. Thomas Groube, John Gaze, William Warden, William Kempthorne, Henry Hart, and former *Indefatigable* lieutenant George Bell, were all stationed there at the same time, in addition to Pownoll and Fleetwood Pellew, who had first served with many of the Indefatigables aboard the *Impetueux* in 1799. Even the unfortunate Richard Delves Broughton was not far away as his regiment was stationed in Madras at the time. This was also a period marked by the next rites of passage in the Indefatigables' private and professional lives: several achieved promotion to commander and post captain, and others met and married their wives while serving on the East India station.[25]

There were several other instances where smaller groups of the 1797 cohort found themselves stationed together with their former shipmates. John Thomson, Nicholas Pateshall, William Kempthorne and James Bray all served on the North American station in 1813, and Jeremiah Coghlan and George Cadogan were both stationed in the Mediterranean in 1814. Earlier in the war, Alex McVicar and James Bray were both stationed in Yarmouth at an important stage in their personal lives: McVicar's first child, Jennet Ogilvie McVicar, was born and baptised there in the summer of 1807, and, in the same church less than two months later, James Bray married his fiancée, Mary Tyler.[26] Another *Indefatigable* shipmate, George Chace, who

---

[22] Kempthorne's grateful remembrance of the Pellew family in his will specifically mentioned Pownoll as well as Lord and Lady Exmouth.

[23] Exmouth Papers, Box 23, Cadogan to Fleetwood Pellew, 12 April 1833. The reference to Pownoll Pellew's state of mind remains opaque. Pownoll died in December 1833, less than a year after his father; however the cause was recorded as scarlet fever, rather than some longer-term illness.

[24] Marriage in high life, *Dublin Monitor*, 16 November 1841.

[25] Thomas Groube, Pownoll Pellew and Henry Hart all married while serving in the East Indies. See Chapter 6 for further information.

[26] LDS C00024-4, record of baptism, St Nicholas Parish Church, Jennet Ogilvie McVicar, born 18 August 1807, baptised 26 August 1807. Ancestry.

served as Pellew's coxswain for many years, was also stationed in Yarmouth at this time.

While it was by no means unusual for former shipmates to be reunited later in their careers, the picture that emerges of Pellew's East India command suggests the existence not just of a professional network, but also of a sociable community sustained by close interpersonal bonds. And it appears that it was Pellew himself who was at the heart of this community. From acting as witness at Henry Hart's marriage, to pursuing justice and restitution for William Kempthorne, and raising the fine memorial for William Warden, Pellew's actions provide evidence of his genuine care and concern for the community of officers and men that had followed him from the frigate school of the Western Squadron to the East India station.

Pellew's concern for his men is also apparent in his correspondence with his close friend Alex Broughton. Although it is understandable that Broughton would appreciate news of his young relative Richard Delves Broughton, Pellew's letters also contain news of other officers to whom Broughton had no relation and whom he would never have met. In a letter to Broughton, Pellew wrote movingly of the death of 'poor young Warden, one of my proteges', and his sadness that he had died just as he was about to have his promotion confirmed.[27]

As the war continued, the rigours of the service took their inevitable toll on the former young gentlemen of HMS *Indefatigable*, and several did not live to see the end of the decade. Those that survived and who lived to see the war through to its conclusion, continued to maintain their network of friendships. Once again, the primary source for these connections is the correspondence of Nicholas Pateshall.

Two letters which are particularly illustrative of the nature of this network were written by Jeremiah Coghlan to Pateshall in 1810.[28] The letters plunge the reader into a conversation *in medias res*, suggesting that they were originally part of a longer ongoing correspondence that has not survived. As mentioned earlier, Coghlan destroyed at least some of his personal papers and correspondence in 1836, and although Pateshall's archive is extensive, it is clearly not a comprehensive collection. In the first letter Coghlan thanks Pateshall for his recent note and promises to keep its contents to himself. He then goes on to wish that Nicholas could have been one of their company at dinner the night before and lists those present as 'Fyffe, Graves, Frazer, Kelly, Litchfield and a mid from *Polly*'. It is evident that Pateshall was familiar with all those named as no

org, film no. 1585963, item 3, p. 156, parish registers of Gorleston Parish Church, 14 October 1807.

[27] Pellew of Canonteign Collection, 7818M/F/1/5-6, 9-10, Pellew to Broughton, 22 July 1807.

[28] Pateshall Papers, A95/V/N/174, Coghlan to Pateshall, undated, and A95/V/N/175, Coghlan to Pateshall, 17 December 1810.

explanation is provided as to their identity. Litchfield would certainly have been familiar, and his presence in Coghlan's letter is a good example of the connections that evolved as naval careers progressed and how the next generation of Pellew's young gentlemen followed in the path of their predecessors. Henry Litchfield entered the navy in 1800 as a midshipman on board the *Impetueux* where he would have been a junior shipmate of several Indefatigables including Pateshall, Coghlan, Hart and Cadogan. He had an impressive start to his naval career and participated in a number of significant actions, including the cutting out of the 22-gun vessel *La Guepe* in Vigo Bay in August 1800, an action which also involved Indefatigables Henry Hart and George Cadogan. Later in 1804 Lichfield was appointed acting master of the *Renard* under Coghlan's command, and two years later in 1806 as second lieutenant aboard the mutinous *Ferret* commanded by George Cadogan. He was serving again with Coghlan aboard the *Elk* in 1809–1810, at the time these letters were written.[29]

Coghlan's second letter to Pateshall is full of the sort of references to people and circumstances known to mutual friends and consequently it is difficult to interpret in any great detail; however Coghlan shares his own pessimism about his current prospects and wishes Pateshall all the best, hoping he has had better news.

> My Dear Nick,
>   Although I am without hope of hearing anything of my own gloomy prospects ... yet believe me I most sincerely hope you have got your rank and we shall see you soon.

Despite his obvious despondency, Coghlan continues with a hospitable offer:

> You must consider the *Elk* as your head quarters whenever you are here whether I am on board or not. You will find Litchfield who will be, I am sure, very glad to show you every attention.[30]

The Pateshall family's penchant for keeping correspondence not only provides a rare glimpse into the personal lives of serving naval officers; it has also preserved for posterity important eyewitness accounts of two of Pellew's most celebrated naval actions: the *Droits de L'Homme* engagement as seen through the eyes of fifteen-year-old Nicholas himself, and the Bombardment of Algiers from Pateshall's friend and former shipmate William Kempthorne. This latter account appears in a letter written to Nicholas Pateshall in 1816.[31] Pateshall, who was still serving in the West Indies at the time that Pellew was assembling his force for Algiers, appears to have written to William Kempthorne to congratulate

---

[29] O'Byrne, vol. 1, pp. 661–2.

[30] Pateshall Papers, A95/V/N/175, Coghlan to Pateshall, 17 December 1810.

[31] Pateshall Papers, A95/V/N/223, Kempthorne to Pateshall, 23 October 1816.

his friend on what Kempthorne referred to as his 'recent very good fortune'. Although Pateshall's side of the correspondence has not survived, it seems certain that this is a reference to Kempthorne's recent promotion to post captain. It also seems likely that Pateshall knew the circumstances of Kempthorne's long struggle to clear his name and regain his commission, and he would have appreciated what a momentous occasion this was for his friend.

It appears that Pateshall had also requested from Kempthorne a first-hand report of the Bombardment of Algiers, 'with the account of the escapes the Admiral had'.[32] Although Kempthorne wrote that he did not know if he could add much to the despatches, he went on to give a detailed account of the action, stressing the meticulous planning and extensive training that had been involved prior to the engagement.[33] Kempthorne also satisfied Pateshall's apparent request for news of the admiral's personal safety by revealing that although Pellew had received no serious injuries, his escapes had been close even for one with his legendary good fortune.

> His Lordship exceeded himself, if possible, with his method of assessing the whole plan, with the execution were equal to the gallantry of the attempt. He had a severe blow on his cheek which knocked out his false teeth ... some wood and iron lodged and left a jagged wound, a musket ball broke his spectacles in his waistcoat pocket, a large splinter struck him in the hip, it made his thigh black to the knee and made a wound, his coat on each side just above the pockets torn in large pieces either by shot or splinters. Thank God he is now quite well and will long live I hope to fight his country's battles; all those who were with him will fight his for him whenever call'd on I am sure.[34]

Kempthorne's vivid letter ends with arrangements to meet with Nicholas in the following weeks, when no doubt they would have discussed the bombardment and the fate of the admiral's false teeth at their leisure.

The years 1816–1818 were watershed years for Pellew and for the former young gentlemen of HMS *Indefatigable*, with the coming of peace and the transition to civilian life. Pellew never went to sea again after returning from Algiers; his fighting days were over, though he continued to serve as Commander in Chief of Plymouth Dockyard, alongside his trusted friend and shipmate, John Gaze. John Thomson, Nicholas Pateshall, Thomas Groube and William Kempthorne also quietly retired from active service at around this time. It is fitting in many ways that 1816 also marked the end for the ship where these men had come together and shared such formative

---

[32] *Ibid.*, p. 1.

[33] *Ibid.*, pp. 2–3.

[34] *Ibid.*, p. 4.

experiences; her service at an end, HMS *Indefatigable* made her last voyage to Sheerness Dockyard where she was broken up.

In 1817, like many of his contemporaries, Nicholas Pateshall took advantage of the first real peace for decades to tour the continent, and like many travelling gentlemen, he commemorated his tour by having his portrait painted, in this case by the school of Domenico Pellegrini. Fleetwood Pellew, who was also abroad at this time, on honeymoon with his new wife Harriet, had his portrait sketched by Ingres.[35] Even Pellew himself was touring the continent, receiving honours from many nations in recognition of his gallantry in saving their citizens from slavery at Algiers. While in Rome, he sat for a portrait bust by acclaimed neoclassical sculptor, Bertel Thorvaldsen, who had a studio there at the time.[36]

Although most of the former Indefatigables retired from active naval service after the war, they continued to meet, socialise and work together through numerous naval circles and charitable societies. Unsurprisingly, maritime charities and benevolent funds were particularly popular causes for retired naval officers and the Indefatigables were no exception. The names of several of the Indefatigables appear in lists of attendees at charitable naval functions and as benefactors to maritime benevolent funds, often standing alongside their former captain, now Admiral Lord Exmouth. For example, in 1819, a fundraising appeal was launched to finance the start-up of a new pilchard and mackerel trade to assist the residents of the Scilly Isles who were living in poverty following the collapse of the kelp industry. Around £13,000 was raised by subscription and among the list of subscribers are the names of Lord Exmouth, Captain Coghlan RN and Mrs Coghlan. Indeed the list notes that Coghlan's contribution came via Pellew.[37] Much later, in the summer of 1849, Henry Hart, George Cadogan and Fleetwood Pellew were all listed among the distinguished guests at a Navy Club dinner given in honour of the new First Lord of the Admiralty,[38] and their names continue to appear regularly as guests at a number of similar events throughout the 1840s and 1850s.

The Scottish members of the *Indefatigable* cohort returned to civilian life in their home country, though John Thomson was eventually to settle in Ireland after being appointed to the coastguard service there. Previously, however, he had been involved, along with former Indefatigable Alex McVicar, in setting up a new company in their home town of Leith, to promote fishing industry sales from the port. These business interests are likely to account for the item in Pellew's domestic accounts concerning

---

[35] Sir Fleetwood Broughton Reynolds Pellew by Jean-Auguste-Dominique Ingres, now in the Metropolitan Museum, New York.

[36] Bust of Admiral Edward Pellew, later First Viscount Exmouth, by Bertel Thorvaldsen, now in the Philadelphia Museum of Art.

[37] *The Morning Post*, 27 March 1819.

[38] *Hampshire Telegraph and Sussex Chronicle*, 23 June 1849.

paying Captain Thomson for fish.[39] John McKerlie's name also appears in these accounts, being reimbursed for unstated items, again suggesting continuing connections between the Indefatigables and their former captain.

Further evidence of the enduring friendship between Pellew and his former officers comes from a series of letters written in the 1820s to his third son George. After graduating from Oxford, George had been ordained as a clergyman with a parish in Yorkshire in 1820, before becoming rector of St George-the-Martyr, Canterbury, and finally Dean of Norwich in 1828. These personal letters reveal a genial domestic side to Pellew, who appears to have thrived on being the centre of a growing family and a wide network of naval friends. Pellew may have had a reputation as a formidable fighting captain during his long career at sea; however in his later correspondence he comes across as benign and bonhomous with a great fondness for his former officers. In this respect, Parkinson's comment that Pellew was not greatly feared in later life has some validity, though in an entirely positive sense.

Forester captures some of this fondness and paternal affection in his fictional portrayal of Pellew in *Hornblower and the Hotspur*. Writing to his protégé, Hornblower, before leaving command of the Inshore Squadron, Pellew comments:

> But Commanding officers are likely to have their favourites, men with whom they are personally acquainted. We can hardly quarrel on that score, since I have indulged myself in a favourite whose initials are H.H.!
>
> Your sincere friend, Ed Pellew.[40]

This affectionate and somewhat indulgent tone is echoed in Pellew's historical correspondence with many of his former officers: for example, in his personal response to John McKerlie's request to join him at Algiers, in his comments about Susan Pellew's affection for Henry Hart,[41] and in the letter to George about Henry Hart and his wife Maria visiting Knaresborough.[42]

The fact that Pellew regularly kept his son George acquainted with news of Henry Hart, John Thomson and others, is evidence of the close

---

[39] Pellew of Canonteign Collection, 7818M/E/2/1/3/1, Right Honorable Lord Viscount Exmouth in Account with Toulmin & Copeland.

[40] Forester, *Hornblower and the Hotspur*, p. 168.

[41] 'At Knaresborough you will find Harry Hart and Maria settled, call upon them and (word illegible) offer my affectionate regards and tell Harry how grateful I am for his letter and I will answer him soon.' Pellew of Canonteign Collection, 7818M/F/3/1/9, Exmouth to George Pellew, September 1828.

[42] *Ibid.*

relationship that continued to exist between these men almost thirty years after they first came together aboard HMS *Indefatigable*. George Pellew was only four years old in 1797 when these young men were serving aboard the *Indefatigable*, yet despite his own career having no connection with the navy, it appears that he came to regard the Indefatigables as close friends and as members of his father's extended naval family.[43]

One of Pellew's letters to his son George, which illustrates the close nature of this extended family, provides news of the impending arrival of John and Constantia Thomson's second child and Constantia's fears about the birth owing to the difficult confinement she had experienced during her first pregnancy.[44] These letters show the Pellews at their most domestic, and reveal Pellew in the role of paterfamilias of a large extended family of children, grandchildren, spouses, friends and former shipmates.

Not all the former Indefatigables maintained an unbroken friendship with their former captain however. Two poignant letters from George Cadogan among the correspondence that Fleetwood Pellew received following his father's death reveal that he and Pellew had had a disagreement or misunderstanding at some point that led to them becoming estranged. Later in his life Pellew had become increasingly influenced by his religious faith, and once he knew he was dying, it appears that he wanted to 'die well' in the sense of mending broken friendships and offering and receiving forgiveness for past grievances and transgressions. Cadogan's first letter is in reply to one from Fleetwood in which he appears to have written on behalf of his father in the hope of reconciliation. In his reply, Cadogan embraces the idea warmly and recalls the kindness and affection he experienced from Pellew as a young man in the service.

> My Dear Pellew,
>
> I must hope and trust in an indulgent and charitable construction having been put both by my poor Lord Exmouth and yourself upon my not having sooner replied to your gratifying tho' melancholy letter of the 11th inst.
>
> I know but of one excuse that such apparent neglect admits of and that is mine. On the very day your letter is dated I left Dover for the continent from whence I am but this moment returned, heaven send in time to convey to my poor old friend your father the assurance not only of reciprocal forgiveness but of all those feelings of I may say affection and gratitude for early kindness which though suppressed for a time never have and never will be erased from my heart and which your considerate and feeling appeal to it have now rekindled with all their former warmth and sincerity.

---

[43] Pinhey also refers to George Pellew's friendship with John Gaze. Pinhey, pp. 1–2.

[44] Pellew of Canonteign Collection, Edward Pellew to George Pellew, 18 July 1824.

You have indeed done me justice in concluding that such interchange of mutual forgiveness and oblivion at such a moment would be most gratifying to me. Convey them I beseech of you my good and worthy friend to your poor father in return with all that can now be acceptable to him in this world the prayers and blessing of a Christian. One who has ever (word illegible) to appreciate the great and good points of his character and fame however unfortunate circumstances may have interrupted their personal harmony.

Finally let me beg you will let me have the gratification of knowing immediately should this communication reach you in time to afford the consolation to your afflicted parent it will be my greatest happiness to have conveyed.

Accept as you (word illegible) my dear Pellew, my best thanks for the kind and charitable part you have taken in this affair and in the hope of seeing you soon believe me always

Very sincerely yours
Cadogan.[45]

Unfortunately, as Cadogan feared, his short absence in France meant that his letter reached Devon too late for Pellew to receive his reciprocal absolution and earnest gratitude. The day after Cadogan wrote his moving letter, the London papers announced news of Admiral Lord Exmouth's death. Despite the melancholy failure of Pellew and Cadogan's heartfelt wish for reconciliation, the correspondence opened the way for the two families to renew their mutual friendship. There appears to have been further correspondence between Cadogan and Fleetwood Pellew, and possibly also with Lady Exmouth.

Cadogan's second letter to Fleetwood Pellew is more positive; he speaks of shared recollections and a planned visit, as well as the hope he might communicate with his old friend Pownoll.

My dear Pellew,
I cannot say how gratified I feel by the flattering testimony your letter of yesterday gives of yours and Lady Exmouth's recollections and regard. It has I assure you a double value in my eyes. First as a pledge of your poor father's reconciliation and forgiveness and secondly as the bond of reunion between myself and your family. I shall ever regret it should have been for one moment interrupted ...[46]

It appears that Cadogan did reconcile with the Pellews following this exchange of letters, as, after this period, his name frequently appears close to Fleetwood Pellew's in lists of guests at ceremonies and dinners with naval connections. Research has not yet identified either the cause

---

[45] Exmouth Papers, Box 23, Cadogan to Fleetwood Pellew, 25 January 1833.
[46] Exmouth Papers, Box 23, Cadogan to Fleetwood Pellew, 12 April 1833.

or the date of the disagreement between Cadogan and Pellew; however, for Cadogan, a very private man who did not share his feelings lightly, the language of both letters is remarkably frank and open in its lament for past estrangements and mourning for a loved mentor whose early influence and kindness he is at pains to acknowledge.

George Cadogan was not the only former Indefatigable to write to Fleetwood Pellew following his father's death. As might be expected, there are other moving condolence letters from those who benefited from Pellew's support and kindness, including John Gaze,[47] Jeremiah Coghlan and William Kempthorne. In an emotional and heartfelt eulogy, Coghlan wrote:

> My dear Fleetwood, the will of God be done. You have lost the best of fathers and I the most generous and kindest of friends who ever lived ... I will mourn in solemn silence for the man who has ever been most dear to my heart.[48]

However it was William Kempthorne who paid the most poignant and eloquent tribute to Pellew's memory. Kempthorne had perhaps more personal reason than most to express his gratitude to his former captain: for the early childhood friendship of the Pellew family, for being taken under Pellew's wing and offered a place on his quarterdeck, and for the indomitable support he received from Pellew in overturning his dismissal, restoring him to rank and securing his future. What is so moving about Kempthorne's tribute, however, is that he speaks not just of his own loss, but on behalf of so many others.

> ... in whom the navy has lost its brightest jewel, your family the best of husbands and fathers, a wide circle of us a matchless friend and the country a stay and defender. We shall look about in vain for his equal.[49]

Kempthorne's elegant eulogy does much to sum up the feelings of many of the young gentlemen who served on Pellew's numerous commands on learning of his death: the sense of having lost an irreplaceable friend and champion. In numerous condolence letters and statements of respect, Pellew's former officers and men regret that his equal will not be found again. While this may be a conventional nineteenth-century idiomatic expression of mourning, that does not make such statements any less authentic. There would be no more conflicts in their lifetime that would

---

[47] Exmouth Papers, Box 28, Gaze to Fleetwood Pellew, 26 January 1833.

[48] Exmouth Family Archive, Coghlan to Fleetwood Pellew, 26 January 1833. Although Pellew's funeral was a low-key event intended for a relatively small circle of family and friends, it is evident that Coghlan would have been a welcome guest as, in the same letter, he effectively apologises for not being present.

[49] Exmouth Papers, Box 28, Kempthorne to Fleetwood Pellew, January 1833.

9 'Mr Pateshall', artist unknown, *c.* 1796. This caricature of Pateshall, possibly by a fellow shipmate, was preserved among his personal papers.

enable a partisan fighter like Pellew to rise to the highest ranks of the service. Pellew's unique mixture of generosity and greed, tolerance and bias, bonhomous welcome and demanding standards, certainly made him remarkable, but his was an age that saw many remarkable captains become successful and capable admirals. It could be argued, however, that Pellew's role as patron, mentor, father figure and, most importantly, friend to the young gentlemen of HMS *Indefatigable*, and many others before and after them, deserves as much respect and recognition as his more spectacular acts of seamanship and daring. Pellew's most recent biographer has memorably described him as a man with 'a gift for friendship',[50] and there is ample evidence that it was a gift he shared freely with his officers and men. The Indefatigables may have lost a 'matchless friend' when Pellew passed away in 1833; however the network of friendships that bound Pellew's former officers together persisted long after his death.

In Nicholas Pateshall's archive there is one further document that, quite literally, provides an illustration of the enduring nature of the friendships forged in the larboard berth of HMS *Indefatigable*. It is a portrait of Pateshall, and though it is a world away from the elegant

---

[50] Taylor, p. 24.

captain in dress uniform painted in Rome in 1817, it is recognisably the same man. The image is a small caricature sketch showing a young man in midshipman's uniform, but also wearing a cook's apron and hat, carrying a rather anxious-looking chicken by its legs; a spiral of smoke trails out from the margin of the page behind them. A banner across the top of the caricature reads simply 'Mr Pateshall'. The sketch seems almost certainly to be a reference to some specific incident known to both the artist and the subject, and for Pateshall, whose letters throughout his life contain references to hunting and shooting for the table, it is rather apposite. There is no evidence in the Pateshall archive or elsewhere as to the identity of the artist, but it seems more than possible that the sketch was drawn by a shipmate of Pateshall's, perhaps one of his fellow messmates, or another of the *Indefatigable*'s young gentlemen. It is tempting to wonder who drew the picture and whether it was perhaps one of a series depicting the other midshipmen and mates. Little is known of the drawing abilities of the young gentlemen of HMS *Indefatigable*; no sketchbooks or other drawings have survived from their formative years in the service; however John McKerlie was certainly a talented cartographer, as evidenced by the maps he later produced while working with Thomas Telford, and artistic talent certainly ran in George Cadogan's family, with three of his children showing a great gift for painting and drawing.[51] The caricature, whilst lightly mocking, is not unsympathetic, and Pateshall clearly attached some sentimental value to it and regarded it as worth keeping. It was still amongst his papers when he died in 1853 at the age of seventy-three, a memento perhaps of his shipmates and the experiences and friendships they shared together.

The small collection of letters that has survived between the Indefatigables and their former captain illustrates the enduring nature of the ties of friendship and camaraderie forged in the 'frigate school' of the Western Squadron. At the same time, the letters provide compelling evidence of the early nineteenth-century ideal of parenthood and friendship combined. The young gentlemen of HMS *Indefatigable* may first have encountered Pellew as captain, patron and mentor, but it is clear that as the years progressed, bringing mutual experience and respect, many of them also came to regard him as their friend. Furthermore, it is clear from the correspondence of the Indefatigables that, throughout his lifetime, Pellew played a pivotal role in maintaining the network of friendship that united his former officers throughout the war and on into their civilian lives.

---

[51] Cadogan's son, General Sir George Cadogan, served in the Crimean War and is well known for his war art, and both his daughters, Augusta and Honoria, were gifted painters.

'No State in Life More Honourable'

ONE factor affecting the Indefatigables, which they shared with the majority of officers and men who served at sea during the eighteenth and nineteenth centuries, was the toll that their naval careers took on their health. In addition to those who lost their lives as a result of shipwreck, disease and wounds sustained in action, a number of them, including Nicholas Pateshall, George Cadogan, Thomas Groube and Henry Hart, suffered from health problems that resulted in them being sent ashore to recuperate for periods of weeks or months. Like many sea officers and men, many of the Indefatigables suffered from the severe rheumatic pains that frequently resulted from years spent in wet clothes and freezing conditions, as well as long-term complications brought on by the destructive nature of earlier wounds. For those that had the means, taking the waters at fashionable spas such as Cheltenham was regarded as a beneficial treatment to alleviate the arthritic and rheumatic pains that were the legacy of the tough living conditions they had endured, and which often became magnified in later life.

In the letter that William Kempthorne wrote to his friend Nicholas Pateshall in 1816 with news of the Bombardment of Algiers, he signed off with the suggestion that they meet at Cheltenham: 'Should I spend a few weeks at Cheltenham as my side sometimes tells me I should, it will give me very much pleasure to meet you.'[1]

Pellew himself spent time in Cheltenham in the late autumn following his return from Algiers, when he was not attending numerous engagements in London. He arrived in the town on 24 October 1816 and was welcomed in grand fashion; *The Morning Post* reported in great detail how his carriage was drawn into the town by a team of beribboned men, preceded by a cheering crowd who escorted him to his town house. *The Post* also noted: 'We are anticipating a crowded ball on the 6th November, under the patronage of Lord and Lady Exmouth at the solicitation of all the naval officers.'[2] It seems quite likely that among the officers making the solicitation there were one or more former Indefatigables, perhaps even Kempthorne and Pateshall.

Cheltenham continued to be a popular retreat for naval officers throughout the 1820s and 1830s. The *Leamington Spa Courier* notes that

---

[1] Pateshall Papers, A95/V/N/223, Kempthorne to Pateshall, 23 October 1816.

[2] *The Morning Post*, 28 October 1816.

Captain John Thomson RN visited the spa in 1825,[3] and we know from Pellew's letter to his son George[4] that Henry Hart and his wife Maria were at Knaresborough, a Yorkshire spa town, in 1828. Writing to George Pellew in 1833, Jeremiah Coghlan also mentioned that his doctors had advised him to visit Cheltenham following a period of severe illness.[5]

Aside from the therapeutic benefits of taking the waters, spas offered welcome opportunities to meet with old shipmates and no doubt to reminisce about past actions and remember lost comrades. Despite the enduring nature of the social networks that continued to unite service personnel long after the end of the war, those of the 1797 Indefatigables who lived on into the middle of the nineteenth century would have spent much of their later years among family and friends who had no direct experience of warfare at sea. Though several, including George Cadogan and Thomas Groube, had sons who served in the army, there were no *Indefatigable* 'grandchildren', as it were, who became naval officers. This is to be expected as the navy had been scaled back considerably since the height of its power during the Napoleonic Wars. There were fewer opportunities for young men seeking to develop a successful career at sea, and no prospect of them winning the kind of prize money that had been such a powerful incentive for previous generations joining the service. Although there were significantly fewer career opportunities within the service, at the same time there were many more civilian career paths open to the sons of the veteran Indefatigables.[6]

Wareham has noted that the popular image, perpetuated by many writers of naval fiction, of retired naval officers getting together to reminisce about their adventures and retrace the courses of famous actions, has resulted in few personal written accounts being left behind.[7] If these social gatherings did take place, and there is some evidence to suggest that they did, the conversations that resulted rarely survived into the

---

[3] *Leamington Spa Courier*, 22 March 1825.

[4] Pellew of Canonteign Collection, 7818M/F/3/1/9, Exmouth to George Pellew, September 1828.

[5] Exmouth Papers, Box 22, Coghlan to George Pellew, 1833.

[6] The sons of the *Indefatigable* veterans benefited directly from the increased social standing that resulted from their fathers' successful naval careers. For example, John Gaze's son, John Pellew Gaze, studied at the University of Oxford and became an ordained Anglican priest, a career path that would not have been open to his father owing to his social class and lack of income. The same is true of Jeremiah Coghlan's son, Sir William Marcus Coghlan, who became a general in the British Army and had a successful diplomatic career. Although their sons' career prospects improved, the same cannot be said of their daughters, although their fathers' successful naval careers would have provided them with additional prosperity and security and improved educational and marriage prospects.

[7] Wareham, pp. 156–7.

historical record. In this context, the correspondence of Nicholas Pateshall and William Kempthorne is even more valuable as it provides frank first-hand accounts of important engagements, which were not intended for publication or for any official record. It is conceivable that the continued references to the *Droits de L'Homme* engagement, both by former officers and in accounts concerning them, resulted partially from an oral tradition that evolved at social gatherings at which such events were repeatedly retold. Certainly the many versions of 'Intrepid Jerry's' dramatic role in the *Dutton* rescue that were printed after both Pellew and Coghlan's deaths bear the hallmarks of an oral tradition that coalesced into printed accounts and written histories.

The trajectory of the careers of the 1797 Indefatigables reflects the times in which they served; after Trafalgar, as the war progressed and Britain asserted its naval superiority, there were fewer opportunities for young officers to make their names in dramatic fleet actions and naval engagements. Many of the Indefatigables were only in their early thirties when the war ended in 1815, and consequently, with the exception of Jeremiah Coghlan, they did not make headlines in the *Gazette* and become household names like many of the previous generation of naval officers. Although the Indefatigables may not have achieved the fame of Pellew's own generation, and most famously, Nelson's 'Band of Brothers', who were celebrated in the national press and feted by the public, it is possible to trace their naval exploits through the small paragraphs and syndicated news reports of Britain's extensive local and regional press. *The Hereford Journal*, for example, carried a brief report of Nicholas Pateshall's appointment to the *Shark* sloop in 1811: 'Lieutenant Nicholas Pateshall is appointed to the *Shark* sloop, in the West Indies, with the rank of Master and Commander.'[8]

It is common to find regional newspapers reporting the promotions and activities of local officers such as Nicholas Pateshall; however he was not the only Indefatigable to feature in the pages of *The Hereford Journal*. The previous year the newspaper had also carried a report of a notable engagement carried out by Pateshall's former shipmate, William Kempthorne, who, in a 'gallant and successful action', defeated a Dutch brig of superior armament.[9] Kempthorne had no connection with Hereford, other than his friendship with Pateshall; however this report is typical of the way in which news items from *The Gazette*, *The Naval Chronicle*, *The Gentleman's Magazine* and other London papers were picked up and carried by the provincial press. There may not have been any significant fleet battles or engagements to report, but there was still sufficient interest

[8] *The Hereford Journal*, 31 July 1811.
[9] *Ibid.*, 19 September 1810.

in the activities of the Royal Navy throughout the regions to warrant the reporting of smaller actions by lesser-known young officers.[10]

As a result of these syndicated news reports it is possible to trace the careers of almost all the Indefatigables through the pages of the regional press. These contemporary news reports may be brief but they add colour and depth to the historical portrait of these young officers. They describe men who were eminently capable of good seamanship, competent gunnery, and commanding the respect of their crews, men who were inventive and resourceful and, more often than not, possessed of considerable courage. As their careers advanced and the former young gentlemen of HMS *Indefatigable* progressed to become commanders of sloops, brigs and frigates, the press reports show that they shared many of the characteristics of their early mentor and, to a greater or lesser extent, had inherited his partisan mentality in their ability to show initiative, independence and gallantry. The account from *The Hereford Journal* of Kempthorne's capture of the Dutch brig is typical in this regard.

> We learn that a most gallant and successful action has been fought by Lieutenant Kempthorne of His majesty's brig *Diana* of 10 twelve-pounders on 11 September 1809, perceiving a Dutch national brig of 16 guns and 47 men, in the Bay of Mazordo, lying under the protection of a fort, he decoyed her out, tacked and brought her to close action, notwithstanding her superior force and the appearance of five gunboats which had been detached in capturing her in most gallant and successful style.[11]

Another example is the account from *The Lancaster Gazette* of Alex McVicar's successful action off the coast of Jutland in 1809 when, as captain of the 18-gun ship-sloop *Rover*, he captured and destroyed eighteen enemy vessels, one of which was carried after the *Rover*'s seamen swam inshore under heavy fire to seize the prize.[12] The characteristics of the engagements that are highlighted in the press reports – the opportunism and inventiveness, the self-belief in the face of superior odds, the combination of bravado and skill – bear all the hallmarks of Pellew's style, but also bear witness to the commitment and bravery of the officers themselves. It is notable that in both cases, commanders and crew also shared in Pellew's famous luck since the engagements resulted in minimal casualties.[13]

---

[10] The British Newspaper Archive reveals that, in addition to the London press, local newspapers from as far afield as Cornwall, Bath, Carlisle and Dublin carried the report of Kempthorne's engagement with the Dutch brig.

[11] *The Hereford Journal*, 19 September 1810.

[12] *The Lancaster Gazette*, October 1809. See Chapter 7 for a full account of the action.

[13] In the case of Kempthorne's action the figures were two killed and none reported wounded, and in McVicar's case one marine killed and the

These young men were far from being merely cut-down copies of their charismatic captain however. As the tone of Nicholas Pateshall's early letters reveals, as youngsters starting out in the service, which he described as 'no state in life more honourable or more pleasant',[14] they may initially have modelled themselves on Pellew; however, as their careers matured, they applied their own personalities, skills and abilities in the service of navy, state, church and community. Kempthorne and Hart both found time for hydrological survey, and Hart later transferred his naval skills into technical innovation. Cadogan, Coghlan and Pateshall were trusted with carrying important personnel and documents, and Coghlan and Hart were both posted on diplomatic missions on behalf of the British government. McKerlie and McVicar both undertook technical trials of ships and compasses on behalf of the Admiralty, and McVicar also represented the Admiralty in an administrative capacity. Pellew was not the only influence to inspire and shape the young gentlemen's careers; a number of them also served as lieutenants and flag officers under other influential captains and admirals, such as Sir John Gore and Sir John Borlase Warren, whom they also came to respect and admire.

As the years brought the Indefatigables seniority and the responsibilities of command, they in turn provided the next generation of young officers with the kind of support and patronage they themselves had benefited from in their own early days. For example, George Thomas entered the navy in 1804 when he joined the *Renard* under Jeremiah Coghlan's command. He followed Coghlan into the *Elk* where he participated in various spirited and dashing actions, and later went on to serve under Pellew in his flagships *Christian VII* and *Culloden*. Thomas also spent many years with Lord Cochrane in South America and Greece, where the skills, inventiveness and daring that he learned during his early days with Coghlan no doubt served him well.[15]

Many years later the Indefatigables continued to receive letters from officers hoping to use their connections as old shipmates to seek support either for their own careers or to find employment or naval preferment for their sons. Among Nicholas Pateshall's papers is a letter written in 1841 by Edward Maxey, a half-pay lieutenant living in Swansea who was hoping to be appointed as dock master. Maxey had previously served aboard Pateshall's 16-gun sloop *Jaseur* in the West Indies in 1816. Writing to his former captain, Maxey explained:

> I am given to understand that the officer who produces the best testimonials from the <u>captains</u> they have sailed with will be elected. I find that the only Captain that I served with thats alive is yourself

boatswain and one seaman wounded.

[14] Pateshall Papers, A95/EB/41/1, Nicholas Pateshall to Edmund Pateshall, 25 November 1794.

[15] O'Byrne, vol. 3, p. 1168.

and Sir A Farquhar. Altho' it is a long time since we were shipmates on board the *Jaseur*.[16]

It is impossible to know what Pateshall made of the rather dubious distinction of being approached by virtue of being the only one left alive;[17] however he himself had had sufficient experience of the hopes and disappointments of naval employment to understand the difficulties Maxey faced as an older lieutenant on half pay. Pateshall willingly provided Maxey with the requested commendation, copying his reply in his own hand, at the bottom of Maxey's letter.[18]

> My dear Sir,
>   It is a very long time since you served under my command as one of the lieutenants of the *Jaseur*, yet I have a perfect recollection of your services and am pleased of an opportunity to express my entire satisfaction in your conduct when so situated, and shall be happy to hear of your success on obtaining your present wishes ...[19]

Despite the exemplary training they had received, the transition to command was not always a smooth process for the Indefatigables, as George Cadogan's experiences with the mutinous crew of the *Ferret*, and later with the troubled midshipman Richard Badcock, reveal. Cadogan was not the only one of this cohort who struggled with troublesome junior officers; correspondence from Coghlan when he was commander of the *Nimble* cutter reveals that he too had a midshipman he was glad to be rid of.[20] Having received confirmation that the midshipman could be discharged at the youngster's own request, Coghlan wrote to the Admiralty: 'I have discharged him by his having furnished a seaman in his room. His conduct while under my command being such as to not entitle him otherwise to any such indulgence.'[21]

Although most of the 1797 Indefatigables retired from active service at the end of the war, their names continued to feature in the national and regional press in a wide range of contexts that reflected their diverse civilian lives and careers; however, only 'Intrepid Jerry' Coghlan was

---

[16] Pateshall Papers, A95/V/N/186, Edward Maxey to Pateshall, 6 September 1841.

[17] Maxey also provided an impressive list of his other commanding officers, many of whom had a connection to Nelson or his home county of Norfolk, including Sir William Bolton and William Hoste.

[18] Pateshall Papers, A95/V/N/186, Pateshall to Maxey, 9 September 1841.

[19] It is unknown whether Maxey was successful in obtaining this post; however he was promoted to the rank of commander in retirement in 1858, and died at Camberwell in 1872 at the age of eighty-two.

[20] ADM 1/2812, Lieutenants' Letters, Surname C, no. 133, Coghlan to Admiralty, 12 September 1802.

[21] *Ibid.*

remembered for his naval exploits. Following Pellew's death in 1833, Coghlan's name appeared in many obituaries, recalling his dramatic first meeting with Pellew on the storm-tossed deck of the stricken *Dutton*, and when Coghlan himself passed away eleven years later in 1844 many newspapers carried stirring accounts of his dashing naval career. Coghlan's was the only name to live on after his death too, at least while the next generation of naval officers lived on to share their reminiscences and write their memoirs. In 1863, almost twenty years after his death, Coghlan's name was invoked as an inspiring example of the navy's finest by Admiral John McHardy, then Chief Constable of Essex, at a dinner for volunteer officers.

> But whether our ships are wooden or iron, England would have confidence in her seamen knowing they would do their duty. [Applause] Who had not heard of Capt Jeremiah Coghlan who, with one boat only cut out the *Cerbère* brig of war within pistol shot of a French battery and within a mile of the French flagship.[22]

This speech was made only two years after HMS *Warrior*,[23] the first iron-hulled warship, had been completed and launched. Wooden men-of-war and much of what went with them, including the kind of cutting out expeditions and boat actions for which Jeremiah Coghlan was remembered, were already being looked on as adventures of a past age. Those Indefatigables who lived on into the 1840s and beyond must have recognised that their experiences of naval service and war at sea were already unfamiliar to their children and grandchildren's generation. However, the fact that Jeremiah Coghlan's name continued to inspire future cohorts of naval officers long after the days of sail had passed shows that men of his generation were still the embodiment of the gallant naval officer.

Coghlan may have been the only one of the Indefatigables who continued to appear in the press on account of his naval service; however there are also a significant number of references to Sir Henry Hart, many of which highlight his ongoing friendship with the Pellew family, and in particular Fleetwood Pellew whom he had first met aboard the *Impetueux* in 1799. In addition to the many occasions where their names are present on the guest lists of naval dinners and society events, they also appear in lists of benefactors of maritime charities and benevolent funds.

As a member of the peerage with a seat in the House of Lords, George Cadogan's name appeared frequently in the national press in the decades between 1840 and 1860. Many reports concern his speeches in the House

---

[22] *The Chelmsford Chronicle*, 17 April 1863.

[23] HMS *Warrior* was built by Thames Ironworks and Shipbuilding Co. in 1859 and launched in December 1860. She was decommissioned in May 1883 and subsequently served as a store ship and oil jetty until she was donated to the Maritime Trust for preservation and restoration in 1979.

10 George Cadogan, 3rd Earl Cadogan, by Camille Silvy, 1860.
Cadogan was about seventy-seven when this photograph was taken,
the last of his generation of the *Indefatigable*'s young officers, and,
as far as is known, the only one of whom a photograph exists.

and the committees on which he sat; however there are also a number of articles that reflect his interest in the arts. *The Morning Post* reported in 1833 that Cadogan presided over the annual dinner held in aid of the Covent Garden Theatrical Fund, which it described as a 'most useful charity' instituted for the purpose of supporting indigent and infirm actors and actresses and relieving their children.[24]

Cadogan remained a man who could be combative and utterly determined, a fact illustrated by the reporting of his opposition to the collection of pew rents in the parish church of Upper Chelsea, an area where he owned considerable property. His complaint was that the surplus funds were being reserved for the personal use of the rector, rather than for the building of a new rectory, and he petitioned the House of Lords to establish a select committee to investigate. The Bishop of London denied any wrongdoing and accused Cadogan of having personal interest in the case, which, as the press reported, 'his Lordship indignantly denied'.[25] This picture of Cadogan, never shrinking from controversy, yet staunch in his defence of his integrity, is entirely consistent with the young captain who had defended his reputation at courts martial in Port Royal and Portsmouth. Cadogan is also the only one of the Indefatigables of whom two photographs are known to exist.[26] Both were taken towards the end of his life and show a physically slight man; perhaps Pellew, who was tall by any standards, had not merely been using a figure of speech all those years before when he referred to 'little Cadogan's' bravery on the night of the *Droits de L'Homme* engagement. Despite Cadogan's small stature, both photographs clearly show a man with a commanding presence and air of determination.

Thomas Groube and Nicholas Pateshall also continued to merit fairly frequent mention in the press, though in both cases it was regional newspapers that carried reports of their involvement in local, civic and church politics. Pateshall made a rare foray into London and the world of royal social circles in 1840 when, as Mayor of Hereford, he presented a

[24] *The Morning Post*, March 1833.

[25] *Dublin Evening Post*, 29 April 1845.

[26] National Portrait Gallery, Ax5079, George Cadogan, 3rd Earl Cadogan, by Camille Silvy; and Paul Frecker, London, cs818, Admiral Lord Cadogan by Camille Silvy. Another curious photograph also exists in the Paul Frecker collection labelled 'Lord Cadogan's Cat', cs817. The photograph shows an elderly woman in outdoor dress standing behind a tapestry chair on which sits an immaculately groomed long-haired black cat. If this is indeed George Cadogan's cat, it is possible that the woman is his wife's 'confidential female domestic', Hannah Hill, to whom the earl left a significant bequest on his death in 1864. Pearman, p. 184. The fact that Cadogan went to the trouble and expense of having his cat photographed, and also that he chose to be painted with his dog Fen earlier in 1830, suggests that he was something of an animal lover.

loyal address on behalf of the city to Prince Albert, the prince consort, and the Duke of Kent. As was his wont, Pateshall wrote a letter to his brother Edmund following the event, which is both amusing and informative. Pateshall tells his brother that he left Hereford at 6.30 in the morning hoping to arrive in time to catch the 1.30 p.m. train in Birmingham. Having narrowly missed that train, he caught a later one, which meant he did not reach his brother Tom's house in Soho Square until midnight. Pateshall appeared to enjoy being a tourist in London and wrote of going to see the skaters on the Serpentine, but he had a somewhat jaundiced view of royal society and complained of the delay in the levee taking place and the regalia he was required to wear: 'I accompany Mr Clive at 3pm to Buckingham Palace, in full uniform and scarlet gown over (how ridiculous) to present the address to Prince Albert.'[27]

Long before, in 1817, as a new post captain, Pateshall had sat for his portrait, resplendent in magnificent uniform with an epaulette he was not quite entitled to wear; however it appears that in his later years he had little patience with pomp and ceremony. Pateshall returned to Hereford, to his local civic duties and charitable activities, interspersed with a little fishing on the Wye, apparently content with a quiet provincial life that was in marked contrast to his dramatic early years in the service of the Royal Navy. Throughout his later years, the local Hereford press continued to carry small news items about Pateshall's civic activities, the reports invariably emphasising his faithful service and the affection and high regard in which he was held by the community.

In Devon, Thomas Groube also continued to make local headlines, though of a very different kind, depending on the political stance of the newspapers in question.[28] He and his fellow radicals were vilified and lauded in turn by rival papers, though, by the time of his death, he was widely remembered as a good man who had lived a life of public service. Groube and his wife Anna Maria raised a large family and, latterly, when his name appeared in the press it was in the context of reports about the activities of his children, their marriages, and their service overseas. As recently as 1932 an article appeared in the Devon newspaper *The Western Times* entitled 'Link with Wooden Walls, Death of a Grand Old Man of Honiton' which reported on the death and funeral of Commander Francis Edmund Groube RN who had retired to Honiton after a distinguished naval career that spanned over thirty years.[29] Commander Francis Groube was one of Thomas Groube's many grandsons and the article reflects on the influence and legacy of the Groube family in Honiton.

The remaining Indefatigables who lived on through the peace made

---

[27] Pateshall Papers, A95/5b/40/7, Nicholas Pateshall to Edmund Pateshall, 28 February 1840.

[28] As discussed in Chapter 6.

[29] *The Western Times*, 17 June 1932.

headlines less frequently than their former shipmates but they still left their mark on the communities where they lived. John McKerlie's name appears most frequently in Lloyd's Register, reflecting his success as the builder, owner and master of several merchant vessels, operating from the busy Galloway port of Garlieston in the 1820s. These included the *Garlies*, a 6-gun, 53-ton smack, operating between Waterford, Liverpool and Garlieston, a route McKerlie had previously surveyed with Thomas Telford.[30] Despite the loss of his right arm during the *Droits de L'Homme* engagement, McKerlie remained a keen shot all his life and occasional reports appear of him attending shooting parties with other prominent local dignitaries. John McKerlie also made one posthumous appearance in the press almost seventy years after his death, courtesy of his only daughter, Lilias Miller Johnstone, who lived on into the twentieth century and wrote to *The Spectator* in 1914, speculating that she was one of the few surviving children of a father who had served in October 1805. True to form, although Lilias's letter mentions her father's presence at Trafalgar, she also notes that he served with Pellew on the night of the *Droits de L'Homme* engagement.

> Sir, I see in the Spectator of February 28th some remarks about descendants of officers who served at Trafalgar. I think I am one of the very few that can say their fathers were among that number. I am the only child of Rear Admiral John McKerlie who died on September 12th 1848. He was Midshipman under Sir Edward Pellew, afterwards Lord Exmouth, and lost his right arm onboard the Indefatigable when she and the Amazon accomplished the destruction of the Droits de L'Homme. After that he became First Lieutenant of the Spartiate under Captain Sir Francis Laforzy; and with him went with Lord Nelson to the West Indies in pursuit of the combined fleet of France and Spain. On return he served, still as First Lieutenant, on board the Spartiate, at the battle of Trafalgar. There is a short account of my Father's services in O'Byrne's Naval Biography, p701.
>
> I am sir &c,
> Mrs Lillias Miller Johnstone, 2 Marchhall Road Edinburgh.[31]

Alex McVicar's appearances in the press relate primarily to his involvement with the fishing and maritime industries of his home port of Leith, where he settled after retiring from active service. In due course, marriage and birth notices for various of his children and grandchildren also start to appear in local newspapers. Like John McKerlie, Alex McVicar was also remembered long after his death on account of his service at

---

[30] *Lloyd's Register of Shipping*, 1823, p. 113. It also seems likely that McKerlie had a hand in naming the Garlieston brig *Lord Exmouth*, owned and captained by one J. Kerr.

[31] *The Spectator*, vol. 12, 1914, p. 645.

Trafalgar. In 1935 a book which includes a section on one of McVicar's grandchildren, who had become a missionary in China, describes him simply as 'Captain McVicar of Trafalgar fame'.[32]

John Thomson is more difficult to track through the press as his name is so common and his surname frequently misspelled with the addition of a 'p'. However he can be identified in press reports relating to social and maritime activities centred around the port of Leith, where his name often appears alongside his former *Indefatigable* shipmate Alex McVicar.

The two warrant officers from the *Indefatigable* cohort did not attract so many references in the press; even at a time when the local and regional newspapers were increasing in number, the interests of the press remained socially stratified. Consequently, George Chace's long naval career and later civilian life went entirely unreported. John Gaze fared somewhat better, primarily as a result of his lengthy association with Pellew, his rise to the top of the career ladder, and his position as Master Attendant of Sheerness Dockyard. The publication of Osler's 1835 biography of Pellew also brought Gaze's name to wider public attention. Many newspapers carried favourable reviews and extracts of the biography, a number of which mentioned Gaze, and in particular his role at Algiers, quoting Pellew's own tribute to him as being 'steady as a rock'.[33]

John Harry, the last remaining of these Indefatigables who survived beyond the end of the war in 1815, appeared in the press only at the time of his death. Following his successful and highly honoured medical career, Harry had retired to his home in Paignton, Devon where he died in 1852. His death warranted only a small announcement in *The Exeter and Plymouth Gazette*, and *The Western Times* did not even get his name right, referring to him as Dr Harris.[34] A few reports did elaborate on Dr Harry's illustrious career however.

> March 8, in the 71st year of his age, John Harry, Esq, MD, who was formerly private physician to her Imperial Highness the Grand Duchess of Oldenburgh and afterwards private physician to her sister, her Majesty, the present Queen Mother of the Netherlands.[35]

The paucity of reports on John Harry's successful medical practice is likely to have resulted from the fact that he spent almost his entire career overseas; in Britain he was remembered primarily for being a local magistrate in his later years. In addition, whereas elderly retired captains

[32] Gammie, p. 21.

[33] Two of the many newspapers that published reviews of Edward Osler's *Life of Admiral Viscount Exmouth* were the *Dublin Observer*, 19 September 1835, and the *Exeter and Plymouth Gazette*, 12 September 1835.

[34] *Exeter and Plymouth Gazette*, 20 March 1852; *Western Times*, 20 March 1852.

[35] *Dublin Evening Packet and Correspondent*, 24 March 1852.

and admirals could be encouraged to recount their heroic exploits for readers' edification and entertainment, a physician, and a court physician at that, would be restrained by professional standards from revealing anything at all.

Five Indefatigables died in service during the course of the war: Bray, Frowd, Reynolds, Warden and Delves Broughton; and although all their deaths were noted in the press, the nature of the reports differed markedly. While several journals carried reports of Robert Carthew Reynolds's heroic engagement with the French brig *Curieux* and the affecting account of his burial on Diamond Rock,[36] Richard Delves Broughton warranted only a single formal death notice: 'Lately, at Poonamalee, near Madras, in the East Indies, Richard Delves Broughton, eighth son of the Revd Sir Thomas Broughton, Bart, of Doddington Hall, Cheshire.'[37] Although Delves Broughton was still a member of the Regiment of Light Dragoons at the time of his death, there is no mention of either his military or naval service. Given the desperation with which his father had once begged St Vincent to prevent the young man's court martial, in order to minimise damage to the family reputation, such a brief death notice, though poignant, is not unexpected.

As all five died young, before they had an opportunity to leave their mark on the service, it might be expected that their names would fade into obscurity, appearing only in the pages of some of the more comprehensive naval histories and biographies. This may be true of Frowd, Reynolds, Warden and Delves Broughton; however the curious exception is James Bray. As the *Plumper* was carrying a valuable cargo of specie when she foundered, there has been considerable interest in the wreck site and in the circumstances of her loss. There was a flurry of activity in the autumn and winter of 1849 when news was reported of divers recovering items including 'a number of silver dollars covered in grey mould, grape shot and bullets, the scabbards of side arms, leathern sheaths and many other articles'.[38] Further attempts have been made to recover treasure from the *Plumper* in the intervening years, resulting in the Canadian government designating the wreck site a Protected Historic Place in 1975.[39] More recently, a number of articles and blogs have speculated wildly about the circumstances of the

---

[36] *The Naval Chronicle*, vol. 12, 1804, p. 423; *The Universal Magazine of Knowledge and Pleasure*, vol. 3, 1805, p. 179; *The Gentleman's Magazine and Historical Review*, vol. 74, part 1, p. 461.

[37] *Manchester Mercury*, 27 October 1807.

[38] *Dundee, Perth and Cupar Advertiser*, 19 October 1849, quoting a syndicated report from *The Times*.

[39] Canada's Historic Places, HMS *Plumper* Shipwreck, Musquash, New Brunswick, E5J, Canada, www.historicplaces.ca/en/rep-reg/place-lieu. aspx?id=7796&pid=0.

wreck, with confusion over whether Bray survived adding fuel to outlandish conspiracy theories.[40]

The increasing number of local and national digitisation initiatives, together with the presence of online archival indexes and resource discovery services, such as the National Archives' Discovery,[41] have significantly expanded the range of resources available to scholars and historians researching both naval and civilian lives during the long eighteenth century. Thus Admiralty and civic records can be supplemented with contemporary press reports, books and journals, and augmented by archives of personal correspondence, to build up a more detailed picture of the maritime careers and later civilian lives of naval officers, while placing them in their wider social context. However a project such as this one, which set out to uncover the lives of the young gentlemen of HMS *Indefatigable*, highlights just how much remains to be discovered. Indexes and finding aids are often incomplete and catalogues may be compiled by archivists with little expertise in naval history, resulting in potentially significant references being missed as other names or topics are highlighted instead. Despite the partial and incomplete nature of the historic record, it has still been possible to identify a wealth of resources relating to this small group of naval officers. The resources that have survived range from the highly systematic, such as the Lieutenants' examination records held at the National Archives,[42] to the completely random, such as a letter found in the online catalogue of an auction room.[43] Although it has been possible to discover a great deal about the lives of the *Indefatigable*'s young gentlemen, inevitably one becomes aware of how much more might come to light as digitisation initiatives continue, and conversely, how much has been lost, including all of George Cadogan's personal archive, some of Jeremiah Coghlan's correspondence, and all the many letters that Edward Pellew sent to his wife Susan.[44]

The evidence that has survived, however, reveals a network of young men whom Pellew was quite right to describe in his protest to Lord Spencer as 'boys grown to manhood' under him.[45] While some of this cohort

---

[40] Richard Geldhof's Blog, Search for Secrets of a Sunken Cannon, http:// richardgeldhof.blogspot.co.uk/2010/05/search-for-secrets-of-sunken-cannon-85.html.

[41] Discovery, The National Archives, http://discovery.nationalarchives.gov.uk/

[42] The National Archives, Records of the Admiralty, Naval Forces, Royal Marines, Coastguard, and related bodies, series ADM7 and ADM106.

[43] Frowd to Taylor, 30 December 1799. Manuscript letter sold by Mullock's Specialist Sporting Auctioneers, www.invaluable.com/auction-lot/ maritime-naval-french-revolution-rare-naval-1-c-t4nu4aarmg.

[44] Taylor, p. 169.

[45] Exmouth Papers, Box 22, MSS/92/027, Pellew to Spencer, no date.

were already experienced seamen when they first came aboard Pellew's frigates, the majority were indeed just boys. However all were to find that their captain would inspire and encourage them in equal measure; his expectations of the service and exacting standards of seamanship were to stand them in good stead. Pellew's reference in the same letter to the loss of 'faithful and attached companions' is likely to have referred broadly to all the officers and men who had served with him between 1793 and 1799 and who had experienced so much together. As a lasting memorial to the 1797 cohort of young officers, it is particularly apt though, as they did indeed grow into companions in arms and friends, both in times of adversity and success. There is no doubt that they were proud of their days aboard the *Indefatigable* and showed loyalty and affection towards the ship, the officers and particularly the captain, through whom they found inspiration, purpose, discipline and a considerable degree of adventure.

These then are the real men who would have been the historical shipmates of the *Indefatigable*'s most famous fictional alumnus, Horatio Hornblower. C. S. Forester first brought Hornblower to life in 1937 as a fully-fledged frigate captain and the quintessential 'Man Alone';[46] it wasn't until 1950 that he went back in time and placed his anxious and awkward midshipman under Pellew's care to oversee the start of his illustrious naval career. Forester was unapologetic for the way he absorbed and manipulated historical details and persons in order to inspire his novels and meet the demands of plot and pacing, commenting 'the student is faced with a choice between history and Hornblower'.[47] But perhaps in studying the lives of these men the choice has become less sharp, the distinction less clear, and history and Hornblower grow closer together.

Forester was well read in the history of the French Revolutionary and Napoleonic Wars, and he chose wisely in placing Hornblower aboard the *Indefatigable* under Pellew's command. However, despite the diligence of his research, beyond Pellew himself, Forester is unlikely to have known anything of the historical counterparts of the fictional characters he created. Yet researching the lives of the historical midshipmen of HMS *Indefatigable* reveals striking parallels with the fictional Hornblower. Like James Bray and John Harry, Hornblower was the son of a doctor; like Nicholas Pateshall, his naval career got off to an unpromising start when he was placed aboard a stagnant ship with a sick captain; like George Cadogan he became embroiled in a scandalous relationship with the Wellesley family; like 'Intrepid Jerry' Coghlan he became feted as the bold hero of ingenious actions and, like him also, he experienced an unhappy marriage; and like all these young men, he was nurtured and encouraged by Edward Pellew.

There have been many attempts to identify the one historical figure

---

[46] Forester, *The Hornblower Companion*, p. 82.
[47] *Ibid.*, p. 64.

who can lay claim to the title of 'The Real Hornblower', to borrow
the title of Bryan Perrett's biography of Sir James Gordon;[48] however
there is in a sense something of Hornblower in all of his historical
contemporaries and, perhaps even more so, something of all of them
in Hornblower. It is the mark of Forester's talent as an author that he
was able to absorb information from a wide range of sources and weave it
together to create such a complex, captivating and believable character
as Horatio Hornblower. As Perrett noted: 'Horatio Hornblower, was not
the swashbuckling sea-dog familiar to earlier generations of readers. On
the contrary, he was a recognisable naval officer with human strengths,
weaknesses, feelings, fears and hopes.'[49]

The time that these young men served together aboard HMS
Indefatigable was a short but significant period of their naval careers. With
the exception of Nicholas Pateshall's remarkable archive and endearing
caricature, we have little day-to-day record of their personal lives and
how they dealt with the realities of living together for long periods in
such close confines. Later in life the Indefatigables clearly had diverse
political and religious views and it is tempting to wonder if these caused
argument and debate around their mess table. Clearly there must have
been disagreements, and certainly for some there were demotions and
promotions that must have temporarily caused jealousy or *Schadenfreude*,
as would be expected of any group of young friends growing up together.

The fact that this particular group of young men had served together
aboard such a fine frigate under a commander whose whole nature and
training made him ideally suited for the requirements of naval warfare at
this time only helped to strengthen the bond between them. In common
with many other young naval officers before and since, they depended
on one another for their very lives while participating in notable
actions, engagements and humanitarian missions, and the skills honed
and emotions matured in those encounters shaped and rounded their
self-identity.

Although these young men have emerged from the examination of the
official archives and private correspondence with their human strengths
and weaknesses laid bare, the majority served their country and community
well and faithfully and their legacy stands the test of time. Central to their
story, in the midst of their hopes, fears and feelings, stands the figure
of Edward Pellew, trusted commander, admired mentor and lifelong
friend, who, together with Susan, drew these young gentlemen into an
extended family in its best and widest sense. The lives of Edward Pellew
and the young gentlemen of HMS *Indefatigable* are testimony to courage,
camaraderie, personal growth and perseverance but above all they are a
testimony to enduring friendship.

[48] Perrett.

[49] Perrett, p. 9.

APPENDIX

The Spencer–Pellew
Correspondence of February 1799

THE remarkable exchange of letters[1] between Sir Edward Pellew and Lord Spencer, First Lord of the Admiralty, relating to Pellew's appointment to the *Impetueux*, has been published in whole and part in many places. It is reproduced in its entirety here as it stands as an eloquent testimony to Pellew's devotion to HMS *Indefatigable* and her crew, the 'faithful, and attached Companions, grown from boys to manhood under him'.

Spencer to Pellew, 15 February 1799

Admt'y 15 Feb: 1799

Sir Ed Pellew Bart.

Dear Sir

The extensive Promotion of Flag Officers which His Majesty has been pleased to authorize me to make brings you so high on the Captains List, that it is no longer consistent with the ordinary Practice of the Service that you should continue to serve in a Frigate: I have therefore given you an Appointment to the Impetueux as being the most active and desirable Line of Battle Ship which the Arrangement on this occasion enabled me to select for you, and I have no doubt but that you will in this new Line of Service continue to gain as much Credit as you have already, by the Acknowledgement of every one who knows you, obtained.

Believe me Dear Sir
your very faithful
humble Servant
Spencer

Pellew to Spencer, no date

My Lord,

I know not how to express my surprize on the receipt of your lordships' very unexpected letter; and had I conceived the intended arrangement of Promotion could have affected my situation in the command of the Indefatigable I should have most earnestly entreated your forebearance,

---

[1] Exmouth Papers, Box 22, MSS/92/027.

215

and shall now feel myself highly gratified if your lordship will permit me to continue in my present situation, amidst officers, and men who have served under thro' the war and who look up to me for protection

I cannot at the same time that I express my wishes, but feel very sensible of your Lordship's attention to me in the selection you have been pleased to make and if my request should not meet your approbation I indulge myself with the expectation of being permitted to remove with me such officers and young gentlemen as I shall point out and I confide in your lordships goodness for throwing me as much into active service as possible.

I have the honour to be my Lord, your lordships most humble and obedient servant, EP.

Spencer to Pellew, 21 February 1799

21 February 1799

Dear Sir

The arrangement by which you are promoted to a ship of the Line is one which considering your situation on the Captain's list cannot but appear very natural and though at first sight it may not present to you as flattering a prospect of service as remaining in the Indefatigable might have done. I think you will not upon consideration look upon it in the light of being laid up on the shelf.

With respect to Officers (I mean Lieutenants) they may be probably some opportunities by degrees of removing some of them who have served with you into the Impetueux though I do not know that there are any vacancies in that ship at present and if you will send in a list of the young gentlemen (bona fides incl) that may fairly be considered your followers I do not think that there will be any objection to their removing with you.

Believe me my dear Sir, your very faithful and humble servant,
Spencer

Pellew to Spencer, 24 February 1799

My Lord

I am too much flattered by the trouble your lordship has taken to reconcile me to parting from my dear Indefatigable not to entreat your acceptance of my best thanks for the kind expressions you are pleased to make use of upon it

And near as it goes to my heart to separate myself from people who certainly for attachment have not been exceeded, yet I will exert myself to be reconciled and use my influence to render the Ship's company so, to their new commander and I place implicit confidence on your Lordship for disposing of me to the best advantage

My thanks are no less due to your lordship for your accommodation respecting my officers when opportunity offers and I enclose a list of Young Gentlemen and some few men who from neighbourhood and long service with me I am very earnest to take and I flatter myself your Lordship will not think me unreasonable in asking this number <u>over and above</u> the usual proportion established by the board, I am my Lord with great consideration and respectful esteem,

Your lordships most obliged and most Obedient humble servant,
Ed Pellew

Plymouth February 24th 1799.

Spencer to Pellew, 26 February 1799

26 February 1799

Dear Sir

The Custom adopted for some time past by the board respecting removals from one ship to the other does not admit of any proportion of men being removed unless in the case of the two ships happen to be together at the same port, therefore the persons for whom you apply (even suppose it should be possible to allow them all to be removed with you) will be the only ones which you can have. I am however rather in doubt that it will be possible to permit so many Petty officers to be at once taken from a ship in commission and in condition for immediate service without risking considerable inconvenience and especially as it is probable that Capt Curzon's followers, if he had any, may have been dispensed with since the loss of the Pallas and his quarter deck may be by that means left wholly destitute which would not be proper. I would however recommend it to you to arrange that matter with Captain Curzon when he joins the Indefatigable and when your two ships meet you may on an exchange of a few men of respectively equal qualities in that its being made the object of an official Application

In the meanwhile with respect to the person you now apply to have removed I will endeavour to procure an Order for the removal of most of them as can be moved consistent with what has been granted to other Officers in a similar situation before.

Believe me dear sir to be your very faithful and humble servant
Spencer.

Pellew to Spencer, 26 February 1799

Adm 26 February 1799

My Lord

On the 10th of Jan'ry 1793 Sir Ed. Pellew commissioned La Nymphe at Portsmouth, and equipped her by 70 Vol's raised by his family in Cornwall, and brought to Port'th at his own expense; when the Ship was ready, he carried her by permission to Falm'th, where he entirely completed her Complement by the same Means, and without any aid from Government whatever. He was permitted from Circumstances, afterwards to carry his Ship's Company into the Arethusa and Indefatigable, but after serving with them for six years and upwards, he is on the 20th of February 1799, taken from his Command, against his inclination, and in a manner, he must say, very Contrary to the former custom of the Service, and without the smallest accommodation, placed in a 74 at Portsmouth, when five Ships of the same Class have been disposed of at the very Port where his ship then lay; he hopes he may be pardoned for having considered, these twenty years past, all 74's to be alike, and when the Article, which still stands a part of the Naval instructions, was laid aside, and a new arrangement made by your Lordships Board, respecting the number of Persons a Captain might be allowed to remove from his Ship according to her Rate; he little apprehended he alone would be excluded from its effect. He therefore does himself the honour to enclose Your Lordship a few precedents appropriate to his case, wherein Commanders have been permitted to carry their Quota of men from one Port to another ...

Had the Boatswain of the Indefatigable been appointed to a Ship at Portsmouth, his servant by rule of Service, would be discharged with his Master by pay Ticket. Sir E.P. – his Commander – is deprived of a desirable and advantageous appointment, after constant employment without relaxation for six years; and sent to a Ship at Portsmouth, amidst INTIRE STRANGERS and without being permitted to take ONE Officer, ONE Man, or even ONE Domestic. It is fair then to presume Sir E.P. has no sensibility, no attachment, no feeling, that his heart must be adamant, that he can part from faithful, and attached Companions, grown from boys to manhood under him, without a sorrowful Countenance, or a Moistened Eye. He grants it may be thought so. But he begs to assert the Contrary. And he dares to say, to those who think thus of him, that language does not furnish words sufficiently strong to express his feelings upon such unmerited hard treatment; nor can time, however soothing on most other occasions, blot from his remembrance, Circumstances so debasing to the reputation of an Officer; to your Lordship he leaves the regret of having occasioned them.

And is with due Respect
Your Lordships
Most Obt Servant
Ed. Pellew

Bibliography

PRIMARY SOURCES

Archives Pyrénées Atlantiques: Fonds Jacques Bergeret
B153 J1, Pellew to Bergeret, 1 January 1809
B154 J1, Bergeret to Pellew, 12 July 1831

British Library:
Aberdeen Papers

MS 43214: 1826–1828, Aberdeen Papers, vol. 176, Coghlan to Gordon, 8
    February 1828, Forte, Rio de Janeiro
MS 43214: 1826–1828, Aberdeen Papers, vol. 176, Coghlan to Gordon, 12
    February 1828, Forte, Rio de Janeiro
MS 43214: 1826–1828, Aberdeen Papers, vol. 176, Coghlan to Gordon, 25
    February 1828, Forte, Rio de Janeiro
MS 43214: 1826–1828, Aberdeen Papers, vol. 176, Otway to Gordon, 1 April
    1828, Ganges, Rio de Janeiro

British Library:
India Office Records and Private Papers

BL-BIND-005137383-00394, Burial Register, Fort St George, Madras, 8
    November 1806
BL-BIND-L-AG-34-29-207-0040, Probate Records, 1807
BL-BIND-L-AG-34-29-211-00136, Probate Records, 1807
IOR/F/4/264/5853, Complaint of Captain De Jean Hilaire of the French
    privateer Les Deux Sœurs regarding the conduct of Captain William
    Warden of HMS Rattlesnake, February–July 1807
L-AG-34-27-388, folio 7, British India Office Records of Inventories and
    Accounts of Deceased Estates

British Library
Peel Papers

MS 40 573, Peel Papers, vol. 393, Hart, H. to Peel, R., 12 September 1845,
    ff. 372–4
MS 38049, Peel Papers, vol. 11, William R. O'Byrne's working notes,
    Pateshall, N., biographical notes, ff. 339–43

Devon Archive and Heritage Centre:
Pellew of Canonteign Collection

7818M, Spencer to Pellew, 9 August 1800

7818M, Spencer to Pellew, 22 May 1804

7818M, Warren to Exmouth, 2 June 1812

7818M, Exmouth to Melville, 24 August 1814

7818M, Edward Pellew to George Pellew, 18 July 1824

7818M, Pellew to Sidmouth, 2 October 1827

7818M, Coghlan to Fleetwood Pellew, 26 January 1833

7818M, Coghlan to George Pellew, 29 July 1836

7818M, Coghlan to George Pellew, 24 August 1836

7818M/E/2/1/3/1, Right Honorable Lord Viscount Exmouth in Account
    with Toulmin & Copeland

7818M/E/2/1/3/2, Right Honorable Lord Viscount Exmouth in Account
    with Toulmin & Copeland

7818M/F/1/5-6, 9-10, Pellew to Broughton, 22 July 1807

7818M/F/1/5-6, 9-10, Susan Pellew to Edward Pellew, 13 March 1814

7818M/F/3/1/9, Exmouth to George Pellew, September 1828

7818M/SS/1, Minute of Admiral Lord Exmouth for Lord Melville's favour,
    'about 24/8/1815'

Herefordshire Archive
Records of the Pateshall Family of Allensmore

A95/5b/40/7, Nicholas Pateshall to Edmund Pateshall, 28 February 1840

A95/AP/7 (1), Nicholas Pateshall to Ann Pateshall, 17 January 1797

A95/AP/17, John Calvert Clark to Ann Pateshall, 16 April 1799

A95/AP/37/7 Nicholas Pateshall to Ann Pateshall, 17 January 1796

A95/EB/40/1, Nicholas Pateshall to Edmund Pateshall, 20 March 1795

A95/EB/41/1, Nicholas Pateshall to Edmund Pateshall, 25 November 1794

A95/EB/42/1 Nicholas Pateshall to Edmund Pateshall, 25 November 1794

A95/EB/42/1 (1), Nicholas Pateshall to Edmund Pateshall, August 1809

A95/EP/40/1, Nicholas Pateshall to Edmund Pateshall, 20 January 1797

A95/EP/40/1, Nicholas Pateshall to Ann Pateshall, 20 March 1797

A95/EP/41/2, Nicholas Pateshall to Edmund Pateshall, 13 March 1803

A95/N/23, Robert Price to Nicholas Pateshall, 31 December 1833

A95/V/EP/5, Nicholas Pateshall to Edmund Pateshall, 18 January 1805

A95/V/DB/6, Nicholas Pateshall to Ann Pateshall, August 1805

A95/V/N/170, Pellew to Pateshall, 25 November 1809

A95/V/N/174, Coghlan to Pateshall, undated

A95/V/N/175, Coghlan to Pateshall, 17 December 1810

A95/V/N/178, Pellew to Nicholas Pateshall, November 1809

A95/V/N/186, Edward Maxey to Pateshall, 6 September 1841

A95/V/N/186, Pateshall to Maxey, 9 September 1841

A95/V/N/223, William Kempthorne to Nicholas Pateshall, 23 October 1816

A95/V/N/287, Freedom of the City of Hereford
A95/V/W/A/2, Nicholas Pateshall to William Pateshall, 26 February 1803
BD 20/9/46, Nicholas Pateshall to Ann Pateshall, 5 December 1795
BD 30/9/1-50, Charles Henry Lane to Ann Pateshall, 2 January 1795
BD 30/9/1-50, Captain Evans, Ann Pateshall and John Davis, February–
    April 1795
BD 30/9/1-50, Nicholas Pateshall to Ann Pateshall, 5 October 1795
BD 30/9/1-50, Nicholas Pateshall to Ann Pateshall, 17 January 1797
BD 30/9/25, Ann Pateshall to Henry Lane, 27 October 1794
BD 30/9/45, Nicholas Pateshall to Ann Pateshall, 12 October 1795
BD 30/9/48, Ann Pateshall to Nicholas Pateshall, 2 March 1799
No reference, Nicholas Pateshall to Edmund Pateshall, 14 September 1801

House of Commons Sessional Papers of the Eighteenth Century

Land Revenue, Prisoners of War, Fisheries, 1797–98, *Report on Treatment
    of Prisoners of War*, pp. 105–6
Reports and Papers 1796–97, Papers relative to the late Expedition of the
    Enemy to the Coast of Ireland

*The Huntington Library:
Francis Beaufort Papers*

FB 1498, Pellew to Beaufort, 25 February 1808
FB 1499, Pellew to Beaufort, 16 November 1809

*The Huntington Library
Grenville Papers*

ST6 Correspondence Box 137(29), George Cadogan to Earl Cadogan, 13
    October 1806
ST6 Correspondence Box 137(28), Earl Cadogan to Spencer, 27 November
    1806
ST6 Correspondence Box 163(73), Spencer to Grenville, 29 November 1806

LDS Family Search

LDS 103101-6, Record of Baptism, St Gluvias, Flushing, Cornwall, 25
    July 1781, William, son of William Kempthorne and Elizabeth, née
    Goodridge
LDS 104589-9, Record of Baptism, St Clement, Cornwall, 30 December
    1782, Robert Carthew, son of Robert Carthew Reynolds and Jennifer
    (Jane), née Vivian
LDS C00024-4, record of baptism, St Nicholas Parish Church, Jennet
    Ogilvie McVicar, born 18 August 1807, baptised 26 August 1807

LDS C01336-7, record of baptism, All Saints, Eccleshall, 28 March 1784, Richard Delves, son of Thomas Broughton and Mary, née Wicker

LDS C05849-1, Record of baptism, St Mary of the Assumption, Market Lavington, Wiltshire, 30 May 1779, Philip, son of William Frowd and Elizabeth

LDS C13105-1, Record of Baptism, St Andrew's, Allensmore, Hereford, 14 October 1781, Nicholas Lechmere, son of Edmund Pateshall and Ann, née Burnham

LDS C13540-3, Record of Baptism, St James, Westminster, 17 May 1784, George, son of Charles Sloane Cadogan, 1st Earl Cadogan, and Mary, née Churchill

LDS C15321-1, Record of baptism, St Michael, Brixton Deverill, 20 August 1779, Philip, son of William Frowd and Elizabeth

LDS C88000-1, Record of Baptism, the British Factory Chaplaincy, Lisbon, Portugal, 2 March 1782, William son of George Warden and Elizabeth, née Barclay

LDS FHL 1526819, item 18, Hickling Parish Registers, John, son of John and Margaret [Fisher], baptised 14 December and John, son of John and Mary [Chase], baptised 10 September 1780

LDS P00172-1, Record of baptism, King Charles the Martyr, Falmouth, 11 January 1775, Thomas, son of Samuel Groube and Catherine, née Boulderson

LDS P00275-1, Records of baptism, St Petroc, Bodmin, Cornwall, 19 December 1781, John, son of John Harry and Elizabeth, née Deacon

LDS P00963-1, Parish registers of St Gluvias and Mylor, Cornwall, baptisms of Emma Pellew, Belinda Kempthorne, Fleetwood Pellew, Mary Anna Kempthorne, Julia Pellew, Renatus Kempthorne, George Pellew and Harriet Kempthorne

Miscellaneous Collections

Edinburgh Sheriff Court Inventories, SC 70/1/59

Gorleston Parish Church, Parish Registers, 14 October 1807

John Harry Papers, Queen's University, Ontario, series 1, numbers 1–6

Parish Church of Charles the Martyr, Plymouth, Marriage Register entry no. 43, John Roach and Elizabeth Colepack, 5 October 1837

Parish Church of Charles the Martyr, Plymouth, Marriage Register entry no. 253, George Chace and Elizabeth Roach, 14 February 1839

Parish of Stoke Damerel, Register of Deaths entry no. 393, Death of George Chace, gunner in HM Navy aged 65, 10 December 1840

Parish of Stoke Damerel, Burial Register, 16 December 1840

Post Office Appointment Books, 1759, 1761, 1764

Staffordshire County Council Digitised Parish Records

St Michael and All Angels, Alphington, Burial Register, 1481A/PR/1/26, 13 April 1835

The National Archives:
Records of the Admiralty, Naval Forces, Royal Marines, Coastguard, and Related Bodies

ADM 1/108/767, Commander in Chief in the Channel Documents, 29 December 1798

ADM 1/176, Pellew to Marsden, January 1805

ADM 1/176, Pellew to Melville, January 1805

ADM 1/2151, McKerlie to Marsden, 6 and 11 March and 10 December 1806, Captains' Letters, Surname M

ADM 1/2314, Captains' Letters 1797, Surname P, nos. 1–150. Enclosed with document 145

ADM 1/2315, Captains' Letters 1797, Surname P

ADM 1/2322 and ADM 1/4799, Memorial from Mr W Kempthorne, late lieutenant HM Navy, sent with a covering commendation from Sir Edward Pellew

ADM 1/2341, Nicholas Pateshall and others to Admiralty, November and December 1811

ADM 1/2400, Captains' Letters, Surname R, letter 142, Reynolds to Nepean, 6 September 1797

ADM 1/2875, Lieutenants' Letters, Surname F, no. 126, Frowd to Admiralty, November 1801

ADM 1/2875, Lieutenants' Letters, Surname F, no. 127, Frowd to Admiralty, December 1801

ADM 1/2766, Lieutenants' Letters, Surname B 238

ADM 1/2766, Lieutenants' Letters, Surname B 239

ADM 1/2812, Lieutenant's Letters, Surname C, no. 133, Coghlan to Admiralty, 12 September 1802

ADM 1/2898, Lieutenants' Letters, Surname G, May and November 1805

ADM 1/2973, Lieutenants' Letters, Surname K, Number 12

ADM 1/3070, Lieutenants' Letters, Surname P

ADM 1/3197, Lieutenants' Letters, Surname W, Warden to Admiralty, 7 March 1801

ADM 1/5336, Skene Court Martial, 1796

ADM 1/5341, Amazon Court Martial, 1797

ADM 1/5349, Impetueux Court Martial, 1799

ADM 1/5358, Records of Courts Martial, 1801

ADM 1/5365, Delves Broughton Courts Martial, 1804

ADM 1/5370, Cyane Court Martial, 1805

ADM 1/5373, Ferret Court Martial, 1806

ADM 1/5395, Cadogan Court Martial, 1809

ADM 1/5438, Colibri Court Martial, 1813

ADM 3/124, Minutes of the Admiralty Board, March 1800

ADM 3/125, Minutes of the Admiralty Board, June 1800

ADM 6/126, Pellew to Admiralty, 21 July 1809

ADM 6/127, George Chace, Gunner's Passing Certificate.

ADM 6/146, John Gaze, Records and Certificates of Masters, Ga-Go

ADM 6/192, Succession books of standing offices

ADM 6/352, Widows Pensions

ADM 9/3/819, Memorandum of the Services of Captain John Thomson

ADM 12/31, Digest, Order in Council reinstating Kempthorne to rank of lieutenant, 4 July 1804

ADM 12/86, Digest for 1800, William Warden promoted and appointed to Decade, 18 January 1800

ADM 12/117, Digest 79:31, Cadogan to Cochrane, 8 July 1805

ADM 29/3, Entry books of certificates of service: Gunners 1817–1839

ADM 35/245, Pay Book of His Majesty's Ship the Indefatigable

ADM 35/1177, Pay Book of His Majesty's Ship the Nymphe

ADM 35/1452, Pay Book of His Majesty's Sloop the Renard, 1800

ADM 35/2806, Pay Book of His Majesty's Sloop the Ferret, 1806–1810

ADM 36/11471, Muster Table of his Majesty's Ship the Arethusa, September 1793–February 1795

ADM 36/128127, Muster Table of His Majesty's Ship the Impetueux, 1799

ADM 36/13143, Muster Table of His Majesty's Ship the Indefatigable, January–October 1796

ADM 36/13144, Muster Table of His Majesty's Ship the Indefatigable, November 1796–October 1797

ADM 36/13145, Muster Table of His Majesty's Ship the Indefatigable, November 1797–August 1798

ADM 36/13146, Muster Table of His Majesty's Ship the Indefatigable, September 1798–April 1799

ADM 36/13161, Muster Table of his Majesty's Ship the Nymphe, 1793

ADM 36/13221, Muster Table of His Majesty's Ship the Phoebe

ADM 36/17385, Muster Table of His Majesty's Ship the Culloden, November 1804

ADM 37/1605–1606, Muster Table of His Majesty's Sloop the Ferret, 1805–1806

ADM 45/12/9, Will of George Chance and pension claim

ADM 51/1171, Captain's Log of His Majesty's Ship the Indefatigable

ADM 51/1197, Captain's Log of His Majesty's Ship the Phoebe

ADM 52/2757, Master's Log of His Majesty's Ship the Ferret, 1806

ADM 102/99, Muster Table of His Majesty's Ship the Bristol

ADM 106/1456, Broughton to St Vincent, Promiscuous Correspondence, Surname B, 1802–1804

ADM 107/21, A. McVicar, Lieutenant's Passing Certificate

ADM 107/23, R. C. Reynolds, Lieutenant's Passing Certificate

ADM 107/23, W. Warden, Lieutenant's Passing Certificate

ADM 107/23, P. Frowd, Lieutenant's Passing Certificate

ADM 107/24, J. McKerlie, Lieutenant's Passing Certificate

ADM 107/26, N. L. Pateshall, Lieutenant's Passing Certificate

ADM 107/27, Richard Delves Broughton, Lieutenant's Passing Certificates

ADM 171/2, Naval General Service Medal Rolls

ADM 171/8, Naval General Service Medal Rolls
ADM 359/47A/208, George Chace, Certificate of Service and Pension
  Record

The National Archives:
Records of the Prerogative Court of Canterbury

PROB 11/765, Will of William Warden Senior, probated 1750
PROB 11/1136, Will of Samuel Groube, Merchant of Falmouth, November
  1784
PROB 11/1468, Will of Richard Delves Broughton, 1805
PROB 11/1507, Will of William Warden
PROB 11/1850, Admon of the Estate of Captain William Kempthorne
PROB 11/2149, Will of John Harry, MD of Paignton
PROB 11/2201, Will of Nicholas Lechmere Pateshall
PROB 11/2910, Will of Jeremiah Coghlan

The National Archives:
Census Returns

HO 107/677/17, folio 8, England, Wales and Scotland Census, 1841
HO 107/1868, folio 196, England, Wales and Scotland Census, 1851,
  household of William Wright, schedule no. 144 for 15 Eaton Place, St
  Sidwell, Exeter

National Maritime Museum, Caird Library:
Manuscripts Catalogue

AGC/26/22, Exmouth to Furling, 25 September 1831

National Maritime Museum, Caird Library:
Letters and Papers of Admiral T. H. Michell

MIC/1, Exmouth to Michell, 30 August 1824

National Maritime Museum, Caird Library:
Papers of Lord Exmouth, Edward Pellew

MSS/92/027, Spencer to Pellew, 25 September 1797
MSS/92/027, Spencer to Pellew, 1 October 1798
MSS/92/027, Box 4, Bell to Pellew, 29 July 1812
MSS/92/027, Box 22, Pellew to Spencer, no date
MSS/92/027, Box 22, Spencer to Pellew, 1 October 1790
MSS/92/027, Box 22, Spencer to Pellew, 25 September 1795
MSS/92/027, Box 22, Spencer to Pellew, 28 September 1795

MSS/92/027, Box 22, Spencer to Pellew, 25 January 1797
MSS/92/027, Box 22, Spencer to Pellew, 18 September 1797
MSS/92/027, Box 22, Spencer to Pellew, 1 October 1797
MSS/92/027, Box 22, Bergeret to Pellew, 16 April 1798
MSS/92/027, Box 22, Pellew to Spencer, no date 1799
MSS/92/027, Box 22, Pellew to Broughton, 7 January 1799
MSS/92/027, Box 22, Spencer to Pellew, 17 January 1799
MSS/92/027, Box 22, Spencer to Pellew, 21 February 1799
MSS/92/027, Box 22, Pellew to Spencer, 24 February 1799
MSS/92/027, Box 22, Spencer to Pellew, 26 February 1799
MSS/92/027, Box 22, Pellew to Spencer, 28 February 1799
MSS/92/027, Box 22, Pellew to Broughton, 1 June 1808
MSS/92/027, Box 22, Susan Pellew to Pellew, 10 April 1814
MSS/92/027, Box 22, Coghlan to George Pellew, 1833
MSS/92/027, Box 22, Coghlan to Pellew, 22 August 1836
MSS/92/027, Box 22, Coghlan to George Pellew, 22 August 1836
MSS/92/027, Box 22, Lacrosse to Pellew, 10 Messidor in the 5th Year of the
    Republic
MSS/92/027, Box 23, Cadogan to Fleetwood Pellew, 25 January 1833
MSS/92/027, Box 23, Cadogan to Fleetwood Pellew, 12 April 1833
MSS/92/027, Box 28, Kempthorne to Fleetwood Pellew, January 1833
MSS/92/027, Box 28, Gaze to Fleetwood Pellew, 26 January 1833
MSS/92/027, Box 28, Alexander Lumsdale to Fleetwood Pellew, 27 January
    1833
MSS/92/027, Box 28, James Weymss to Fleetwood Pellew, 28 January 1833
MSS/92/027, Box 28, Bryan Sneyd Broughton to George Pellew, April 1833

Private Collections

Kempthorne to Roberts, 4 July 1829
Pellew to Keith, 7 October 1816
Pinhey, F., Comments on Edward Osler's *Life of Admiral Viscount Exmouth*

Scotland's People:
Old Parish Registers

OPR Birth 692/01 0030 0276, Leith North, Record of baptism, North Leith
    Parish Church, 6 September 1774, John son of John Thomson and Jean,
    née Redpath
OPR Birth 692/02 0060/0271, Record of Baptism, South Leith Parish
    Church, 1 November 1768, Alexander, son of William McVicar and
    Marjory 'May', née Berry
OPR Birth 894/00 0010 0104, Record of baptism, Glenluce Parish Church,
    Galloway, 12 August 1775, John McCarlie (sic) son of John and Agnes
    Wallace, Old Luce

Southampton Archive:
Smith Collection

D/CB/4/14/2, John Smyth to Rev. John Gee Smyth, 3 May 1803
D/CB/4/14/3, John Smyth to Rev. John Gee Smyth, 14 May 1803
D/CB/4/14/5, John Smyth to Rev. John Gee Smyth, 14 April 1803

SECONDARY SOURCES

Books, Journals and Periodicals

Alexander, L. M., *Women, Work, and Representation: Needlewomen in Victorian Art and Literature* (Ohio, 2003)

Armstrong, F. C., *The Naval Lieutenant: A Nautical Romance* (London, 1865)

The Asiatic Annual Register, vol. 9 (London, 1807)

Bailey, J., *Parenting in England 1760–1830: Emotion, Identity and Generation* (Oxford, 2012)

Bath Chronicle and Weekly Gazette, 26 October 1786 (Bath, 1786)

Beck, J., *A History of the Falmouth Post Office Packet Service 1689–1850* (Exeter, 2009)

Blackburn, S., *A Fair Day's Wage for a Fair Day's Work? Sweated Labour and the Origins of Minimum Wage Legislation in Britain* (Aldershot, 2007)

Blessington, M., *The Idler in France* (Paris, 1841)

Bourchier, J. B., *Memoir of the Life of Admiral Sir Edward Codrington: With Selections from His Public and Private Correspondence*, vol. 1 (London, 1873)

Bowen, T. R., *Mutiny* screenplay, 2001

Boyd, M., *Reminiscences of Fifty Years* (New York, 1871)

Brenton, E. P., *The naval history of Great Britain: from the year MDCCLXXXIII to MDCCCXXII* (London, 1825)

Brighton, J. G., and P. V. B. Broke, *Admiral Sir P. B. V. Broke: A Memoir* (London, 1866)

Brimnes, N., *Constructing the Colonial Encounter: Right and Left Hand Castes in Early Colonial South India* (London, 1999)

Bury and Norwich Post, and East Anglian, 20 March 1844

Byrn Jr, J. D., *Crime and Punishment in the Royal Navy, Discipline on the Leeward Island Station 1784–1812* (Aldershot, 1989)

Caledonian Mercury, 15 October 1825

Cavell, S. A., *Midshipmen and Quarterdeck Boys in the British Navy, 1771–1831* (Woodbridge, 2012)

Cobbett, W., *Cobbett's Weekly Political Register*, vol. 10 (London, 1806)

Collyer, J., *Reports of Cases Decided in the High Court of Chancery: By the Right Hon. Sir J. L. Knight Bruce, Vice-chancellor*, vol. 2 (London, 1853)

Corbett, J., *The Private Papers of George, 2nd Earl Spencer*, Volume I, Navy Records Society, vol. 46 (London, 1913)

Courtney, N., *Gale Force 10. The Life and Legacy of Admiral Beaufort* (London, 2002)

Crawford, A., *Reminiscences of a Naval Officer, During the Late War*, vol. 1 (London, 1851)

Derozario, M., *The Complete Monumental Register: Containing All the Epitaphs, Inscriptions, &c. &c. &c. in the Different Churches and Burial-grounds, in and about Calcutta* (Calcutta, 1815)

Devonshire Association for the Advancement of Science, Literature and Art, *Reports and Transactions*, vol. 19 (Plympton, 1887)

Dublin Evening Packet and Correspondent, 24 March 1852

Dublin Evening Post, 29 April 1845

Dublin Monitor, 16 November 1841

Dundee, Perth and Cupar Advertiser, 19 October 1849

The Elgin Courant and Morayshire Advertiser, 29 March 1844

The European Magazine: And London Review, vol. 34 (London, 1798)

The Examiner (London, 1813)

Exeter Flying Post, 31 January 1850

Exeter and Plymouth Gazette, 12 September 1835; 20 March 1852

Ferguson, P., 'Sir Henry Hart – some new perspectives', in *Hindsight*, vol. 5 (Uckfield & District Preservation Society, 1999)

Firth, C. H., *Naval Songs and Ballads*, Navy Records Society, vol. 33 (London, 1903)

Fitchett, W. H., *How England Saved Europe: The Story of the Great War (1793–1815), Volume I: From the Low Countries to Egypt* (London, 1901)

—— *How England Saved Europe: The Story of the Great War (1793–1815), Volume II: The Struggle for the Sea* (London, 1909)

Forester, C. S., *Mr. Midshipman Hornblower* (London, 1951)

—— *Lieutenant Hornblower* (London, 1959)

—— *The Hornblower Companion* (London, 1964)

—— *A Ship of the Line* (London, 1970)

—— *The Commodore* (London, 1973)

—— *The Happy Return* (London, 1975)

—— *Flying Colours* (London, 1975)

—— *Hornblower and the Hotspur* (London, 1979)

The Freemans Journal, 11 March (Dublin, 1844)

Gammie, A., *Duncan Main of Hangchow* (London, 1935)

Gardiner, R., *Fleet Battle and Blockade: The French Revolutionary War 1793–1797* (London, 1996)

—— *Frigates of the Napoleonic Wars* (London, 2006)

The Gazette, 17 January 1797; 9 August 1800; 2 October 1804; 20 August 1805; 4 November 1806; 9 November 1806

Gazette Nationale ou Le Moniteur Universal, No. 126, Sexti li, 6 Pluvoise, l'an 5 de la Republiqué Française une et indivisible, mercredi 25 jànvier 1797, vieux style (Paris, 1797)

Geggus, D. P., *The Impact of the Haitian Revolution in the Atlantic World* (Columbia, SC, 2001)

The Gentleman's Magazine, vol. 67, part 1, 1797; vol. 74, part 1, 1793

Gronow, R. H., *Captain Gronow's Last Recollections: Being the Fourth and Final Series of His Reminiscences and Anecdotes* (London, 1866)

Gutteridge, L. F., *Mutiny: A History of Naval Insurrection* (Annapolis, MD, 2006)

Haight, M. V. J., *European Powers and South East Africa 1796–1856* (New York, 1967)

The Hampshire Advertiser, 30 March 1844

Hampshire Telegraph and Sussex Chronicle, 23 June 1849

Hay, M. D., *Landsman Hay. The Memoirs of Robert Hay 1789–1847* (London, 1953)

Hazard, S., *Hazard's United States Commercial and Statistical Register*, vol. 5, 1841–1842 (Philadelphia, 1941)

Henderson, J., *Frigates, Sloops and Brigs* (Barnsley, 2005)

The Hereford Journal, 19 September 1810; 31 July 1811; 29 January 1834

Hill, J. R., *The Prizes of War: The Naval Prize System in the Napoleonic Wars* (Portsmouth, 1998)

James, L., *Mutiny: In the British and Commonwealth Forces, 1797–1956* (London, 1987)

James, W., *The Naval History of Great Britain from Declaration of War by France in 1793 to the Accession of George IV*, vol. 1 (London, 1837)

—— *The Naval History of Great Britain from Declaration of War by France in 1793 to the Accession of George IV*, vol. 2 (London, 1837)

The Kentish Gazette, 25 February 1851

The Ladies' Cabinet of Fashion, Music and Romance, vol. 26, second series (London, 1865)

The Lancaster Gazette, October 1809

Laughton, J. K., *Dictionary of National Biography, 1885–1900*, vol. 29

Leamington Spa Courier, 22 March 1825

Le Fevre, P., and R. Harding, B*ritish Admirals of the Napoleonic Wars: Contemporaries of Nelson* (London, 2005)

Lewis, R., *The Even Chance*, screenplay for Meridian Broadcasting (1998)

Lloyd's Register of Shipping (London, 1823)

The London Literary Gazette and Journal of Belles Lettres, Arts, Sciences, Etc (London, 1829)

The London Quarterly Review (London, 1835)

Lower, M. A., *The Worthies of Sussex: biographical sketches of the most eminent natives or inhabitants of the county, from the earliest period to the present time* (Sussex, 1865)

Maclay, E. S., *A History of American Privateers* (New York, 1899)

Mahan, A. T., *The influence of Sea Power upon the French revolution and Empire 1793–1812* (Boston, 1894)

Manchester Mercury, 27 October 1807

Marryat, F., *The King's Own* (Ithaca, NY, 1999)

Marshall, J., *Royal Naval Biography*, vol. 1, part II (London, 1823)
—— *Royal Naval Biography*, vol. 2, part II (London, 1825)
—— *Royal Naval Biography*, vol. 3, part II (London, 1823)
—— *Royal Naval Biography*, vol. 4, part II (London, 1835)
—— *Royal Naval Biography Supplement*, part I (London, 1827)
—— *Royal Naval Biography Supplement*, part II (London, 1828)
—— *Royal Naval Biography Supplement*, part III (London, 1829)
—— *Royal Naval Biography Supplement*, part IV (London, 1830)
McGrath, J., and M. Barton, *British Naval Swords and Swordsmanship*
    (Barnsley, 2013)
The Medical Register, 1783
The Metropolitan Magazine, 1835
Mitchell, F. T., *Personal recollections of the expedition to Algiers in August,
    1816* (Totnes, 1865)
M'Kerlie, P. H., *History of the lands and their owners in Galloway: With a
    historical sketch of the district*, vol. 1 (Edinburgh, 1870)
The Morning Chronicle, 14 August 1801; 23 November 1819; 20 March 1823;
    29 September 1848
The Morning Post, 28 October 1816; 27 March 1819; 29 July 1830; March
    1833; 28 January 1833; 22 June 1849
Morriss, R., *The Channel Fleet and the Blockade of Brest, 1793–1801*
    (London, 2001)
Mullié, C., *Biographie des célébrités militaires des armées de terre et de mer
    de 1789 à 1850*, vol. 1 (Paris, 1851)
*The Nautical Magazine: A Journal of Papers on Subjects Connected with
    Maritime Affairs*, vol. 4 (Glasgow, 1835)
The Nautical Magazine and Naval Chronicle, vol. 4 (London, 1837)
The Naval Chronicle, vol. 4, 1801; vol. 12, 1804; vol. 18, 1807; vol. 28, 1812;
    19 July 1841
Newport Mercury, 25 July 1812
The New York Tribune, 19 July 1841
Norie, J. W., *The Naval Gazetteer, Biographer, and Chronologist:
    Containing a History of the Late Wars, from Their Commencement
    in 1793 to Their Conclusion in 1801; and from Their Re-commencement
    in 1803 to Their Final Conclusion in 1815; and Continued, as to the
    Biographical Part, to the Present Time* (London, 1827)
Northcote, J., and W. Hazlitt, *Conversations of James Northcote* (London,
    1830)
O'Byrne, W. R., *A Naval Biographical Dictionary: Comprising the Life and
    Services of Every Living Officer in Her Majesty's Navy, from the Rank of
    Admiral of the Fleet to that of Lieutenant, Inclusive* (London, 1849)
One Who Has Served, *Facts versus fiction; or, Sir Wm. Symonds' principles
    of naval architecture vindicated by a compilation of official and other
    documents; with intr. Remarks* (London, 1845)
Osler, E., *Life of Admiral Viscount Exmouth* (London, 1841)

Parliamentary Papers, *A collection of papers relating to the expedition to the Scheldt, presented to Parliament in 1810* (London, 1811)

Pawlyn, T., *The Falmouth Packets 1689–1851* (Truro, 1803)

Parkinson, C. N., *Edward Pellew: Viscount Exmouth, Admiral of the Red* (London, 1934)

—— *The Life and Times of Horatio Hornblower* (Stroud, 1997)

Pearman, R., *The Cadogans at War 1783–1864* (London, 1990)

Perrett, B., *The Real Hornblower: The Life and Times of Admiral Sir James Gordon, GCB* (Barnsley, 2013)

Pipon, E., 'Narrative of the terrible shipwreck of the French ship, Droits de L'Homme, of 74 guns, driven on shore the 14th of January 1797', in *The Mariners Chronicle or Interesting Narratives of Shipwrecks* (1826)

Pitt, W., *The Cabin Boy: Being the Memoirs of an Officer in the Civil Department of H.M. Navy, Well Known by the Name of "Billy Pitt", and who Died at Malta in the Month of August, 1839* (London, 1840)

Pollock, A. W. A., *The United Service Magazine*, part 1 (Colburn, 1836)

Rae, M., 'Sir Edward Pellew, First Viscount Exmouth, 1757–1833', in *British Admirals of the Napoleonic Wars: Contemporaries of Nelson*, ed. P. Le Fevre and R. Harding (London, 2005)

The Repertory of Arts, Manufactures, and Agriculture: Consisting of Original Communications, Specifications of Patent Inventions, Practical and Interesting Papers, Selected from the Philosophical Transactions and Scientific Journals of All Nations, vol. 23 (London, 1813)

The Repertory of Patent Inventions Enlarged Series, vol. 13 (London, 1849)

Robson, M., *A History of the Royal Navy: The Napoleonic Wars* (London, 2014)

Rodger, N. A. M., '"A little Navy of your own making", Admiral Boscawen and the Cornish Connection in the Royal Navy', in M. Duffy, *Parameters of Naval Power 1650–1850* (Exeter, 1992)

—— *The Command of the Ocean: A Naval History of Britain 1649–1815* (London, 2004)

Rostul, B., *Retribution* screenplay, 2001

Sharp, J. A., *Memoirs of the life and services of Rear-Admiral Sir William Symonds, Surveyor of the navy from 1832 to 1847 with correspondence and other papers relative to the ships and vessels constructed upon his lines, as directed to be published under his will* (London, 1858)

Smallwood, A. L., 'Shore Wives: The Lives of British Naval Officers' Wives and Widows, 1750–1815', a thesis submitted in partial fulfilment of the requirements for the degree of Master of Arts (Wright State University, 2008)

The Spectator, vol. 12 (London, 1914)

The Sporting Magazine, vol. 34 (London, 1809)

Stanhope Lovell, Vice-Admiral W., *Personal Narrative of Events from 1799 to 1815 with anecdotes* (London, 1879)

Starkey, P. and J., *Travellers in Egypt* (London, 2001)

Stephen, L., *Dictionary of National Biography*, vol. 6 (London, 1886)

Stuart, V., and G. T. Eggleston, *His Majesty's Sloop-of-War: Diamond Rock* (London, 1978)

Taylor, S., *Commander: The Life and Exploits of Britain's Greatest Frigate Captain* (London, 2012)

Telford, T., and J. McKerlie, *Report from the committee appointed to examine into Mr. Telford's report and survey, relative to the communication between England and Ireland, by the North-West of Scotland*, House of Commons (London, 1809)

The Times, 29 July 1830; 15 July 1843

Tipping, M., *Nicholas Pateshall: A Short Account of a Voyage Round the Globe in H.M.S. Calcutta in 1803–1804* (Victoria, 1980)

Troude, O., *Batailles Navales de La France*, vol. 3 (Paris, 1867)

Uckfield Visitors Guide (Uckfield, 1869)

The United Service Journal and Naval and Military Magazine, part I (London, 1836)

The United Service Magazine and Naval and Military Journal, part III (London, 1864)

The Universal Magazine of Knowledge and Pleasure, vol. 3, 1805

University and City Herald, 2 December 1860

Voelcker, T., *Broke of the Shannon: And the War of 1812* (Barnsley, 2013)

Walker, C. F., *Young Gentlemen. The story of Midshipmen from the 17th Century to the present day* (London, 1938)

Wareham, T., *The Star Captains: Frigate Command in the Napoleonic Wars* (Annapolis, MD, 2001)

The Western Times, 17 June 1932; 15 February 1850; 20 March 1852

The Westmorland Gazette (no date)

Woolmer's Exeter and Plymouth Gazette, 23 September (Exeter, 1848)

Internet Retrievals

Boulderstone Family of Falmouth, Cornwall, England, retrieved from http://freepages.genealogy.rootsweb.ancestry.com/~jray/boulderson/index.htm

Canada's Historic Places, HMS *Plumper* Shipwreck, Musquash, New Brunswick, E5J, Canada, retrieved from www.historicplaces.ca/en/rep-reg/place-lieu.aspx?id=7796&pid=0

Frowd to Taylor, Manuscript letter sold by Mullock's Specialist Sporting Auctioneers, December 1799, retrieved from www.invaluable.com/auction-lot/maritime-naval-french-revolution-rare-naval-1-c-t4nu4aarmg

Memorials at St Peter's Church, Port Royal, Jamaica, retrieved from www.jamaicanfamilysearch.com

O'Donnell, M., *A Walk Round Fethard*, retrieved from http://fethard.com/people/more_web_articles/walk_around_fethard.html

Quinan, A. and G., *To Annoy the Enemy. The careers of Commander John Thomson R.N. (1751–1803) and of his son Captain John Thomson R.N. (1770–1835)*, retrieved from www.pellew.com/Family%20Tree/Thomson.htm

Richard Geldhof's Blog, Search for Secrets of a Sunken Cannon, retrieved from http://richardgeldhof.blogspot.co.uk:2010:05:search-for-secrets-of-sunken-cannon-85.html

Surman Index, Dr William's Centre for Dissenting Studies, retrieved from www.english.qmul.ac.uk/drwilliams/surman/intro.html

Index

The seventeen men who are the subjects of this study, together with Sir Edward Pellew, are shown in **bold**. Page numbers in *italics* refer to illustrations. Ships are British, unless stated otherwise.